Gospel of the Absurd

Gospel of the Absurd

Assemblies of Interpretation, Embodiment,
and Faithfulness

r. scot miller

Foreword by Andrew William Smith

WIPF & STOCK · Eugene, Oregon

GOSPEL OF THE ABSURD
Assemblies of Interpretation, Embodiment, and Faithfulness

Wipf & Stock
An Imprint of Wipf and Stock Publishers
199 W. 8th Ave., Suite 3
Eugene, OR 97401

www.wipfandstock.com

PAPERBACK ISBN: 978-1-4982-9646-5
HARDCOVER ISBN: 978-1-4982-9648-9
EBOOK ISBN: 978-1-4982-9647-2

Manufactured in the U.S.A.   JUNE 19, 2017

For Jennifer L. Seif,
who brings life and light into the world

Contents

Foreword

Andrew William Smith

ONE OF SCOT MILLER'S many important premises in this important book invigorates the claim that biblical narrative has on members of the Christian community. By virtue of our baptisms and our shared commitment to faithful Christian discipleship, Scot Miller and I believe we are a part of a bigger story of God's radical actions for justice and peace in a world broken by personal and communal idolatry. Learning about our respective participation in our particular Christian communities and ministries occurred when we reconnected as aspiring public theologians around 2011. But the roots of our friendship have very different beginnings.

Scot Miller and I used to party together in Detroit's Cass Corridor and Woodbridge neighborhoods. We were white activists and young dads in over our heads with our own personal battles with drug and alcohol addiction. Even though we both had roots in church, I don't ever recall our many discussions touching on theology. But our own epic fails were undoubtedly connected to the Fall and our arrogant repudiation of grace reflected a sinister kind of white privilege.

Those were heady times of late-1980s counterculture for us, where the economic and cultural stain of the Reagan-Bush years sparked in us a strain of creative resistance thick with thoughts of Marxism and anarchism. For moments, we would meet at the corner of Cass and Palmer in a vegan cafe or at the corner of Second and Prentis outside the basement offices of the *Fifth Estate*, a legendary anti-authoritarian journal. Each in our own strange way, we dipped our feet into the Motor City lineage for white radicals at the music-fired intersection of hippy, hip-hop, and punk rock rebellion.

Although I wanted to commit "class suicide" in the sense that I imagined the Black Panthers once did and thus shed the imaginary shackles of my white guilt, the cunning nature of addictive acting out meant I was more hell-bent on suicide itself. The throes of an addict's euphoria can feel like kenosis, but it is a far too selfish form of fake selflessness to sustain the kinds of commitments to radical social change that we liked to pontificate about. Scot and I were close enough that I occasionally had a front-row seat to his vulgar version of this story of white leftist rebellion, and it turned out to be a losing battle for both of us. We could not save ourselves from ourselves and were both too intoxicated to make a true lasting impact on the marginal communities in and out of which we floated. With each daily reprieve that clean and sober living grants us, we have another opportunity to submit to the will of Christ in our daily lives and communal vocations. Finally, we might be blessed to experience another kind of kenosis, where God uses us to help others, to hurry up and wait for the "kingdom" come.

But my intellectual odyssey into anarchist counterculture had a spiritual, religious, and theological component. I was on the run from a calling to serve the poor through Catholic Worker–style urban hospitality, which is why I told myself I dropped out of college and moved to a rough and integrated inner city. The cost of radical discipleship was too much for this bohemian, who was also on the run from a suburban upbringing of white privilege, and at twenty years old, I traded the Holy Trinity for the all-too-American trinity of sex, drugs, and rock 'n' roll. After attending Easter services high as a kite on April 3, 1998, I renounced my spiritual allegiance to Christ and traded the transcendent God of the universe for an immanent New Age pantheistic hodgepodge common for intellectual hippies of my ilk, loosely based around the neopaganism popularized by feminist radicals like Starhawk.

Decades later, Scot Miller and I found our way to a personal faith in the resurrected Christ and to a public commitment to do social witness in our respective contexts. Our intellectual and pastoral styles are different as are our ecclesiologies and theologies. Scot is more of a systematic philosopher, and I am more of a mystic poet; he is an Earlham-trained Quaker, and I am a Vanderbilt-trained Presbyterian. But our deep Detroit roots and our specific journeys away from substance abuse and secular radicalism into long messy journey of vibrant church work binds us. We are kinfolk in our shared commitment to proclaim the gospel of Jesus Christ in the context of narrative communities practicing the prophetic teachings of Scripture in everyday life. It's an honor to introduce readers to his first book, *Gospel of the Absurd*.

Scot Miller roots his ethics in his exegesis in such a way as to point us toward participation in the inaugurated eschatology of God's radical reign. He writes, "Indeed, either the poor are blessed and the humble will inherit the earth or, for all intents and purposes, the cross is little more than a storied failure, a myth for the conquered and miserable to revel in as they await reward in the future but avoid the pursuit of justice and righteousness in the present." In the honest reflection and hindsight God has granted us, we can see how our radical postures of those past protests were merely pointing us to Christ's upside-down kingdom. God was there in those decadent and disconcerting bohemian encounters we had back in Detroit; we were just too caught up in the arrogance of our positions to see that. Today, we at least have the option to entertain some sanctified sanity that the evaporation of our past emotive and egocentric ways provides.

In a world where fundamentalist Christians could bless and sanctify the entire capitalist circus of American shame without irony or apology in the amen chorus of trite tweets, at a time when the cultural crisis in American Christianity that has been percolating since World War II reaches a new pinnacle of idolatrous insult, a book of gospel absurdity like this one is surely absurd. It's our hope that theologians, pastors, and Bible-reading radicals will find food in this text that will feed their communal readings of gospel radicalism at a time when right-wing Christianity has gone all-in for denouncing the poor and marrying mammon.

For white, academically trained thinkers to do more radical theology at this juncture is a leap of faith and feels somewhat fanatic. But when I look at Scot's practice and my own, I know a little bit about the brokenness from where this comes. Despite the hamstring of our race-gender positionality, the scars we've endured through overcoming addiction and relinquishing at least a portion of our patriarchal privilege in the process are a mark of this absurd gospel. Unlike some allies trying to mansplain how to be an ally, Scot is a writer-activist-pastor-theologian who admits his white male baggage before he abandons it, and he is a Christian who understands that we are all broken sinners in need of redemption, regardless of social location. By the grace of God, the redeemed bodies of a sober drunk and a clean addict reunited at the absurd intersection of unconditional gospel love, genuine communal interactions, and grassroots nonviolent interventions.

By listening to radical black theologians and participating in shared witness with members of the black church tradition, we learn how to be conversation partners and allies in the kinds of religious communities for whom a hopeful hermeneutic is a matter of communal survival. Reading Scot's manuscript and meditating on the risks of his ministry, I am reminded of a fellow Tennessee maverick, the late Will D. Campbell. Campbell's

Christian radicalism made him friends with fellow travelers on the fringes of the 1960s civil rights movement and the rural rednecks of his culture alike, a strange incongruous unity that made him a perfect mentor for the outlaw country singers of Nashville who would visit him in his office. I suggest that Scot Miller's sense of religious vocation and vagabond cultural fluidity could help him lean into being a kind twenty-first-century continuation of Campbell's radical legacy for the folks of rural and urban Michigan communities that neoliberal economics has forgotten.

Like Campbell, Miller rejects the ideologically presumptive stance of pretentious left and liberal activisms. Scot's ministry is neither left nor right, neither liberal nor conservative, but the ways in which his witness will be offensive to progressives can be clearly seen from my vantage point in my adopted home in small-town Tennessee. For Scot, there is just too much Bible and too much Jesus at the core of the belief and practice to appease a liberal audience. This book is for people rooted in the strange gospel contract that makes us slaves to God's grace, participants in Christian tradition, and rebels to the American gravy train. Essential humility in light of God's authority makes us anti-authoritarian in relation to worldly idolatry.

As an academically trained theologian and lay preacher working in a small-church congregational context, I identify with the challenges that Miller faces with this book and in his ministries to make the absurdity of the gospel accessible to friends seeking liberation, especially in the context of situations like the ones facing Scot's neighbors in Flint, Michigan. For real, why do people living and fighting in the trenches of social struggle against institutional sin need to read academic theology?

Perhaps it will only be our fellow preachers and professors who have the time or the vocabulary to fully wrap themselves in this text and the intense mission I believe it passionately professes. But whether this book is read by preachers, taught by teachers, studied in Sunday school, borrowed by your mother's book group, or shared like a war story around the campfire at a revolutionary revival on the shores of Lake Michigan, it will hopefully satisfy a hunger and meet a real need. We all need some gospel absurdity in our lives.

Acknowledgments

THERE ARE A LOT of people to thank, and many of them don't know how much they have contributed to the writing of this book. Of course, my wife and family, Jenn, Emma, Rosa, and Micah, have patiently accommodated books, index cards, and angry searches for lost bits and pieces of information relevant only to me that were scattered about the house. The willingness of my two older sons in Detroit to embody the sacrifice of privilege though they confess no gods has been a joy to observe. Of course, our family has been as understanding as necessary to support writing, ministry, and the frustrations and joys of church life that pulls in so many different directions.

Andrew William Smith has been an important conversation partner. I rely on the professor and preacher to ask the challenging question, and test my temperament. If Andrew can handle my self-righteous attacks on his politics despite his obvious and significant faithfulness (and self-professed liberalism), I can feel like I have not crossed a line that should not be crossed. Andrew is a good interpreter of my work because he has understanding and empathy for my past. The book is best understood in light of my life experience in Detroit's Cass Corridor, Brush Park, and Woodbridge neighborhoods.

I have gratitude for the work that Joy Milano, a former colleague at Kuyper College, performed for me. She edited the first half of the book, and gave me some solid writing tips to continue forward. It was Kuyper College that made grace real to me. For this I am grateful.

It was my experiences at the Earlham School of Religion that strengthened my faith and provided me with the kind of minds necessary to the development of a theology of faithfulness, no matter how absurd. It is folks like Matt Hisrich and ESR dean Jay Marshall that invested in the kinds of supportive discussion necessary to moving forward with a book idea. My old seminary mates Brian Young and Julie Rudd, Mark Walker and Nate Polzin, have done much to support my ministry of writing, blogging, and outreach in Flint. I cannot forget the relationship I forged with the Hammond family and all whom they have taken in as an example of messianic faithfulness. Samuel (B.B.) Smith and Mulondo and Angelo Echols are the kind of Flintstones that made me eager to go to Flint each week. They are vessels of living water.

Special thanks to Kyle Small of Western Theological Seminary; Josh Hendershot; Charles O'Grady; the Gramze's, both Jim and Cathy; Mike and Dorothy Wolfe; Paul Crumback; and Greg Scott and Judi Meerman of Kuyper College. Finally, grace and peace reciprocated to Common Spirit Church of the Brethren in Grand Rapids, Michigan; Joanna and John Willoughby; Roya Stern; and Amy Gardine. I am indebted to the Religious Society of Friends (Quakers) and all who came before me as a community of embodied faith.

CHAPTER 1

The Failure of Christian Ethics

It is time for communities of faith to read the Bible together as a community of faith. It is time for congregations to challenge the ghosts of the academy and eschew the "hermeneutics of suspicion" in favor of a hermeneutic of faithfulness.[1] It is time to return to prioritizing the biblical text in the practice of Christian ethics. At the same time, congregations should recognize that Scripture is not a transcendent text; it cannot be authoritative for those who do not believe and it does not contain any hidden truths or plain meanings, nor hold universal moral authority. It is a text in which understanding is contingent upon a belief that Jesus of Nazareth is a focal point of God's acting in history. It is a text that can only have meaning once accorded to it by readers and interpreters. It is a text that can be interpreted in unlimited variety and thus support the meanings given to it by a diverse collection of communities. Its chief paradox might be that it is an authoritative text without authority.[2] Finally, whatever the Bible might represent to one person or

1. Mudge, introduction to Ricoeur's *Essays in Biblical Interpretation*, 5. Mudge writes: "Any new articulation of faith must pass through and beyond the 'hermeneutics of suspicion,' not slide around it." I interpret the following statement by John Caputo to complement Mudge's assertion: "We are trying to restore the difficulty of life, not to make it impossible." Caputo, *Radical Hermeneutics*, 209.

2. Caputo, *Radical Hermeneutics*, 161. Concerning the work of Jacques Derrida and textual authority: Derrida's "point is to expose the limitations, to delimit the authority of every assertion which does not set itself up as authoritative. And this is not that there are no authorities, but there are no absolute authorities, that authorities are always suspect, that they are only as good as the results they produce . . ." Ibid. See also Lyotard, *Postmodern Condition*. Lyotard is wary of any claims to universal or transcendent authority by a text and believes that we should no longer turn to "grand narratives" as a primary source of a universal knowledge. "But," he writes, "the little narrative remains the quintessential form of imaginative invention." This coincides with Caputo's and Derrida's concern with claims of universalism and transcendent authority. Little narratives produce a valuable knowledge that values "open systems, local determination,"

1

another, it cannot reasonably be ignored by those concerned with a specifically Christian moral vision.

Fundamentalists and conservative Christians will not only disagree with the above statements, but insist the Bible has unquestionable authority (*sola scriptura*) and is inerrant. The first response to such assertions is that the existence of Protestantism and its denominations indicate that the Bible is open to a variety of interpretations (all of which are socially and historically contingent) and is authoritative in a variety of ways (but not universally so). Consider: there are not only never-ending disagreements over which kind of baptism is biblical, but over the biblical representation of creation, authorship of various books and epistles, the meaning of the Revelation to John, and the role of women in the church. Simply, facts betray the fundamentalist argument that there is a universally appropriate way to understand the biblical text, because the Reformation responded to Roman Catholic claims of authority the same way fundamentalism in turn questioned the theological claims of many reformers in their development of dispensationalism, second-coming apocalypticism, and biblical inerrancy.

Secondly, the only matter of concern over fundamentalist and conservative interpretations of Scripture is that such readings have become politically conservative. It is increasingly evident that conservative readings of the text are not, in reality, theologically conservative, but are instead politically conservative and motivated by the intellectual and emotional need to have the Bible underwrite political agendas. Such interpretations become concerned with power and control and are inherently oppressive when used as propositional devices. Maladaptive exegesis is not limited to the political right, however.

Christians who favor the politics of the left tend to view the Bible in much the same way as their counterparts, insisting on parallel fundamentalist readings focused on the declaration that there are no virgin births, that Jesus could not have walked on water, and that there are no resurrections. It seems that "liberal" views of the text will use the hermeneutic of suspicion as the natural "literal" counterbalance to the supposed literal reading attributed to their political enemies.[3]

---

and is "anti-method." Lyotard even questions the efficacy of consensus by referring it to a "tool of power." Lyotard, *Postmodern Condition*, 60. Gadamer states it most succinctly: "Meaning is not fixed." Gadamer, *Truth and Method*, 156.

3. MacIntyre, *After Virtue*, especially chs. 2–7. He states that moral discourse is competitive, won by the individual who "displays the greatest appearance of a clear, undoubting conviction," which in turn lends to the appearance of the victor's access to universal truth, and reflects a false sense of reasoned authority through an appeal to an objective and impersonal criterion but in reality is simply a display of rhetorical skill (p. 19). He suggests that "the most striking feature" of modern argumentation is that, despite appeals to rationality and universal truths, the argument can never end.

Consider that neither of the above illustrations of textual understanding are illegitimate. Instead, such interpretations are suspect because they are used to grasp hold of and maintain political power. The use of the text to control the behaviors and choices of others has made the Bible a weapon in the hands of Christians who are not so much stuck in the Middle Ages as they are stuck in the failed philosophical project of modernity.[4] Liberal Christians use the text for similar purposes. They may not be caught up in the downward spiral of modernity (though social sciences serve their criticisms well), but in what appears to be a lack of faith in the God of the Bible, instead turning to a transcendent universalism that mocks the narrative with every proof-text used to buoy the call for social welfare programs, food pantries, and anti-war demonstrations. Some have decided that the Bible, and all of its particularity, is an embarrassment, a technical document for moral discourse, or simply problematic.[5] The problem of Scripture can be located in the very real difficulty of how Americans in particular have come to view the construct of community; the Bible can only be a meaningful text of faith when it is read

"There seems to be no rational way of securing moral agreement in our culture" (p. 6). Regarding specifically Christian claims of universality, he points out the relationship between emotivism and evangelism. "The sole reality of distinctively moral discourse is the attempt of one will to align the attitudes, feelings, preferences, and choices of another with his own. Others are always a means, never ends" (p. 24).

4. Ellul writes, "Nothing is left. And this nothing is increasingly aggressive, totalitarian, and omnipresent." Ellul, *Anarchy and Christianity*, 22. Lyotard adds much to the discussion: "Scientific knowledge does not represent the totality of knowledge." Lyotard, *Postmodern Condition*, 7. Consider the Bible as an authoritative text in our contemporary intellectual environment as related to Lyotard's proposal that emotivism is coincidental to the self-justifying nature of reasoned propositions. Lyotard understands bureaucracy to be a primary example of self-justifying reasoning, but it reflects the nature of denominational religious structures, and the political uses of the biblical text. The Bible must be declared the text of transcendent universal truth in order to justify the political desires of the individual or organization that relies upon it as a supportive, transcendent truth. Moral discourse in Western democracies often depends on making truth claims that necessarily support the needs of an established economic, legal, or social class, "or it is dysfunctional." Such "dysfunctional claims," like the Bible teaches that participation in war is not a Christian behavior, is relegated to the status of "not-credible." Credibility, according to Lyotard, is granted solely to those universalist propositions and the findings of hard sciences or well-reasoned outcomes within a boundaried moral discourse that promote the success and progress of the major stakeholders of a system, and maintain its stability and supremacy as an overarching regulatory structure. Lyotard, *Postmodern Condition*, 12.

5. Cartwright, *Practices, Politics, and Performance*. Cartwright follows the use of the Bible in Christian ethics and draws a line from the rise of modernity to the present. "By 1965," he writes, "the use of the Bible in Christian ethics was a problem to be solved." He writes further that if the Bible was to be authoritative for Christian ethics "there is little agreement concerning how it is authoritative." Ibid., 40, citing Long Jr., "Use of the Bible in Christian Ethics."

together by congregations. The *problem* of the Bible as an informant of moral vision or ethics is not, in fact, a problem. It is best interpreted by a community in a manner through which the biblical ethic is made credible by no other means than through the embodiment of the biblical narrative in the lives of the interpretive community. Prioritizing individual growth over corporate faithfulness can only result in a lack of accountability for how one uses the text to his or her advantage, or to the disadvantage of others.

The Bible was not written by individuals and is never about individuals. Instead, it describes the faith and faithfulness (or lack thereof) of a people and those communities that have confessed that YHWH is the one true God, and that Jesus is the full representation of God. Yet, the Bible can only be interpreted properly within the context of a community that has no concern for finding a universally held transcendent truth spelled out within it. If we can take Derrida seriously enough to know that he has something to contribute to theology, then we can acknowledge not so much that there is no truth, but more aptly that humans will construct a plethora of truths in order to suit their immediate and long-term needs. Derrida calls for the liberation of humanity from all oppression by identifying many texts as oppressive by their very nature while, at times, calling for the liberation of the text. Much of the world must be liberated from the bonds of Scripture that are as much shackles of the empire as representative of Western truth.[6]

The Bible, however, needs liberating as much as humanity does from its bondage to those constituents who insist it is an overarching arbiter of truth. It needs liberating from dogma and systematics and the aggressive contentions that the text has absolute authority. Any authority given to the Bible can only be legitimized by the embodiment of the interpretive twists and turns that produce positive outcomes regarding its moral vision. These outcomes will vary, as will the comparative moral vision of any community who comes together in the name of Jesus as the Christ.[7] There can be no *a priori* authority assumed, but instead faith in an interpretive body that participates in repeated readings, enjoys the challenges of new understandings, and then promotes actualizations that lead back to reading the text through fresh hermeneutical lenses, once again ready to be acted out and

6. Caputo, *Radical Hermeneutics*, 156. He paraphrases Derrida by writing, "we create as many truths as we require . . . It has to be liberated from the illusion of a single truth. It is to be liberated from dogmatism and hermeneutics and to adapt a strategy of writing . . ." Ibid. I now add a disclaimer gleaned from Ruf, *Postmodern Rationality*, 13. He writes: "One can only write for one's own rhetorical purposes in response to Derrida's writing."

7. This claim is representative of the work of many Christian theologians and ethicists, beginning with MacIntyre and including much of the work of Hauerwas, *Peaceable Kingdom*; and Yoder, *Politics of Jesus*. See also Yoder, *Priestly Kingdom*.

reviewed by others. Reading the Bible, as Fee says, "for all its worth,"[8] means that it must be read not so much by every individual as much by individuals together as part of a community that prioritizes corporate faith. Otherwise, readings of the text, understandings of Jesus as Christ, and the mission of the church will inevitably stagnate. The proof of such stagnancy, so to speak, is evident in the post-Enlightenment pudding that we call the contemporary church.

To begin this project, we must consider the nature of twentieth-century liberal religion and the tendency of major theological thinkers to relegate the Bible to the periphery of Christian ethics. While conservative preachers certainly enjoyed a significant amount of control, it does not appear that those thinkers contributed much to the contemporary discussions of American morality and ethics. However, integral characteristics of the religiously conservative political public face were patriotism, the promotion of American democracy, and anti-communist sentiments. After WWII, a now-legendary preacher named Billy Graham fomented the anti-communist fears of religious conservatives and forged a new role for the church as a significant voting block. Jerry Falwell and others grabbed hold of Graham's coattails and launched their own very public, and politically aggressive, ministries. The effects on American politics were realized very quickly.[9]

During the 1980s, through political power struggles and emotional manipulation, political conservatives seemed to hijack Scripture as their own. They followed Rauschenbusch in an important and familiar way—an insistence that the Bible contained universal truths, and that Jesus could be fully represented in the realm of liberal democracy. Yet, there is also a difference. Political conservatives came to insist that they had special access to this truth and a divine mandate to legislate a universal moral vision, much of which was left over from the anti-communist crusades that served to counter anyone who might interpret the stories of Jesus in a manner that prioritized kenosis, sacrifice of privilege, and the eschewing of power as a reflection of the cross. Additionally, conservatives have relied upon a marginalization of those communities that understand the text to be saying something different by publicly questioning the legitimacy of that community's faith.[10]

8. Fee and Stuart, *How to Read the Bible for All Its Worth.*

9. Barker et al., "Of God and Caesar." Note also, former United States Vice-President Dick Cheney sent out Christmas cards in 2003 that quoted, in handwriting, Benjamin Franklin: "And if a sparrow cannot fall to the ground without His notice, is it probable that an empire can rise without His aid?" Quoted by Noah, "Imperial Vice Presidency"; cited in Rieger, *Christ and Empire,* 63.

10. For an excellent example of populist-style writing that provides evidence to support my assumption, please see Hawkins, "Seven Non-Political Differences between

Conservatives have commandeered biblical language to the point that many Christians avoid any reference to central biblical themes, such as sin and redemption, forgiveness and salvation. Embarrassment keeps many from embracing their readings of the Bible as a basis for ethics, and prevents them from being vocal about their beliefs. There are some who perhaps do not want to risk being confused with their political opponents and what they believe to be "magical thinking" about God and America.[11]

But consider this: there are very few groups or individuals who concern themselves with the lives of the Amish, the Bruderhof, the Hutterites, or most Pentecostal congregations. It is pertinent to the conversation to note that these groups do not vote or run for public office. Such Anabaptist or Radical Reformation groups practice an ethic that is closely bound to very conservative interpretations of the biblical text. However, not only do they not engage the world through ballot boxes, but they are also generally known to be pacifist groups who self-marginalize. Because of their perceived harmless political status, or their eschewing of the electoral process, these groups are rarely scrutinized for their religious beliefs. However, they are generally considered to be positive, if not somewhat enigmatic, communities.[12]

Conservative groups who work to elect politicians that will insist on ordering school texts that contain information on biblical "science," or teach that same-sex intimacy is sinful, or want to make access to abortion

Liberals and Conservatives," para. 12. He writes: "Conservatives are better Christians than liberals: Certainly there are debates about social conservatism and Christianity on the conservative side of the fence, but Christian conservatism is considered to be an honorable and important part of the Republican base. People are going to hate to hear this, despite the fact it's absolutely true, but Christianity and liberalism have become largely incompatible. That's because there are so many liberals who are implacably hostile to Christianity that liberal Christians are left with one of two unpalatable choices. Either they can water their Christian beliefs down into thin gruel so as to be compatible with liberalism or liberal Christians can choose to be cringing dogs and keep their mouths shut while their beliefs are regularly insulted, demeaned, and attacked by their fellow liberals. Neither option should be acceptable to someone who has a strong Christian faith."

11. Mark Sandlin, "I Want My Religion Back," para. 2.

12. Compare Yoder's *Priestly Kingdom*, part 3, "The Public Realm." Yoder argues assertively for Christian participation in democracy and the overcoming of "American civil religion" through the introduction of Christian commitment to reconciling democratic leadership to the gospel. Contra Ellul, who writes that Christian anarchy is an "absolute rejection of violence. Should anarchists vote? For my part, like many anarchists, I think not." Ellul also states that conscientious objection to militarism is an important witness, and states that anarchists should "avoid taxes, and compulsory schooling . . ." Ellul, *Anarchy and Christianity*, 11. Ellul, in direct contrast to Yoder, believes that Christianity is the first form of anarchism, and suggests aggressively that the church should embody anarchy as its witness to the gospel message.

illegal come to be viewed as political threats and labeled as cranks. These groups are often mocked and vilified because they attempt to coerce specific religious beliefs onto others. It is the insistence that morality should be legislated onto the lives of others that is in turn used to indict, with a broad stroke, the whole of Christianity as an aggressive, oppositional, and oppressive constituency.[13]

I suggest that the failure of Christian ethics is related to Christianity's continuing quest for power as a political force, because it is perceived to be a coercive force in people's lives. Yoder wrote that the good news cannot be good unless it is perceived as such.[14] The failure of Christian ethics is in fact the failure of the church to be Christlike. The downfall of Christendom is its insistence upon maintaining political relevance at the expense of embodying ethics in a manner that makes claims about Jesus and the Bible credible to others. Human history shows that political power and the ethics of power are, if anything, in-credible. Such is the case for the contemporary church and its insistence upon making universal claims of transcendent truth, biblical inerrancy, and divine right to rule (often, the right to rule and control social and economic expression politics). What can be done?

The answer to the problem of discredited Christian ethics is to deconstruct the church, yet not to some primeval state that wishes to return to a sort of first-century purity. Many might agree that postmodern thinkers like Jacque Derrida go too far in asserting that all texts are inherently controlling and oppressive. Derrida is a primary proponent of a literary process that strips away layers of what are referred to as historically privileged meanings that have been applied to authoritative texts. This process assumes that popular interpretation and privileged meanings occur with the intention of underwriting a maintenance of a privileged social, economic, and political class. Racism, sexism, and ethnocentrism are interpretive filters often stated to be at the core of such privileged meanings, among other institutionalized cultural assumptions. Such themes are at the root of the understanding of texts as inherently controlling and oppressive.[15]

A text will, I believe, be inherently oppressive when any group asserts that it is transcendent and universally authoritative. Usually, those who make the claim that universally valid meanings are present in a text want control over which way such meanings are applied to social or political

13. For an example of one such conservative lobbying entity, please see the website of Focus on the Family.

14. Yoder, *Priestly Kingdom*, 55.

15. Armstrong, "Deconstruction," 138. While reliance upon a dictionary citation for an explanation of deconstruction and Derrida's major themes is certainly suspect of intellectual laziness, the work of Derrida plays a minor role.

discourse in order to ensure favorable outcomes. Writers such as Yoder and Cartwright have rightly proposed that the text is liberating when it is read and interpreted by communities who eschew any stake in coercive political activity. The focus on Matthew 18 and the nature of how a congregation practices binding and loosing is important to communities of interpretation, as it allows the hermeneutical process to play itself out.[16]

Interpretations are always contingent, and so it follows that each community must interpret according to its historical and social place in time, and then within the greater context of a world community.[17] This is an ancient practice, and is evidenced in the four canonical gospels, each of which use the sayings of Jesus in a manner that suits the context of that community. For example, the gospels were written by members of a Jewish sect that insisted God's messiah had come and changed the nature of the relationship between Jews and Gentiles. As such, first-century messianic Jews interpreted the Hebrew texts in a manner that supported their claim.[18]

There is much evidence that displays how competing Jewish groups contextualized the Hebrew narrative according to localized concerns (obviously, groups such as the Pharisees and Sadducees, interest groups like the Scribes and Hasmonians, and messianic pretenders on either side of the time of Jesus' ministry). There was also the larger political context. The promised land was occupied by the Romans, who propped up Herod's regime, which was considered illegitimate. The Romans demanded sacrifices to the emperor, and taxes were paid by the temple elites with the funds collected from Jews via the temple tax. Taxation is claimed to have been around 30–40 percent of all earnings, and there were no social services outside of slavery.[19]

There was also the context of Hellenistic philosophy and literature, the Hebrew and Greek texts of the faith, and all the other realities of first-century life. In other words, the gospels are all a product of the first-century and are social, political, and religious documents intended to make sense of their times and legitimize the specific claims of small communities. The very same realities and contingencies apply to any twenty-first century community that reads and collectively interprets the text. All of a congregation's

16. Yoder, *Priestly Kingdom*, 116; and Cartwright, *Practices, Politics, and Performance*, 71.

17. MacIntyre, *After Virtue*. "The extraction of theological or philosophical statements from their contemporary context lends to a 'false independence' which in turn attempts to make such statements universal truths" (11). Understandings and interpretations are also contingent upon the inescapable agenda of the interpreter. See Ruf, *Postmodern Rationality*, 68–69.

18. Wright, *New Testament and the People of God*, 456.

19. Herzog, *Jesus, Justice, and the Reign of God*, 122.

social situation, both positive and negative, is going to influence the way the Bible is understood, the way it should be embodied, and the manner in which a congregation uses it as a community rule.

As the readers wade through the canon, a few things become evident. Christian communities will read the Hebrew texts through specific religious lenses that support the belief that God has acted incarnationally in Jesus. Whatever the understandings of Judaism might be—and Jewish commentators will rightfully be cited to inform interpretive maneuvers—the Christ is necessarily at the center of a hermeneutic rooted in very particular first-century religious claims. Contemporary Christian communities will also read the text through lenses tinted by church history and tradition, the social and economic standing of the community, and the material resources that each congregation might have access to; this will be the baggage that it is necessary to unpack during the interpretive task. Primarily, the readers of the text will interpret it through the unshakable lens of a contingent though contemporary *zeitgeist*.

Two things are of primary importance. The first is the recognition that we cannot interpret first-century texts with any understanding of the author's particular intention. We can assume general circumstances, but making more than general assumptions prioritizes academic exercises that are consistently evolving as new information comes to light. Academic advances should be used as critical guides for a community's reading, but the reading should not prioritize such exercises. The second item of importance is a firm recognition that we can only interpret the text in light of our own understanding of what is real, what values or virtues are meaningful to us, and why they are meaningful. Considering the above few paragraphs, I engage in this project with the idea of promoting just one way (of many) to interpret the text and restore the Bible to its rightful place as the authority of Christian ethics. Of course, according to all that has been written above, this cannot be *the* way, but only *a* way. By this example, I hope to provide some insights to the notion that the Bible can be authoritative without having any claim to transcendence, or used to support propositional claims, which by default would make the text a tool of oppression.

An important place to begin is back at the top. The concept of a "hermeneutic of suspicion" was introduced by Paul Ricoeur, who also introduced the concept of "second naiveté." In his book *Symbolism of Evil*, Ricoeur suggests that it is not possible to properly interpret first-century texts because they concern themselves, for the most part, with particular and singular outcomes. A text will describe this particularity in metaphor and symbols that cannot be interpreted because we cannot relive this past or recreate the particulars. Ricoeur believes that modern readers can only approximate first-century conditions, concerns, and possibilities. The concept of second naiveté can be especially useful to moderate-to-liberal communities who get caught up in gospel narratives that include miracles, angels, satans, and virgin births.[20]

The main function of the hermeneutic becomes its place as the facilitator of belief, because we begin to interpret the text with an understanding that it is we who give meaning to the text. Ricoeur writes that interpretation is belief. While those who lived within the historical and social place in time in which the text was first written and edited could perhaps exegete meanings that were in fact extensions of authorial intent, all the twenty-first-century interpreter can do is read the Bible "as if." A modern reader can interpret the text, despite a wealth of possible outcomes and multiple meanings, by practicing a reenactment of the text that is in sympathy with the particular narratives.[21]

While we cannot possibly know what Jesus meant when he claimed that if he wished, twelve legions of angels could drive out the oppressors, we can sympathize with the text and understand it in a manner that suggests nonviolence as the Christ-centered response to evil. Properly stated, a community can interpret the text in any manner that suits its own reality.[22] The key to second naiveté is that an ethic held in sympathy with the text will lead to the performance of the interpretation. Interpretation becomes belief, which is then lived out in faith—a faith that believes such activity will later be vindicated in a manner imagined by the interpretive community, regardless of whether that truth is represented by metaphor or literal belief in heaven, etc.[23] It is "as if" we access meaning in the text and, through our hermeneutical lenses, live the meaning out in the manner that makes it intelligible to ourselves and our contemporaries. We live as though, for example, when practicing non-violence, despite our privileged position of living within the safety of the empire, we will not make use of the strength of the empire but empty ourselves of privilege in order to live in sympathy with the text and with Jesus. Of course, such an interpretation is contingent

20. Ricoeur, *Symbolism of Evil*, 18. In his introduction to Ricoeur's *Essays in Biblical Interpretation*, Mudge writes this interpretive maneuver is necessary to read the text through modern lenses: "Any new articulation of faith must pass through and beyond the 'hermeneutics of suspicion,' and not slide around it" (5).

21. The main function of the hermeneutic becomes its place as the facilitator of belief, because we begin to interpret the text with an understanding that it is we who give meaning to the text.

22. Caputo, *Radical Hermeneutics*. "We create as many truths as we require . . . it has to be liberated from the illusion" that there exists a single truth (156).

23. Hauerwas, *Peaceable Kingdom*. "God's story is not merely told; it must be lived" (45). "By learning to 'imitate' Jesus we in fact become part of God's very life and therein find our true home. We become citizens in God's kingdom . . ." (67).

on any number of realities and truths that are manipulated to serve the goals of the interpretive community. Every interpretation can only be as much.

It must be stated that some interpretive twist, much like beliefs in general, will be deemed not credible, which is different than saying they are in-credible. An in-credible practice might suggest that the imagined outcomes are not realistic, or that the practices of a community are the result of magical thinking, misguided or unreasonable assertions of reality, or simply unrealistic according to the observable nature of human activity. Certainly, many liberal-to-moderate thinkers will deem the resurrection event in-credible. Other potential responses to an ethic as constructed by biblical interpreters is that the public performance of interpretation by its believers proves to be unfruitful, oppressive, or destructive. Walking on water is in-credible, but such a narrative can be interpreted and embodied through sympathetic performances that provide meaning that facilitates understandings of stories that are productive and beneficial in the lives of others. It is a matter of a community interpreting the event at the Sea of Galilee and in some way applying Ricoeur's "sympathetic imagination"[24] in order to make sense of it. Might walking on water indicate something greater than the sum total of the words on paper? Only an interpretive community can suggest a meaning, and then must make the claim credible through public performance of the attributed meaning.

On the other hand, if a community insists that walking on water is a literal miracle, indicative of Jesus as a divine being capable of altering the reality expressed by physics, and then uses this interpretation to underwrite militarism in the name of the divine, an observant public might be forced to consider whether such an ethic is credible at all. As Lindbeck wrote, it is incongruous to claim that God is love "while cleaving the skull of an infidel."[25] Militarism of this sort may be appropriate for nation-states in the defense of citizenry or the conquering of another people, but if a congregation claims that God is love, it may be hard-pressed to use the Bible to underwrite holy war as being Christian or biblical. To claim God is love while hating one's enemy is simply not a credible claim, for Jesus instructs disciples to love enemies and pray for persecutors. It can be deemed credible for the nation-state to use military force, but a government's claim that God is love would, in most every instance, have little credibility.

Liberation theologians and philosophical thinkers refer to the embodiment of beliefs as praxis.[26] The concept of praxis best describes the concept

24. Mudge, introduction to Ricoeur, *Essays in Biblical Interpretation*, 6–7.

25. Lindbeck, *Nature of Doctrine*, 64.

26. Gutierrez, *Theology of Liberation*, xxx. Lindbeck states that intelligibility is a

of biblical ethics. A biblical ethic is the intentional behavior of a community whose public performance of particular texts are intended to define and make credible the claims about a specific moral vision. If a community of interpretation has a moral vision based on the theme that they should love God, and love their neighbors as themselves, the public performance would intentionally enact the drama of, say, feeding the hungry or visiting the prisoner that is found in Matthew. The stories of the Bible provide narratives that the congregation can reenact with sympathetic imagination—like understanding the story of the good Samaritan as an indicator of what it means to love your neighbor and to love your enemies. Since these practices are public, they are both witness and drama to be observed by outsiders, thus, open to critique. Herein lays the hermeneutic circle.

Hermeneutics act as a community's preunderstanding of reality. It is through this understanding—perhaps "prejudice" is an apt word—that individuals, communities, and societies interpret events and the rest of the world. The hermeneutic is what one (or more) brings to the text to begin the interpretive process. All hermeneutics contain meanings that are socially and historically contingent meanings; they are inextricably linked to a person or community's time and place in history, their shared experiences, shared language, self-understanding, and corporate concepts of truth. It is through the hermeneutic that individuals and congregations interact with the text, interpreting the text or historical events in accordance with their reality. This is the act of interpretation of text or event. Once the event occurs, or the interpretation of the biblical text has been engaged through the hermeneutic vision, a community will gain new understanding of truth, of self, and of "the other." This interpretive move marks the beginning of Caputo's process of "repetition."[27] With every opportunity to interpret comes an opportunity to develop deeper relationships with the text and one another. Also, the repetitive act of interpreting facilitates a firmer grasp of old and present truths and, potentially, even a radical change in such understandings, e.g., the life, death, and resurrection of Jesus as events that were interpreted in such a manner that Jesus became identified as the messiah of Israel. This was a radical change in understanding of truth that could have only been accomplished by a Jewish community of belief who used the Hebrew Scriptures to both understand the ministry of Jesus and his death, and witness to others how God had acted to change the world through

---

"matter of skill, not theory, and credibility comes from good performance, not adherence to independently formulated criteria." Lindbeck, *Nature of Doctrine*, 131. See Wright, *New Testament*, 233.

27. Caputo, *Radical Hermeneutics*, 196.

resurrecting him. The matter of Jesus in history makes absolutely no sense when taken out if its ancient Jewish context.

The next aspect of the hermeneutic circle is praxis. This point of repetition depends upon a community's ability to experience new possibilities and test these new understandings and possibilities through the process of sympathetic imagination. This is an important part of hermeneutical repetition because a community anticipates publicly performing new actualities as a means of testing and meaning making. Also, it displays a witness to the public so that the matter of credibility may be established, and then further self-reflection occurs. The last aspect of repetition is the reinauguration of the circle, as new understandings of the text and truth become an interpretive group's new preunderstanding, discursive language, and understanding of truth. The process, as stated, is continuously repeated, and it is only through this repetition that old narratives can be continued and passed down and new understandings can develop. There can be no actualization of praxis without a process that allows for consistent reevaluation.

It is now time for applying meaning to the hermeneutical process described above. Herein lays the possibility that the text cannot be universally authoritative due to the contingent nature of all understanding, but is still authoritative because it provides a community with textual discourse by which the world and truth claims can be evaluated in faith. One of Yoder's biggest fears was that others would interpret his work as sectarian to the point that it would be dismissed as anarchistic.[28] I contend that there is no hermeneutical catastrophe lurking behind dark interpretive corners if the biblical constructs of a community lead to both sectarian understandings and even the sort of anarchy in which the community may indulge a nation-state's claimed monopoly on authority. But the congregation is free to test and challenge laws and demands of the state through a hermeneutic process that is wholly contingent on the biblical narrative and not upon the fear of consequences. Such praxis can sometimes result in martyrdom or imprisonment. Yet, such are the consequences of maintaining an ethic that intends to make sense of reality in a manner that is dependent upon the interpretation of Scripture and believes that God is the final arbiter of history. Returning to Derrida, an interpretive community must discard the need to make the Bible universally true or universally authoritative. This begins the deconstructive process that allows for the hermeneutical theme of repetition to be fully engaged. The point of deconstructing the text is "to expose limitations, to de-limit the authority of every assertion which sets

---

28. Yoder, *Priestly Kingdom*, 25. Just one example of many where Yoder uses the theme of anarchism in a pejorative sense.

itself up as authoritative."[29] Removing any propositional claims about the contents of the biblical text reduces the opportunities for interpretations to become oppressive when embodied by believers. Yet, Derrida does not want to destroy all authority, as Yoder fears, but instead he wishes to eliminate absolute authority; he further supposes that all authority is suspect, being *only as credible as the results they produce!*

We then turn to Yoder to identify how the text can be authoritative and to his discussion of the believer's church practice of binding and loosing as gleaned from Matthew 18:15–22. The text gains its authority through the meaning given to it by an interpretive community that reads the gospel together and corporately enacts the interpretation. The authority lays in the text as it provides a boundaried discourse through which church understandings are developed, dialogue takes place, and forgiveness for interpretive disagreements can be a priority. Discipline is not the primary result of the Matthean pericope, but rather a means of reconciling voluntary members of the congregations who have disagreements or hurt one another. Where two or three are gathered, the praxis of a community can be established through engagement with the hermeneutical circle. Whatever a community binds together becomes a new possibility or a deeper understanding of tradition and ongoing praxis. Whatever is loosed by the community means the repetitive process has led to the rejection of a particular interpretation, and the members of the community may choose to leave or to continue with behaviors and be continuously forgiven upon repentance.

Caputo suggests that repetition and hermeneutics are important due to the following: the church, and its adherence to a truly biblical ethic, represents an attempt to "restore the difficulty of life, not to make it impossible."[30] Faithfulness is a difficult proposition. The difficulty lays in reading the text "for all its worth." The impossible part may be using a text that has little meaning despite attempts to make it universally authoritative so that any use of the text in the discussion of social, religious, or controlling narratives makes the text, and the Christian ethic, unintelligible—and a rather empty and in-credible witness at best.

29. Caputo, *Radical Hermeneutics*, 196
30. Ibid., 209.

Chapter 2

Dark Shadows of the Enlightenment

"The Good Book says . . . ," recites Tevye the milkman, as he considers a matter of spiritual import in the musical *Fiddler on the Roof*. "As the Good Book says, when a poor man eats a chicken, one of them is sick."

Mendel retorts, "Where does the book say that?"

"Well, it doesn't say that exactly, but somewhere there is something about a chicken."[1]

Popular culture is a reliable source of biblical amusement, with its various appeals to the authority of Scripture. Television sitcoms of the 1970s offer plenty of examples. Consider this theological nugget from the character of Archie Bunker in Norman Lear's *All in the Family*.

Archie states, "Now, no prejudice intended, but, you know, I always check with the Bible on these here things. I think that . . . I mean if God had meant for us to be together, He'da put us together. But look what He done. He put you over in Africa, and put the rest of us in all the white countries."

Sammy Davis Jr. responds, "Well, He must've told 'em where we were because somebody came and got us. You know, they had work for us . . ."[2]

The above illustrations are only two of the variety of ways in which popular culture relies upon an assumed public acquaintance with Scripture. They provide examples of the way the arts develop stock characters for the purpose of humor. Some characters will cite the authority of sacred texts in the belief that it will somehow add legitimacy to their often-absurd claims. Additionally, this existential fallacy creates levity when the plot calls for such a maneuver, as in *Fiddler* when Tevye attempts to make sense of his lack of fortune or, similarly, when Archie attempts to address the issues of

---

1. Jewison, *Fiddler on the Roof*.
2. Lear, "Sammy's Visit."

racism from his hopelessly prejudiced perspective while in the presence of a successful African-American.

Yet, while appeals to Scripture are often a vehicle for the amusement of Americans, the use of the Bible to buoy moral claims that are otherwise not seaworthy is a concern for those persons and communities that attempt to generate a faithful, biblically informed ethic. More serious is the ever-increasing number of moral constructs of human agency and ethics that claim a foundation in Christian thought, yet often avoid supporting such moral vision with the resources of the canon.

It might be presumed that Christian ethics are necessarily biblical in nature, and that Christian ethics and biblical ethics are one and the same. Not surprisingly, academics from all corners take issue with this assumption. However, the greater issue is the probability that the "stock characters"[3] of our own communities not only assume that an unarguable authority exists in religious texts, but that the moral claims they may or may not have gleaned from Scripture are universally valid. The contemporary problem of staking out a claim for the Bible's place in constructing Christian ethics has often been predicated on the absurdities of populism or self-righteous piety or—often more to the point—that all such appeals to religious texts as a resource for moral assumptions are inherently detrimental to the exercise of doing ethics, Christian or otherwise.[4]

3. MacIntyre, *After Virtue*. MacIntyre fully develops a theme of the "stock characters" of narrative and community self-understanding. MacIntyre "chooses the word 'character' . . . because of the way it links dramatic and moral associations" (27). Also, "Characters are masks worn by moral philosophers" (28), yet he states that "the requirements of *character* are imposed from the outside, from the way in which others regard and use *characters* to understand and evaluate themselves" (29). It should not be surprising that many political "conservatives" somehow identified with Archie Bunker as a legitimate character who could sympathize with their "suffering" during a time of radical upheaval. The radical social elements of *All in the Family* were characterized by a daughter and son-in-law who always acted as a liberal foil to Archie's conservative assumptions.

4. Jessica Taylor of National Public Radio covered a political event that provides an excellent example of how the Bible and an individual's assumptions can produce chaos in some circumstances, if not more simply a comedy of errors. On January 18, 2016, the populist candidate Donald Trump, while running for the Republican Party's nomination to the office of President of the United States, spoke at Liberty University, a fundamentalist Christian educational institution founded by the politically conservative evangelist Jerry Falwell. The professional and electronic media paid special attention to what were considered to be religious or theological missteps attributed to Trump's convocation speech. He showed a certain lack of biblical familiarity by referring to Second Corinthians as "Two Corinthians," citing 3:17 ("Now the Lord is that Spirit: and where the Spirit of the Lord is, there is liberty") while saying, "that's the whole ballgame . . . Is that the one you like?" Taylor wrote, "There were a few stumbles during Donald Trump's sojourn to Liberty University on Monday. He mispronounced a book of the Bible. He cursed—twice. And on Martin Luther King Day, the GOP presidential candidate said

Consider the late James Nash's 2008 contribution to discussions of the Bible and bioethics.[5] Nash writes candidly about his belief not only that Scripture is rather non-committal on the issue of environmentalism, but also that even the Christian proponents of earth care fail to produce credible biblical support for prioritizing the maintenance of biodiversity in any way. Nash does not believe this indicates a moral quandary, insisting rather that "Christian ethics is not synonymous with biblical ethics. Much more than Scripture is needed to do ethics." In fact, Nash does away with Scripture altogether as the potential informant of Christian contributions to bioethics.

For many who identify as Christians, the Bible is anxiety-producing in matters related to articulating a vision to address the moral dilemmas of the United States. As indicated in the article by Nash, there are people of faith that write about Christian ethics without citing biblical support. Yet, for more than a century there have been ongoing ethical constructs that address the issue of Christian morality and ethics; and while being welcome contributions to the discipline (especially, as I will show is the case with individuals such as Reinhold Niebuhr), they remove the task from any biblical center. There is evidence that the Bible is now considered by many to present a problem for Christian ethicists. First, the Bible as an authority is as contingent as the interpretation of its meaning by diverse communities of faith. Second, the Bible has become enough of a political force in the United States that interpretation of the text is often undertaken with a latent authority given to political preferences and economic realities. Finally, the fact that systematic readings of the Bible, attempts at systematic theologies, and systematic ethics have all failed to actually produce a systematically biblical anything often leaves those who would otherwise cite it as an authority embarrassed at its contents.

---

he was honoring the slain civil-rights leader by dedicating to him the record crowds he says he drew for the school's opening convocation. (Students are required to attend.) 'We're going to protect Christianity. I can say that. I don't have to be politically correct,' he thundered at the beginning of his speech at the conservative evangelical university." Taylor, "Citing 'Two Corinthians,'" para. 3–4.

5. Nash, "Bible vs. Biodiversity," 215. Nash's criticism of "biblical ethics" is fully developed and indicting. The article focuses entirely on the whether the Bible authorizes earth care and the protection of biodiversity. He writes, "the Bible, on the whole, fails the test as one should expect when ancient texts are used . . . to legitimate contemporary concerns." Also, Nash claims to be "a Christian ethicist . . . who is deeply troubled by the misuse of Scripture," and somewhat disingenuously applies his criticism of the use of the Bible to his allies concerned with passion for bioethics as well as his enemies. Nash will not accept any positive contributions supported by the text, regardless of the hermeneutics involved in the construction of a bibliocentric earth care mandate. He states, "I know of no coherent hermeneutical process or principle that can transform this neutral or negative outlook into the justification of bio-responsibility."

However, there is also evidence of problematic dogmatism in the secular world as it attempts to articulate a moral code that can be applied universally to any apparent dilemma before an individual or community. While Christian ethicists have moved away from the biblical text as a primary informant of ethics, they have accepted the assumptions of secular thought. As such, a Christian ethic may be difficult to discern when used to achieve the goals of secular ethical concerns.

Reason, Ethics, and Emotivism

One of the first demands of the Age of Enlightenment and later modernist thought was that individuals move beyond looking to Scripture or religion as primary resources for backing moral truth claims. Because the Bible and its assertions of morality, history and science, and truth were all historically and socially contingent—reflecting ancient knowledge and an unscientific worldview dependent on religious myth—it was not a trustworthy authority. Truth claims, it was proposed, gain their credibility through navigating the process of empiricism.[6] The scientific method became the anchor of moral discourse. Reason took the place of the Bible as the foundation for moral discernment and universal truth claims for most in the Western world. Interestingly enough, the same claims that Christians made about the Bible and the notion of a god revealing itself in history were made by the Enlightenment and modernist philosophers themselves—that there must be a universal truth that is not contingent on any human construct but stands alone as an existential authority unconstrained by the boundaries of historical time and place, or social understandings. The differences are dependent upon how one discerns such truth—through reason and scientific method, or supernatural revelation.[7]

6. Thiel, *Nonfoundationalism.* "Enlightenment thinkers cited the irreconcilable inconsistencies in Scripture as evidence that the sacred text was at best a reasonably defensible collection of moral dictates, at worst, poor history, and by no means what the Christian tradition claimed it to be—the divinely revealed world of God" (44). Modernism, being the offspring of Enlightenment ideals, operates according the following epistemological claim: "Modernists believe that there are asocial and ahistorical moral principles and that these principles are necessary if the moral appraisal of social practices is to be possible." Ruf, *Postmodern Rationality,* 34. Ruf writes that modernist thinking demands that contingency-free "concepts, propositions, and meanings do exist. Furthermore, they argue that the socially invariable and the timeless must be postulated in order to account for socially different people at different times being able to say the same thing, for one person's ability to deny what another person says . . ." (33).

7. Some of the basic assumptions of the Enlightenment reflect the same basic assumptions of religious dogmatics. For instance, the Enlightenment was concerned with

The aims of Enlightenment and later modernist agendas, negatively stated, remain to marginalize regional and localized narratives of truth in hopes of "liberating" individuals from the baggage of their own provincialism. What has occurred over time, and perhaps sooner than one could imagine, is that the Enlightenment, while promoting democracy as the most reasonable means of liberating humanity from the tyranny of religion and myth, has had to settle upon utilitarianism as the philosophy that stakes out the claim as being most democratic in its aims and outcomes.

Also called consequentialism, the thinking is that moral vision should be driven by the ability to produce outcomes that are favorable to a majority of stakeholders, in terms of increased happiness or absence of pain. (Some definitions prefer the term "welfare" over "happiness.") Consequentialism is described as a "theory of responsibility," meaning that consequences alone should be taken into account when making judgments about right and wrong.[8] More briefly, utilitarianism/consequentialism aims to achieve results that produce favored outcomes for the majority with the hope that the unfavorable consequences are minimized for others. Perhaps another term is "situational" or "contextual" ethics.

Such a manner of "doing ethics" is not only contrary to the assumptions proposed by proponents of biblical ethics, but presents obstacles for

---

establishing universal truth, though such truth was based on logic such as evidenced by the rules of mathematics and physics rather than the "whims" of culture and myth. As we stand in the long shadow cast by science since the Enlightenment, Hauerwas writes that "we accord to science the primary status for the nature of truth. Subjected to sciences verification criteria, religion seems to be merely opinion. While science cannot establish the truth of certain hypotheses, it at least has tests for falsity . . ." Hauerwas, *Peaceable Kingdom*, 14. Modernity insists upon data that is verifiable, or falsifiable, as a means to arrive at truth. As such, modernity has led to the discipline of science demanding a place of primacy as a means of asserting and legitimizing all truth claims. "One is a scientist if one can produce verifiable or falsifiable statements about referents accessible to the experts." Lyotard, *Postmodern Condition*, 25. Lyotard would identify religious claims as narrative claims. As to the authority or legitimacy of types of knowledge, while science appeals to itself as an authority, it holds all other knowledge to scientific standards if those narratives are to be considered for discussion, even when the subject is morality or ethics. However, since religious narratives are neither verifiable or refutable, science refuses to legitimize religious claims, and in the process, makes the scientific method just as self-legitimizing as religions, myths, or any other contingency-based claims. Ibid., 25. As such, science establishes itself as what Lyotard refers to as a "metanarrative," an epistemological proposal that insists it is the center of all knowledge and relevant discourse.

8. Mautner, *Dictionary of Philosophy*, 636–67, 119–20. Ogletree describes Consequentialism as challenging individuals "to calculate the likely result of their actions, and to access their relative goodness (or badness) for human well-being. They drive home the point that the quality of the overall outcome of action is what counts, however that outcome may be achieved." Ogletree, *Use of the Bible in Christian Ethics*, 20–21.

most Christian ethicists who favor a firm and universal moral "justice" to an ethic based upon the realization of widespread happiness.[9] Nevertheless, it has become difficult to discern between Christian ethics and secular ethics, as the criteria for both has become a practice in personal preferences over a practice in reasoning or democracy. As MacIntyre writes, such a moral discourse was doomed to fail—and it has failed. The result, presented by postmodern thinker Lyotard as well, has been the replacement of moral discourse with emotivist argumentation, a manner of promoting a specific value over another based not upon evidence but upon the achievement of an individual's favored outcome. Both secular and Christian thinking have fallen victim to this "error."[10] Additionally, in light of the individualism demanded by the proponents of empiricism and utilitarianism, any other ethical practices that assume an overarching or existential truth exists are bound to be frustrated.[11] MacIntyre writes in *After Virtue* that "all moral judgments are *nothing but* expressions of preference, expressions of attitude or feeling, insofar as they are moral or evaluative in character."[12]

Also, there is more to utilitarian moral vision and ethics than facts and numbers, upon which empirical reasoning and utilitarianism base their actions. The morality of emotivism is always to be differentiated from what is factual. Writes MacIntyre, "We use moral judgments not only to express our own feelings and attitudes, but also precisely to produce such effects in

9. Hauerwas, *Peaceable Kingdom*, 117. For Christians, situational ethics demands that one ought to ask themselves the question of what should be done in response to a particular event that demands a response. Hauerwas writes that this question "tempts us to assume that moral situations are abstracted from the kind of people we are and the history we have come to be" (ibid.). Also, "Our society seems to generally think that to be moral, to act in a responsible manner, is to pursue our desires fairly, that is, in a manner that does not impinge on anyone else's freedom" (9).

10. MacIntyre, *After Virtue*, chap. 3; Lyotard, *Postmodern Condition*, 12. Hauerwas writes that "Protestants could only assume that Christian ethics was little different from the consensus of whatever culture they found themselves a part. This is most strikingly illustrated by Protestantism's inability to be more than a national church." Hauerwas, *Peaceable Kingdom*, 52.

11. Lyotard, *Postmodern Condition*, 9–10. He should be understood as stating that all contemporary moral discourse is emotivist, and is therefore competitive. Lyotard cites Ludwig Wittgenstein's premise of language games. Moral discourse is the game board upon which participants calculate and persuade others by verbalizing preferences in a way that can trump another's argument with a final word that either wears down an opponent or wins new adherents to one's own side as a participant in the game. Such argumentation is most always reliant upon claims or statements intended to take advantage of another's emotions concerning a specific topic, which in turn excludes reasoning from the process.

12. MacIntyre, *After Virtue*, 12. Italics original.

others." [13] Excellent examples are found in debate over "hot topic" issues like abortion, capital punishment, war, same-sex marriage, and a plethora of other "dilemmas" in the church. Christians often appeal to God's universal and undeniable moral authority, despite the consistent disagreements that often occur between Christians themselves. More interestingly emotivist is the process by which Christians pursue public policy with appeals to religious moral assumptions while basing their arguments upon empirical data or a manner of reasoning that conflicts with the very definition of faith.

More often observed but often less grasped by participants in moral debate is evidence that contradicts the view that reasoning (scientific method or empiricism) or democratic vision (emancipation from provincial narratives and contingencies) can deliver a universally held agreement on what is morally sound and what is not. Also, at least in the Western world, emotivism is a practice not only in individual self-justification, according to Lyotard, but in the continuing justification of present economic, legal, or class systems. He writes that any other claims that fail to justify the *status quo* are considered "dysfunctional."[14] In such an environment, the matter of ethics can hardly be discussed in a manner that can be deemed "liberating."

There is a latent aspect of emotivism-*qua*-utilitarianism that should be acknowledged. As is especially true of the social sciences and the discipline of philosophy, it appears as though, despite all of the promises of reasoning and the liberation of individuals from their provincial loyalties, modernism has marginalized the opportunities for outcomes that can ever be recognized as universal truths, even by a majority of persons in many cases.[15] Hauerwas writes:

13. Ibid. MacIntyre further states that moral discourse is competitive (like the language games of Lyotard and Wittgenstein before), won by the individual who displays "the greatest appearance of clear, undoubting conviction," which in turn leads to the appearance of the victor's access to universal truth." The problem of utilitarianism is that moral discourse contains little more than a false sense of reasoned authority through an appeal to "an objective and impersonal criterion but in reality is simply a display of rhetorical skill." Ibid., 17.

14. Lyotard, *Postmodern Condition*, 12. He believes self-justification in Western culture is epitomized in "bureaucracy." To sum, Lyotard believes that that which passes for moral discourse in the Western world must anticipate projected outcomes that somehow serve or benefit the "establishment." Contributions to mainstream moral conversations are not allowed status of credibility if it suggests a challenge to the metanarratives of the hard sciences, social sciences, or political and economic processes that are currently practiced by the authoritative political regimes.

15. Ruf, *Postmodern Rationality*. He writes, "Modernist theorists, it seems, can't be moved by someone else to end their philosophical projects . . . Their reasons may be nothing but unexamined pictures that are forcing their reasoning to move along pre-channeled lines, but this is something they must find out for themselves" (94). In *After*

attempts to secure such an [universal] ethic inevitably results in a minimalistic ethic and often one which gives support to forms of cultural imperialism. Indeed, when Christians assume that their particular moral convictions are independent of narrative, that they are justified by some universal standpoint free from history, they are tempted to imagine that those who do not share such an ethic are particularly perverse and should be coerced to do what we know on universal grounds they really should want to do.[16]

Think about contemporary moral debate, or better yet, persuasion, in terms of the Christian call to evangelize. Emotivism is a primary tool, not reluctantly used, of many Christians who prioritize sharing themes of eternal "damnation" as a primary means of bringing non-believers to "faith," or of provoking others to affirm the favored moral stance so as not to offend God. Writes MacIntyre, "The sole reality of distinctive moral discourse is the attempt of one will to align the attitudes, feelings, and preferences and choices of another as its own." For MacIntyre, utilitarianism and emotivism reduces relationships with others to the point where "others are always a means, never ends."[17]

Democracy, Christendom, and Reality

Just as consequentialism and situational ethics would seem to be at odds with Christian ethics, it is a common course run by many who believe the church must display an ethic that is relevant to contemporary secular concerns and secular society. For the church to be relevant, its ethicists often decide to take up moral issues according to terms established by public policy makers, secular sociopolitical professionals, and those parties committed to the

---

Virtue, MacIntyre writes, "The most striking feature of modern moral argumentation is that moral disagreements are expressed in their interminable character. I do not mean by this just that such debates go on and on . . . but also that they apparently can find no terminus. There seems to be no rational way of securing moral agreement in our culture" (6). He later adds, "contemporary moral argument is rationally interminable because *all* moral . . . [and] evaluative argument must be rationally interminable. Contemporary moral disagreement of a certain kind cannot be resolved because *no* moral disagreement in any age, past, present, or future, can be resolved" (11). Though this successfully reasoned positive outcome is the promise of the Enlightenment, it has never shown it can be delivered. Since "writers cannot agree . . . ," he writes, "on the character of morality," and participants in moral discourse "cannot secure agreement on the formulation of principles from colleagues who share their basic philosophical purpose and method, there is . . . *prima facie* evidence that their project has failed" (21).

16. Hauerwas, *Peaceable Kingdom*, 61.

17. MacIntyre, *After Virtue*, 24.

maintenance of liberal democracy as the corporate arbiter of moral imperatives. Such consequentialist accommodation is evident, for example, in the
work of Reinhold Niebuhr, the foremost proponent of "Christian realism."

Lovin's summary of Niebuhr's ethics provides an in-depth overview of
Christian realism. He writes that "we may begin to understand Christian realism . . . by taking it seriously as a version of political realism. The reality in
question is the multiplicity of forces that drive the decisions that people actually make in situations of political choice."[18] Lovin rightly states that Niebuhr
was highly influential in the realm of politics and policy, and was considered
the premier Christian ethicist for many decades. For Christian realism, one
must "not rely on moral argument alone . . . nor should we overestimate the
power of moral suasion to determine the course of events."[19] An illustrative
narrative that puts Christian realism and Niebuhr's ethics in perspective is his
stance on war. During the early part of the twentieth century, Niebuhr was
a Christian pacifist. In response to World War I and the attending violence
leading up to the war, he turned away from the pacifist witness, hoping that a
victory by democratic nations could bring a lasting and just peace.[20]

While Niebuhr instituted a new Christian ethical standard, his prede-
cessor, Walter Rauschenbusch, provides an ideal example of emotivist ethical reasoning in the establishment of his "social gospel" movement. Prior
to Niebuhr's concern with *realpolitik*, Rauschenbusch had also prioritized
the propagation of democracy as the foundation of his own work. His assumptions about democracy were obvious but the nature of his focus on the

18. Lovin, *Reinhold Niebuhr and Christian Realism*, 4. "To be 'realistic' . . . Niebuhr
suggests, is to take all realities into account. None should be overlooked and each
should be assigned a weight that reflects its real effect on the course of events, rather
than its place on our own scale of values."

19. Ibid. Lovin believes that Niebuhr's influence in Washington, DC, was so significant because the consequentialist ethic supplied space for "political leaders and
diplomats, who were caught between the idealism of democracy and the brutal realities
of international politics." Ibid., 4–5.

20. Reinhold Niebuhr, "Must We Do Nothing?" See also Niebuhr's WWII article,
"Why the Christian Church Is Not Pacifist." Another defining element of Niebuhr's
theological journey is his rejection of the continuing pacifist stance of a theologian
that was integral to his own development. Walter Rauschenbusch continued to preach
pacifism well into the First World War as part of his Social Gospel movement. Many of
Rauschenbusch's Social Gospelers abandoned pacifism as well as Niebuhr, and this turn
of commitment led to the establishment of his theology of Christian realism. According
to Lovin, Niebuhr's major criticisms of Rauschenbusch are that his "writings shared . . .
sentimental piety's one fundamental confusion: the moral vision of the New Testament
is treated as a 'simple possibility.' It becomes a key point of Christian realism that the
ethics of Jesus cannot provide a social ethic." Lovin, *Reinhold Niebuhr and Christian
Realism*, 5.

gospels as the informant of Christian ethics tends to make the commitment to democracy seem more nuanced than it really is.

Rauschenbusch wrote as though he had one foot in the sixteenth-century Reformation debate, or perhaps in the library of Wycliffe. "The Bible hereafter will be 'the People's Book' in a new sense . . . directing religious energy by scientific knowledge [so] that a comprehensive and continuous reconstruction of social life . . . is written within the bounds of human possibility." And later, "Where religion and intellect combine," he wrote in *Theology for the Social Gospel*, "the foundation is laid for political democracy."[21]

One can interpret Rauschenbusch's work as an attempt to bring the gospel into the twentieth century by applying the hermeneutical lenses of human reasoning and the methods of the social sciences to biblical interpretation. However, the hermeneutic seemed less focused on interpreting Scripture in a way in which it could inform and guide the social gospel movement than on fitting the appropriate proof-texts into the foundation of an already established, well-reasoned theology. What followed was an implicit proposition that democracy is in some way a divine construct and thus carries out the will of God—and perhaps resulted in a preference to articulate the will of God in the more private confines of ballot boxes. This reduced the use of the Bible to those proof-texts that seemed to underwrite the nation-state's priorities or, more likely, the priorities of those Christians who were most invested in the manner in which the nation-state was to be governed.[22]

21. Hauerwas, "Democratic Policing of Christianity," 217. He writes, "According to Rauschenbusch the new social sciences have discovered the plasticity of human society as well as the inherent organic character of social relations. For example, through the new biblical sciences and historical method we are being put in the position of the original readers of each book, thus making the Bible more life-like and social. "We used to see the sacred landscape through allegorical interpretation as through a piece of yellow bottle-glass. It was very golden and wonderful, but very much apart from our everyday modern life. The Bible hereafter will be 'the people's book" in a new sense. For the first time in religious history we have the possibility of so directing religious energy by scientific knowledge that a comprehensive and continuous reconstruction of social life in the name of God is within the bounds of human possibility." In short, Rauschenbusch writes, "Where religion and intellect combine, the foundation is laid for political democracy." Rauschenbusch, *Theology for the Social Gospel*, 165.

22. I here follow Cartwright, *Practices, Politics, and Performance*, 59. He quotes *Rauschenbusch's Christianity and the Social Order*: "Democracy aids in Christianizing the social order by giving political and economic expression to" Christianity's "fundamental view of the worth of man." Rauschenbusch uses the Bible as providing historical legitimacy for the claim that Jesus is representative of the Christian ethic, and tends to view American liberalism as the natural extension of Jesus' unchallengeable authority." Read Gary Dorrien's "Rauschenbusch's *Christianity and Social Crisis*," which states in a generally positive review that Rauschenbusch's supporters were "sentimental,

Thus, three distinct occurrences of thought have had a major impact upon the manner in which the Bible is used to inform a specifically Christian ethic. First, the intellectual turns brought about by the Enlightenment, and the subsequent marginalizing of story and myth as tools of human understanding by modernist philosophers, who insisted the text be viewed with suspicion as a credible contributor within discussions of moral vision and reasoned ethical constructs.

A second occurrence was the application of modern reasoning and a sort of scientific method to the practice of biblical ethics. Rauschenbusch is considered by many as a primogenitor of modern biblical hermeneutical method. We might consider, however, that Rauschenbusch's interpretive move (which, we will see, cannot and should not be done away with) had more to do with making Christendom a relevant voice in an always-progressing American social milieu and within the realm of American democracy, which for many "social gospelers" might have been viewed as the divinely mandated *zeitgeist.*

Thirdly, we have the work of Niebuhr, who had reached a point in the drive for theology to be relevant to American geopolitics, where the biblical narrative was not only unrealistic, but the ethics exemplified by the gospel accounts were deemed by Niebuhr to be counterintuitive and delusional. The very premise of Christian realism was that the realities of the contemporary world were far beyond the scope of any moral considerations of the early Christians trying to adhere to a new messianic ethic.

The above intellectual movements, beginning in full force after the American Civil War and finally leading us to the Christian ethics exemplified by Nash, are the product of more than a century of modernist thought and the practice of emotion-laden, interminable argumentation—interminable because of the very nature of what both modernity and American religious commentators believe to be absolute: that there somewhere exists, whether in reason or divine revelation, a universal and totally non-contingent truth. In pursuit of this truth, modernity has produced its own dogma to counter the propositional claims of religion, and the practitioners of religion have

---

moralistic, idealistic and politically naive. [The book] preached a gospel of cultural optimism and a Jesus of middle-class idealism. It was culturally chauvinist and thoroughly late-Victorian. It spoke the language of triumphal missionary religion, sometimes baptized the Anglo-Saxon ideology of Manifest Destiny, and usually claimed that American imperialism was not really imperialism, since it had good intentions . . . It created the ecumenical movement in the U.S., but it had a strongly Protestant, anti-Catholic idea of ecumenism, and Rauschenbusch was especially harsh on this topic. Most social gospel leaders vigorously opposed World War I until the U.S. intervened, whereupon they promptly ditched their opposition to war (with the brave exception of Rauschenbusch)." Dorrien, "Rauschenbusch's *Christianity and Social Crisis*," para. 11.

claimed for their own use the basic assumptions of empiricism to argue against a relative upstart of an opponent—"pure reason."

To consider the current state of Christian contributions to the discourse of moral vision and ethics, one must consider the concerns put forth above. All of those concerns have resulted in a church that strives to influence secular moral discourse through the pursuit and maintenance of political power, emotionally charged rhetoric, and continuing claims of universally valid propositional truths that are revealed by the God of Abraham and Sarah, and Scripture. While Scripture is often used in a questionable manner to promote or support either side of an ethics discussion, that fact remains that such references to the text hold weight with many individuals who do not otherwise read or interpret the Bible with a critical eye or listening ear. As such, the Bible is often an emotionally charged means to justifying a politically favorable end within the democratic process, as opposed to being the primary interpretive tool by which the church can realize its anticipated end as a revelatory body through which the kingdom of God might be fully realized.

Presently, I will address each of the problems that serve as obstacles to the realization of a credible ethic, or more aptly put, a plurality of meaningful Christian ethics. I will also respond to the growing absence of the use of Scripture to articulate and support an ethic that is considered credible by secular scholarship and public policy standards. Additionally, I will deliver an account of a Christian ethic that will provide an example of how such an ethic, or such ethics, can be constructed and embodied with the purpose of bearing spiritual, moral, and loving fruit.

The Concern for a Universal Truth

The logic of many contemporary moralists—that a fundamental, universal, transcendent truth or reality exists—is not limited to propositional claims about gods or religion; the same insistence exists in the world of science and in many modern philosophical projects. While it might be assumed that most attempts to construct a Christian or biblical ethic might rely upon overarching propositional claims,[23] it may seem surprising that secular ethical or moral

---

23. Lindbeck, *Nature of Doctrine*, 64–66. Lindbeck believes, in contrast to thinking represented below, that the possibility that a propositional truth must exist must be allowed for. He defines propositional claims as those statements "which function as informative propositions about objective realities" (16). Lindbeck rightly suggests that such claims illustrate an Enlightenment preoccupation with "the cognitive and informational meaningfulness of religious utterances." He also differentiates between his definition of propositional truths and those truth claims that he regards as

formulations are also founded upon some claim of unsurpassble authority or universal truth that is deemed to be transcendent of diverse cultural and linguistic particulars. Such claims were thought to be possible to realize through a process of reasoning and the administration of the scientific method.[24]

A brief example of this notion is evident in a randomly chosen peer-reviewed journal article entitled "A Short List of Universal Moral Values." The 2000 article is the product of psychology and counseling professionals who seek to show that, in a world that is increasingly unwilling to accept universals, there are some propositions such as "the Golden Rule" that are held true across the wide spectrum of ethical guidelines, from fundamental religious beliefs to secular statements of moral vision. At the end of the article, the social science academics propose a "short list" of transcendent values that are witnessed across religious and secular expressions. To be brief, the authors state that it is universally held that individuals should commit to something greater than one's self. Individuals should display healthy self-respect, which should be tempered by humility, self-discipline, and accountability. The article lists the act of treating others as you would have yourself treated as the third universal, and then further delineates ethical standards that flesh out this "Golden Rule" more formally. Finally, it is stated that human beings should show respect for other animals and for the environment.[25] The assumptions operating in the article are that treating

"noninformative and nondiscursive symbols of inner feelings, attitudes, or existential orientations" and calls "experiential-expressive" claims. Thirdly, Lindbeck offers a hybrid of "cognitively propositional and expressively symbolic," which he submits is favored by Catholicism. The nature of creedal and dogmatic religious expression often mandates that once a truth is stated, it must always be defended as truth, and that all meaning and understanding must be built upon the foundations of statements originally intended to transcend their historical context.

24. Gadamer, *Truth and Method*. Gadamer implicitly supports Lyotard's view that "The old principle that the acquisition of knowledge is indissociable from training of minds, or even of individuals, is becoming obsolete . . ." by declaring that hermeneutics and the acceptance of historical reflection and criticisms "demolished the claim of classical antiquity to be normative." Gadamer, *Truth and Method*, 156; and Lyotard, *Postmodern Condition*, 4. I suspect that Lyotard's critique of science and academia are implicit in Gadamer's thinking. Just as Lyotard states that the sciences both physical and social are self-legitimating, Gadamer proposes that classical thought can no longer be identified as a "normative" springboard for modern historical criticism's distaste of postmodern "technique," or individual intellectual itinerary, as it were.

25. Kiner et al., "Short List of Universal Moral Values." This article is by no means intended to represent any cross-section of literature, but more to the point I use it to represent the idea that there are universally held truths, and at least in the case of this article, those universals are purported to be of use to therapists and other helping professionals in stabilizing or introducing a sense of reasonable means and ends in the minds of those seeking help. MacIntyre is particularly harsh on the social sciences and the manner in

others well, respecting all, and serving the other represent themes that have an easily understood nature and are capable of producing a fixed meaning across any cultural divides.

Yet, as Gadamer states in *Truth and Method*, meaning is *not* fixed. Any idea or statement can be no more than a product of its own unique time and place in history. Historical inquiry reveals that the literature of the past and the claims about truth made in such literature reflect the peculiarities of time and location. Most hermeneutical methods include the use of historical criticism to "properly" interpret texts, ancient or otherwise. However, there is even an important caveat to this apparent universal "technique." The interpreters must access and be aware of their own techniques, their own particular "understandings," and their own relationship to the text. As such, the meaning drawn from the text or truth claim is contingent upon the epistemological and ontological moorings of the interpreters. One cannot come to the text void of such "baggage."[26]

Might it be said that even a text written specifically for and about a specific time in history may at least provide indisputable claims about that sociological setting? Gadamer illustrates an issue that is common to the interpreter who fails to understand her own subjectivity. He cites Schleiermacher as conceiving of hermeneutics as a "reconstructive completion of the production" of a text. Implicit is the sense that the interpreter can access, through the

---

which this discipline seeks to self-justify its therapeutic practices through the presentation of data and empirically based predictable therapeutic outcomes. Reading the Kiner et al. article, one may not get the sense that empirical data was used at all in arriving at conclusions, but rather, as I will show below, was more reliant upon cultural narratives than scientific method. Contra MacIntyre, *After Virtue*, ch. 6, "Some Consequences of the Failure of the Enlightenment Project." He not only challenges the claims of social sciences and management science as self-justifying, but illustrates the failure of emotivist-as-such concerns like "human rights" as indicative of universal claims that have as yet to be realized as being true, let alone transcendent truths. I mention this because the authors of "Universal Moral Values" cite the United Nations document *A Universal Declaration of Human Rights* as an example that universally held concepts are valid as moral claims—an assumption MacIntyre refutes due to the fact that any account of rights themselves is historically and culturally contingent. There is no real concept of human rights prior to the Enlightenment, nor is there a real concept of individual rights that must be protected by the nation-state prior to feudal contracts and later democratic regimes.

26. Gadamer, *Truth and Method*, 156–57. MacIntyre recognizes this and writes, "we moderns—that is, we seventeenth-century and eighteenth-century moderns—had stripped away interpretation and theory and confronted fact and experience just as they are. It is precisely in virtue of this that those moderns proclaimed and named themselves the Enlightenment . . . This conceit of course, as such conceits always are, is the sign of an unrecognized transition from one stance of theoretical interpretation to another. The Enlightenment is consequently the period *par excellence* in which most intellectuals lack self-knowledge." MacIntyre, *After Virtue*, 81.

process of historical inquiry, the meaning the author intends the text to have for others. The reader simply writes an additional, or as it may be, the final chapter to the text so that the original meaning transcends time. [27] In a search for the transcendent truth of a given text, one might simply need to recognize the author's intentions and apply them to modern circumstances.

However, "the artist who creates something is not the ideal interpreter of it," writes Gadamer. The author has no "automatic priority as an authority over the [one] who is receiving [the] work. *The meaning that [the author] gives is not authoritative."* While the issue of interpretation or truth is no closer to resolution at this point than at the beginning, one should be aware that the challenges of critical thought have reduced the need to stand by transcendence or universal understandings as necessary to either the effectiveness that a claim may have on moral vision or ethics, or to the necessity to have claims reasoned according to the fundamentals of the scientific method or objective interpretive structures.[28]

The proposal that facts and observed data alone can lead to the realization of distinct universal understandings of truth indeed undermined an important means of humans gaining and transmitting understandings of those facts and observed data. It is here that we find what an utter loss is suffered in allowing the sciences to marginalize storytelling, mythic memory, and meanings grounded in local understandings as being at least unreliable, if not an obstacle to the promises of liberating humanity that are articulated by so much of the Western world. Modernity and its monopolization of truth once relegated to religion and cultural mores have not only carried on the tradition of demanding universal understandings of reality, but have also succeeded in squeezing out all other prisms of meaning. Yet, the promises of liberation and unity continue unrealized and the credibility of Christian truth claims is often lacking as it becomes mired in just such reasoning.[29]

---

27. Gadamer, *Truth and Method*, 169.

28. Ibid., 170. Italics original.

29. See Godzich, afterword in Jean-Francois Lyotard, *Postmodern Explained*, 127–28. Prior to modernity, humans were bound to nature and one another through knowledge. "And this knowledge," Godzich writes, "one which individual and collective identities depended, was guaranteed by some divine instance or by some constitutive homology between humans and the world. Such knowledge permitted humans to act, to build a world of human relations that increased the sum of knowledge—that is, their set of relations, their mode of being in the world. With the advent of modernity, a change begins to take place in this economy: the old guarantees of knowledge cease to be true, and we are threatened with individual meaninglessness and collective tyranny, the latter understood as the arbitrary exercise of power . . . now knowledge is becoming autonomous from us instead of anchoring us in the world, of insuring stability of our being in the world . . ."

CHAPTER 3

Ethics of Babel and a Confused Faith

Imagine standing on the sidewalk at 11 Wall Street. You are in the middle of a crowd of passionate radicals gathered there to hold the New York Stock Exchange responsible for an economic downturn that has left much of the nation in financial dire straits. Whether the charges levied against the Stock Exchange are reflective of real or perceived malfeasance, the mood of the crowd, and much of the United States citizenry, is one of insurrection. Often repeated by the lips of more than a few activists is a quote from Thomas Jefferson:

"The tree of liberty must be refreshed from time to time with the blood of patriots and tyrants."

This quote originates with a letter sent by Jefferson to William Smith, an American diplomat in London. It is in reference to the conscripting of government militias to put down a Massachusetts armed uprising in 1787 known as Shay's Rebellion.

"God forbid," wrote Jefferson, "we should ever be 20 years without a rebellion. Let them take arms."[1] It is hard telling whether Jefferson's quote was tongue-in-cheek or he meant it to be taken literally. It really depends on whom, and how, one is interpreting it and, of course, what they want it to mean.

Individuals from the crowd are making speeches and exhorting the crowds to take political matters into their own hands. "The ballot box is failing us," one of the speakers shouts. "It is time to restore power to the people."

And then, a rather unkempt individual walks through the crowd and stands at the foot of the Golden Bull of Wall Street. The crowd sits at the foot of the stage, and men and women who are apparently "comrades" of this speaker are passing out leaflets that declare a new age of politics was dawning.

This man stands apart from the other speakers, however, as he does not use the aggressive language of the revolutionaries that spoke before him.

1. Horwitz, "Thomas Jefferson and the 'Blood of Tyrants,'" para. 4.

Listening to the speaker, he sounds more like a preacher and his references to God make you uncomfortable. Few people in this crowd of radicals have time for gods of any kind. They want to change and tear down everything. Yet, something he says catches your ear, though no one else seems to be moved by it despite the fact they hear the same words.

"But I say to you, love your enemies and pray for those who persecute you, so that you may be the children of your Father in heaven," he says, and his next statement seems directed at your inner being: "Be perfect, therefore, as your heavenly Father is perfect."[2]

It is evident that there are two very different narratives at work in the above act. Both, however, are easily identifiable to most Americans, whether they believe them to represent basic truths or otherwise. Despite evidence that each saying represents "polar opposite" points of view, many Americans have been comfortable collapsing the two historic possible responses to human conflict into a single, uniquely American narrative. For many, it is the ideals of democracy that place the commandments of Jesus beyond the contemporary context. In the twenty-first century, militarism is often considered noble, especially when it is undertaken in defense of innocents. As such, to oppose what the culture decides is a "just war" is to risk being a traitor to America. Hauerwas believes that American civil religion demands of the faithful that "whatever kind of Christian they may be or not be, their faith should be in harmony with what it means to be an American."[3]

Such civil religion has led Christendom to assume the following: Democracy is a political system that is divinely wrought so that differing religious beliefs are "subordinated to their common loyalty to America." As the story above points out, it has been rather easy for Americans to dismiss such biblical tenets as love for enemy in favor of the canon of American democracy. Hauerwas writes, "War is a moral necessity for Americans . . . [it is] America's central liturgical act necessary to renew our sense that we are a nation unlike other nations."[4] And, as is commonly said, and perhaps just as commonly believed, the United States identifies itself as a "Christian nation."[5] In this sense, can it be possible to understand the gospel in

2. Matt 5:43, 48 (NRSV).

3. Hauerwas, *War and the American Difference*, 4.

4. Ibid.

5. For an example of this view as related to conservative American political claims, especially in light of Hauerwas's assumptions, see Starnes, "Are We Still One Nation Under God?," para. 17, 25, 26. The article takes issue with a statement by President Barack H. Obama during a speech in which the author assumes that Obama declared that the United States in no longer "just a Christian nation." Starnes cites President George Washington to support his claim: "'While we are zealously performing the duties of

a manner that does not underwrite the policies and actions of Western democracies?

What appears to have occurred is that, as pragmatism desires, the institutional Christendom of the United States has come to insist that the only credible, legitimate, or perhaps reasonable interpretations of the Bible are those that do not bring to light the ways in which the biblical text, and the ethics we see embodied by Jesus' ministry, actually challenge or stand in outright conflict with American militarism, economics, politics, and social distinctions. It has become a matter of fact that the nation-state can almost count on American churches to read, preach, and proof-text the Bible in a manner that may or may not agree with government or capitalism or criminal justice, but certainly defends or actively works to maintain the status quo.

The relationship between American democracy and Christendom has produced a critical error in the project of constructing a contemporary biblical ethic. Presently, much of what is presented as Christian ethics fails to reflect both the manner in which God has worked through Jesus the Christ and, just as importantly, how Christians should act in order to reflect God's call to embody the life of the Christ. Proposing, or preaching and teaching, the supremacy of a peace and/or love ethic has proven to be a difficult task provided the Enlightenment and modernist assumptions that continue to undergird American Christendom's subjugation to the demands of liberal democracy.[6] The difficulty stems from what I identify as a core inconsistency between an ethic centered in Scripture and the very nature of democratic republicanism.

The beginning of the twentieth century provides an example of how modernist philosophical thought and politically liberal religion were combined to overcome the problems that the Bible apparently created for the articulation of Christian ethics. The Second Great Awakening had much to contribute to social progress during the first half of the nineteenth century. Yet, the church's support of women's rights and suffrage, the abolition

---

good citizens and soldiers, we certainly ought not to be inattentive to the higher duties of religion. To the distinguished character of Patriot, it should be our highest glory to add the more distinguished character of Christian." Sterns himself adds quotable statements to his essay: "And while the winds of change may sweep across the nation's capital—there stands a beacon of hope—a reminder that this nation of immigrants was built, not on sinking sand, but on a firm foundation, girded by Almighty God," followed with, "on this Fourth of July, the first ray's [sic] of morning light will shine down upon these United States of America—illuminating an eternal truth and a grateful nation's prayer-praise be to God!"

6. This statement is based on the work of a number of theological writers. The following list is intended to provide a cross-section of theological thinking that has been critical of Enlightenment and modernity as it relates to Christian ethics and the biblical text. Caputo, *Radical Hermeneutics*; Thiel, *Nonfoundationalism*; Ruf, *Postmodern Rationality;* Hauerwas, *Peaceable Kingdom*; MacIntyre, *After Virtue*; Yoder, *Priestly Kingdom*.

of slavery, the temperance movement, and care for the poor ebbed after the Civil War. Modernism heightened the level of skepticism concerning the credibility of Christian claims, and secular movements were growing in numbers and began to replace religious organizations as champions for social change. Socialist and communist movements gained footholds in American cities following the Civil War, and anarchists such as Emma Goldman were both highly sought after political speakers as well as candidates for exile or imprisonment. In the case of Goldman and many others, an all-out attack on Christianity was thought by them to be necessary to the liberation of humankind. Christian "activists" were either deemed too naive and lacking in reasoned approaches, or their theology was attacked by many churches who did not want to be suspected as anti-American socialists or union supporters.[7]

There was an additional problem for Christian ethics at the turn of the century, and it was identified as Scripture itself. The problem of the Bible was that content which was interpreted to underwrite slavery, subservience to rulers, war, and the continuing subjugation of women.[8] Such issues made up the bulk of leftist criticism. Conservative Christian congregations preached wholesale the themes of patriarchy, the righteousness of American war efforts, segregation, and the elimination of socialism.[9]

Walter Rauschenbusch inaugurated a response to this apparent problem of Scripture. He reprioritized Scripture and made it more appetizing for many Christian liberals through the application of historical and literary criticism. He consistently promoted the modern literary and interpretive concepts of hermeneutics as a manner in which references to the Bible's authority could coincide with contemporary advances in the social sciences. As such, reading his work can often make one feel as though she is reading a Marxist treatise or an early volume of liberation theology.[10]

That said, the "Social Gospel" movement was not only successful in winning over many Christians who might otherwise leave a religion that apparently had little to say about the matters of poverty, class, and gender, but it also initiated an attempt to legitimize the gospel as a contributor to the

7. For an excellent example of the relationship between religiously conservative Christians, the socialist movement in the United States, and union struggles, see the movie *Matewan*, directed by John Sayles. Based on a coal mining strike and union organizing in 1930s West Virginia, stock characters reflect the attitudes of conservative Baptists, social gospel Baptists, socialist union organizers, and an exploited working class. Interestingly, the socialist organizer is portrayed as an atheist, while the workers are portrayed as rather ambivalent toward religion.

8. Cartwright, *Practices, Politics, and Performance*, 8.

9. Powers, *Not Without Honor*, 51.

10. Rauschenbusch quotes Engels' *Condition of the Working Class in England* (1845). Rauschenbusch, *Christianity and the Social Crisis*, 216.

discussions of ethics and politics within the realm of modernist discourse. Whether or not Rauschenbusch succeeded in this, he certainly pioneered attempts to make Christian ethics relevant to public moral discourse. He interpreted the Bible as the main informant of American democracy. "Where religion and intellect combine," he wrote in *Theology for the Social Gospel*, "the foundation is laid for political democracy."[11] What followed was an implicit proposition that democracy is in some way a divine construct and thus carries out the will of God—and perhaps resulted in a preference to articulate the will of God in the more private confines of ballot boxes. This reduced the use of the Bible to those proof-texts that seemed to underwrite the nation-state's priorities or, at the very least, the priorities of those Christians who were most invested in the manner in which the nation-state was to be governed.[12]

It may be suggested that Rauschenbusch should be credited for reestablishing an American religious concern for the poor and exploited, and there is most likely little interest in highlighting his work as representative of negative contributions to Christian theology. However, the work he dedicated to the Social Gospel movement initiated an epistemological shift that resulted in the need for Christian ethics to prioritize political power and acquiescence to the supremacy of American narratives of individualism and democratic ideals. Later, this same type of shift was necessary to accommodate free-market economics over and against self-sufficient communities.

One of Rauschenbusch's biggest critics is in fact indebted to his work. Reinhold Niebuhr was a proponent of the Social Gospel while pastoring in Detroit. After growing a small congregation into one of the city's larger and

---

11. Hauerwas, "Democratic Policing of Christianity," 217.

12. I here follow Cartwright, *Practices, Politics, and Performance*, 59. He quotes Rauschenbusch's *Christianity and the Social Order*: "Democracy aids in Christianizing the social order by giving political and economic expression to" Christianity's "fundamental view of the worth of man." Rauschenbusch uses the Bible as providing historical legitimacy for the claim that Jesus is representative of the Christian ethic, and tends to view American liberalism as the natural extension of Jesus' unchallengeable authority. Read Dorrien's "Rauschenbusch's *Christianity and Social Crisis*" which states in a generally positive review that Rauschenbusch's supporters were "sentimental, moralistic, idealistic and politically naive. [The book] preached a gospel of cultural optimism and a Jesus of middle-class idealism. It was culturally chauvinistic and thoroughly late-Victorian. It spoke the language of triumphal missionary religion, sometimes baptized the Anglo-Saxon ideology of Manifest Destiny, and usually claimed that American imperialism was not really imperialism, since it had good intentions . . . It created the ecumenical movement in the U.S., but it had a strongly Protestant, anti-Catholic idea of ecumenism, and Rauschenbusch was especially harsh on this topic. Most social gospel leaders vigorously opposed World War I until the U.S. intervened, whereupon they promptly ditched their opposition to war (with the exception of Rauschenbusch), para. 14.

more influential churches, he became well known for his commitment to the labor movement, the plight of the working class, and his pacifism. However, while Rauschenbusch maintained his commitment to non-violence, Niebuhr's pacifism was challenged during World War I, and he supported the war effort against Germany as a possible step toward a lasting peace.[13] Niebuhr naturally followed Rauschenbusch closely in his thinking about democratic ideals; yet, he later called the Social Gospel movement naive and utopian, writing in 1944 at the height of World War II that American democracy was more realistic: "Man's capacity for justice makes democracy possible; but man's inclination to injustice makes democracy necessary."[14]

Reinhold Niebuhr bears witness to Rauschenbusch in two equally important ways: a concern for the Social Gospel, and a commitment to liberal democracy as the primary vehicle through which the good intentions of the church could be realized. Hauerwas writes that, "ironically, Niebuhr's justification of democracy turns out to be a legitimation of Protestant liberalism. His views appear less religiously specific than those of Rauschenbusch, but that is only because his account of Christianity had already been well policed by the requirements of sustaining democracy as a universal achievement."[15]

Another aspect of Niebuhr's theology bears mentioning. The more one explores Niebuhr's writing, the less it becomes possible to find references to the Bible as an informant of Niebuhr's ethics. In his quest for realism and relevancy to the American political system, the former proponent of the Social Gospel ostensibly found Scripture to be less than helpful. He was vague concerning the importance of the Bible to ethics, other than the text's capacity to articulate universal truths and assist in providing religious metaphors for reality. Niebuhr's prioritizing of democratic ideals and what he termed to be "Christian realism"[16] is evident in his work concerning the American civil rights movement of the fifties and sixties. One can observe the concern for relevance within the context of the ongoing discussions of civil rights and the mobilization of resources in the pursuit of the movement's goals, as Niebuhr's writing increasingly lacked references to the biblical text. Siker writes that "when one examines Niebuhr's work as a whole, one finds that he tends to make more frequent references to specific Bible texts in overtly theological writings, even if often in passing . . . in his more socially and politically oriented writings, however, Niebuhr rarely cites scripture, perhaps

13. Chrystal, "Reinhold Niebuhr and the First World War."
14. Niebuhr, *Children of Light and Children of Darkness*, xi.
15. Hauerwas, "Democratic Policing of Christianity," 228.
16. Niebuhr, *Children of Light and Children of Darkness*, xi.

because of the more public forum he was seeking to influence."[17] Siker goes on to state that Niebuhr's primary community "was not so much the church as it was the forum of national and international policy debates addressed in light of his Christian convictions."[18]

Though Niebuhr was not alone in his decision to rely on the nation-state to exact or promote justice during the 1960s, I consider him representative of what the white establishment came to be during this time of crisis. The answer to the question of what it is that we ought to do tends toward finding ways to legislate and enforce justice. The question of how we ought to do it is less clear. A quick (perhaps unfairly so) read of some of Niebuhr's essays in the sixties reveals that he strayed from articulating faith-based responses to what he referred to as the "racial crisis" and relied instead on the ability of the nation-state to resolve the issue of injustice as it related to segregation and voting rights. His writing suggested that political power is the appropriate means for achieving preferred outcomes, and he can be interpreted as believing that appropriate use of such power occurs when the state has the monopoly on enforcing morality. "It has been said," wrote Niebuhr in "The Crisis in American Protestantism," "that perhaps the weakness of American Protestantism reveals itself in the fact that it is 'captive to the power structure.'"[19]

It is Niebuhr, as we read through some of his work in the mid-sixties, that favors political and military power. He avoided the suggestion that it is the imbalance of power and the human tendency toward domination that makes his own, and often our own, understandings or moral crises captive to the power structure. Just as when he could see no alternative to the

17. Siker, *Scripture and Ethics*, 10.

18. Ibid. See also the editorial note in the *The Christian Century* that describes Niebuhr as "one of Protestantism's most renowned figures." Niebuhr, "Crisis in American Protestantism," 1498. Stanley Hauerwas identifies this manner of "doing Christian ethics" as rooted in the church's insistence on being taken seriously in an increasingly secular American society. He writes, "Christian ethicists [have] come to think that, if they wish to remain political actors, they must translate their convictions into nontheological idiom. But once such translation is accomplished, why is the theological idiom needed at all?" Furthermore, Hauerwas states that this secularism has presented theological ethicists with an irresistible temptation. Even if theologians cannot "demonstrate the truth of theological clams," Christians attempt to insist on maintaining a place in ethical discourse by making the argument that religious "attitudes" are necessary "to the maintenance of our culture . . . If religion is to deserve allegiance, so the thinking goes, it must be based on what can be agreed upon universally." Such is the case for Niebuhrian ethics that indicate a trajectory moving from pacifism to militarism, and from sacrificial kenosis to dependence on the coercive forces of the government. Hauerwas, "On Keeping Ethics Theological," 68, 52.

19. Niebuhr, "Crisis in American Protestantism," 1498–1501.

fascist threat outside of militarism, Niebuhr could see no response to racial injustices without supporting the use of power by the American government to enforce civil rights laws at gunpoint. He wrote in 1965 that it was necessary for Lyndon Johnson to federalize the Alabama National Guard so that Martin Luther King Jr.'s march on Birmingham could receive appropriate protection.

In a brief column entitled "Civil Rights Climax in Alabama,"[20] he adds a telling observation concerning revolution and the matter of hope. Niebuhr believed Marx had it all wrong—that Marx believed revolution is motivated by "pure desperation." Niebuhr quoted Proverbs 13:12 to make his point: "Hope deferred maketh the heart sick [but when desire cometh it is a tree of life]," suggesting that having hope, yet not seeing it realized, is the greater motivator.[21] That may be true, yet there is something troubling here. While he quotes Proverbs, Niebuhr did not suggest that hope for African-Americans comes from the gospel narratives or from an experience of the risen Christ. Niebuhr used Scripture to locate the hope of the black cause in the Supreme Court, and its deferment in the unrealized implementation of desegregation laws. Whether or not Christ gives hope of any justice is not so much the issue, but that hope is placed elsewhere, which indicates a failure of Christian ethics to be Christian any more. Niebuhr published his article in a Christian journal. The level of writing suggests that the readership has some academic training. In this context he implicitly states that hope and justice are found solely within the realm of government, government courts, and government military force. Niebuhr's only mention of the church comes with his possibly condescending affirmation of the black church. He identified white Protestantism as a problem rather than a solution to the civil rights struggle, rightfully indicating the black church as a locus of the movement. He singled out King for honors as a contributor to rectifying wrongs. Yet, in his articles during the mid-sixties, identifying the black church as the response to racism is lacking. He seemed to find the solutions originating with the federal government. Did he believe the black church to be powerless in the struggle for anything outside of the moral support it might supply to activists? He certainly found white Protestantism to be lacking, outside of a few prophetic voices.

An observer might believe Niebuhr had no room for particularly Christian or Christ-centered propositions to provide foundation for his ethic, even though he wrote as a Christian. He did not write with an eye toward reforming Christian congregations, other than rightfully stating that

---

20. Niebuhr, "Civil Rights Climax in Alabama," 61.
21. Niebuhr, "Mounting Racial Climax," 121–22.

white churches were lagging behind in the cause of civil rights. "We may all be racists at heart," he wrote, "but we have some limits of humane concern that distinguish us from the Nazis." Who is the "we" that Niebuhr writes of, and how could he overlook the very real "master race" organizations that existed all over the North and the South? Racial superiority was at the heart of slavery and Jim Crow, and was prevalent even among those whites who supported abolition before the American Civil War. Instead of proposing a well-interpreted scriptural mandate for justice by appealing to Galatians 3:27–29 as a warrant for participation in justice movements, Niebuhr in effect overlooked the truly racist realities of the American democracy in order to commend hope to American institutions. He is really saying, "at least we're not Nazis."

Niebuhr in effect writes to relax any tensions that would potentially ask too much of white Protestants by asking them to participate in greater numbers in marches, civil disobedience, or boycotts, though he must have somehow supported such action. It appears in the limited scope of my reading that he simply trusted whites to acquiesce to the federal government as the legitimator of black civil rights claims instead of calling for more participation from those who need to be most changed—white Protestants. It is remarkable that he calls for federal troops to protect participants in a non-violent movement. Siker sums Niebuhr's nod to realism as such: "With regard to the love ethic, it is . . . crucial for Niebuhr to argue that the love ethic of Jesus is an impossible ethical ideal."[22] Thus, his apparent trust in the coercive abilities of government over the biblical mandate to love one's enemy distinguishes the Bible as an informant of solely personal ethics from more universally authoritative civil laws, and the ethic of Christ as inad-

---

22. Siker, *Scripture and Ethics*, 13. Also Yoder, *Politics of Jesus*, 4–8. Yoder writes that there are six assumptions that are argued in opposition to the credibility of the so-called "love ethic" as a normative Christian ethic. Those assumptions are: 1) "The ethic of Jesus is an ethic for an 'Interim' which Jesus thought would be very brief." 2) "Jesus was, as his Franciscan and Tolstoyan imitators have said, a simple rural figure . . ." and he had no intention of speaking to the "complex problems of complex organizations," etc. 3) "Jesus and his early followers lived in a world over which they had no control . . . they could not conceive of the exercise of social responsibility in any form other than being a faithful witnessing minority." 4) Jesus "dealt with spiritual and not social matters, with the existential and not the concrete." 5) Jesus "pointed people away from the local and finite values to which they had been giving their attention and proclaimed the sovereignty of the only One worthy of being worshiped." 6) "Jesus came to give his life for the sins of humankind . . . but should never be correlated with ethics." In *The Priestly Kingdom*, Yoder adds to his list of common errors concerning a Christ-centered and biblical ethic a list of arguments that are often invoked to cut any discussion of radical ethics short. They are the tendency of mainstream pastors or church members to ask "'how far' should we go, or 'at what point' it needs to be buffered or diluted by 'realistic,' or 'pastoral' or 'ecumenical' considerations" (16).

equate for Christian contributions to moral discourse. This seems to be an important manner in which Christian ethicists could have prioritized both the Bible and the life of Christ as the primary informants of Christian ethics. The leading theologian of the time chose a different row to hoe.

I believe Niebuhr is truly on the side of justice. It is more likely that, especially in light of the crisis of World War II, Niebuhr could not see the power that is inherent in the weakness—in lovingly changing the heart of your neighbor and enemy—of the cross. He interpreted Christ through the lenses of democracy because he could only interpret the achieving of justice as occurring through the gears of power and control. And, because he trusted solely in the power of democracy, he initiated an ethic that renders the Christian narrative and its canonical texts peripheral contributors, because it otherwise has the ability to challenge democracy's assumed truth of righteous coerciveness. Even with the civil rights victories that so many like Niebuhr worked for, there has been no real change in theological perspective. We still have an overwhelmingly racist and sexist society—and church—that pretends incremental achievement will someday bring us to that final, overarching moral perfection. In the end, there seems to be a general rejection of the cross as a means of realizing justice. Why would white Christians choose to experience marginalization *en masse*—like those experiences of the Freedom Riders or participants in lunch-counter sit-ins—if government can enforce desegregation at gun point? Niebuhr refused the messianic challenge toward cross-bearing in favor of what Yoder and others call the Constantinian option.[23]

I hope this will not be misunderstood as a criticism of civil rights legislation. It is to point out that, in the process of seeking justice with as little effort or self-reflection as possible, we lose sight of the biblical mandate to love our neighbors and enemies. It is not that the nation-state should resist enforcing legislation—the question is far different. The question is: what are Christians called to do differently? Niebuhr did not ask white folks to sit at lunch counters or march on Birmingham, though he knew that some did. He did not ask them to walk away from their congregations to start new ones that supported justice through the embodiment of Galatians 3. He instead called for the support of militarism; and Jesus, no matter how you nail him to the cross, rejects that notion. As such, there is no real christocentric contribution to the discussion—no non-violent alternative; for even though the marchers and demonstrators were non-violent, Niebuhr could not help but to call for their defense at gunpoint instead of sitting down next to them. He simply had to dictate the terms, the time, and the means despite the best

---

23. Yoder, *Priestly Kingdom*, 135–37.

arguments of those he supports. I am sure Niebuhr commented consistently on the righteousness of non-violence. It seems he didn't believe it would work, which was a wholesale exclusion of faith.

Perhaps a biblical ethic is an ethic of absurdity. The gospel is absurd on its face when one reads the claims made in the Sermon on the Mount, or the manner in which Jesus feeds crowds of five thousand from a few loaves and fishes. Stories of resurrections may or may not be absurd, but belief in such stories most certainly is. Yet, if an ethic is to be Christ-centered, I propose that it must have two qualities at the very least: the particulars of the Christian ethic must be gleaned from a faith community's reading and discussing Scripture together, and those communities must be brave enough to have faith that even the absurd produces possibilities, and the most radical kinds of faithfulness are the most fruitful. If one believes in the resurrection of the messiah, one must live as though it is true and embody the meaning of such an event for both church and world.

The evidence above, however, indicates that the church, both laity and leadership, has found it increasingly difficult to embody a Christian moral vision according to an ethic that others will agree is produced by a thorough reading of the text. Love of enemies is an absurdity, especially during war, so much so that it is rare that one will hear prayers for enemies during services. Of course, it seems right to pray for healing of relatives and safe travels. Yet, if we are biblical in our thinking, why not pray for blessings to be bestowed upon our enemies and the enemies of the nation-state?

Then, we must ask how our reading and interpretation of the Bible are so thoroughly embedded in cultural understandings, and even more so in our social and economic well-being, that any reading that suggests the absurdities of the Sermon on the Mount are normative for Christian ethics are rejected out of what we all recognize as "common sense." Yet, this is exactly what we must be aware of—how culture and stability get in the way of reading the text in a manner that prioritizes faith over pragmatism. Therese Okure leads the way by recognizing that "culture is one aspect we must look at when we talk about finding truth in Scripture. Truth does not mean what is true as opposed to false. It means that which *is*, what is real."[24]

What is real is, of course, contingent upon how we perceive reality. In a world that insists on universals in order to convince others of the propriety of specific behaviors or the favorability of specific outcomes, it seems nearly impossible to allow a specific Christian community the leeway to read the text according to what it perceives is real, because we see alternative understandings as a threat to our political and social stability. This is related as

24. Okure, "What Is Truth?," 406. Italics original.

much to human sin as it is to liberal democracy and political conflict. Davis provides a perfect example, however, that might help us understand two ideals. First, there are readings that are radically different from my own, and the circumstances justify those readings. Second, any biblical ethic must be one of voluntary association and never be intended to manipulate or author public secular policy.[25]

Consider the very real opposition of African Christianity to liberal American views of homosexual behavior. What happens when we understand the manner in which our interpretations of the text are contingent upon cultural understandings and our understanding of history? Davis quotes Sudanese Episcopalian Archbishop Daniel Beng Bul as stating, "We live in the Old Testament." Bul shares how his Sudanese students so readily identify with Exodus and Leviticus; such legal codes are rooted in the very kinship-based agrarian society that exists, if not in the communities of some contemporary Sudanese church communities, readily in the narratives of their very identity. While Levitical laws might seem incomprehensible to an American reader of the Bible, the settings of the Hebrew Bible are standard to many African readers.[26]

Americans find Ugandan laws condemning gays and lesbians to death a violation of a basic biblical concept of mercy. Americans must understand, however, not only that the laws of Israel are easily contextualized for Ugandan Christians, but that fewer than 150 years ago, a story of national heroism placed such prohibitions directly into the contemporary context. Old-Testament prohibitions of homosexual activity inform Ugandan law because it is considered to be an act of dominance and aggression related to war and military defeat or the coercive demonstration of superiority by one man over another. In 1886, a Ugandan leader was martyred for his refusal to submit to sexual demands of a conquering king who wanted to force himself on the Ugandan. Such stories close the gap between recent biblical interpretations of human sexuality and ancient Hebrew law codes.

Does such understanding threaten gays and lesbians? Absolutely. This is why one common foundation for biblical ethics must arrange agreement on a non-coercive embodiment of truth claims. While one can state the case for a biblical prohibition against same-sex physical intimacy, there is not biblical evidence that the church is called to legislate or create policy that pushes the ethic onto others who live outside the sphere of the church. A biblical ethic is for a community that voluntarily accepts the conditions prescribed by a corporate interpretation of the text. There is no indicator in the

25. Davis, "Reasoning with Scripture," 512.

26. Ibid., 514

New Testament that anyone was held liable to Christian ethics if they were not members of the church. Finally, there is absolutely no biblical example of messianic violence or violence as a means of preaching the gospel in the New Testament.

My alternative is to explore how we answer the question of Christian ethics from a biblical standpoint instead of a perspective that prioritizes a pragmatic way of reading the Bible so that we produce ethics that do not only make sense exclusively and intentionally to protect the normative assumptions of liberal democracy and electoral politics. The question of what we ought to do can be answered with, "We ought to reflect the love of Jesus Christ, if we call ourselves Christians." The answer to how we ought to do it must be framed much differently than it has since World War II. Yet, perhaps the question simply needs to be qualified: "How can we reflect the voluntary suffering of the cross in our pursuit of a justice that may be unlike anything we can describe?" In this we may find our response to the dichotomy between the options presented in the introduction, and we can find it in the Gospel of John, chapter 6. Consider the following:

Many of the young folks that were demonstrating on Wall Street came from, or met at, Columbia University in the heart of Manhattan. It was at this college where revolutionaries from both the faculty and from the surrounding urban chaos made plans for the overthrow of the Stock Exchange and the realization of true democracy. The preacher from Wall Street walked over to Columbia intending to preach to the revolutionaries who were forming themselves into affinity groups in order to carry out their next action.

The followers of this preacher who taught "love of enemies" noticed that many in the crowd of revolutionaries were hungry; some of them had not eaten in days. The people had no money, as many had lost their jobs. Others were students, and still others simply left their jobs to join the movement. The preacher of love had called upon his followers to do the very same, and he understood the angry masses before him. His followers said to him, "How can we feed these hungry people? We have no more than $200."

The preacher calmed them and instructed the entire mass of people to sit and be fed. Together, the disciples went to urban gardens, outdoor markets, pushcarts, and around the mass of people themselves, collecting enough food that everyone could have second helpings. The preacher told his students, "You need not spend the money of the Stock Exchange when we have resources in our own community. We need not spend what is valued over people when we can provide an alternative that renders the money of Wall Street valueless."

Yet, the people in the crowd could not understand. They wanted to elect this preacher as a leader and creator of consensus. They decided to march to Wall Street and declare him as the new face of the movement. But the preacher knew that they still planned to use force, and he would not give up his love ethic. Feeding people from the resources available was preferable to killing and redistributing mammon. He withdrew to a nearby building, away from the crowds, in order to pray.[27]

During prayer, he knew other sacrifices would be necessary to show the masses what God expected of the church to bring about a new realm on earth. He asked for guidance, yet set his face toward Wall Street to preach love yet again.

What is it that your ears will hear in these competing narratives? How will you embody the ethics that each moral vision offers? The choice is not only difficult; the two options cannot be conflated into one without doing murder to both. Yet, contemporary ethics and moralizing insist Christians are given such choices. Democracy and economic realities often make the decision not only far too easy for followers of Jesus, but it becomes much easier to conflate the competing assumptions into an ethic that gives lip service to Christ, yet honor to power.

27. John 6:1–15.

CHAPTER 4

Who Would Dirk Willems Torture?

Most Protestants are not familiar with Dirk Willems. In 1569, this Dutch Anabaptist was imprisoned for heresy for receiving adult baptism. The story of Willems' martyrdom has significance among the many narratives of Christian suffering for the faith because of the intensity of its witness. It is not just that Willems died for the sake of conscience, but he saved the life of the jailer that was chasing him during an escape attempt. The jailer fell through the ice that covered the moat surrounding the jail. Willems, who was running to save his own life, turned back to rescue his pursuer. While his action saved the jailer's life, Willems was nonetheless burned at the stake.

Unless the hearer of this narrative is a member of an Anabaptist church, the response to this story is incredulity. Yet, it is just such a story that should be retold by every congregation who takes the gospel seriously. For it is in the gospel that we are made aware of Jesus' command to love our enemies, and that is exactly the command that is embodied by Willems' action. While few would find it difficult to applaud Willems' faithfulness, a majority of Christians would not say his way of loving an enemy is normative for the Christian faith.[1]

Of course, there is no "normative Christianity."[2] However, Christendom seems to have become stagnant since the climax of the Second Great Awakening. Following the American Civil War, during which both sides appealed to divine providence, the church seems more closely aligned with democratic ideals than the performance of Christ-centered ethics. It is difficult to distin-

1. Yoder, *Priestly Kingdom*, 16; idem, *Politics of Jesus*, 4–8.

2. Sykes, *Identity of Christianity*, 3. "Christianity is an essentially contested concept." John Caputo, however, states that it might be possible to entertain the notion of a foundation upon which to build a way of "doing" Christian ethics. He writes that a good starting place is the attempt "to restore the difficulty of life, not to make it impossible." Caputo, *Radical Hermeneutics*, 209.

guish the American church from the American project and propagation of democracy.[3] To this end, the church has tended to identify the nation-state as a sort of *Fidei Defensor* and seems not to concern itself with matters of policy outside of those negotiated through the ballot box. If there *is* any kind of normative American Christianity, it is characterized by its relationship to sociopolitical power and the means by which certain religious leaders might influence public popular support, and politicians, to win legislation in favor of a particular moral, political, social, or economic agenda.

It is in this context that Christians are able to debate the use of torture as a tool of war. This should not be a one-sided criticism of right-wing religious leaders and organizations. I will propose that the political left wing of the church, indeed the church as a whole, has strayed from its purpose despite many opportunities to embody the gospel during the so-called war on terror. For nowhere is there evidence of mass resistance on the part of American Christians to any part of the war—or the use of torture—outside of participation in public marches of sorts. Furthermore, many if not a majority of Christians show overt support for the war on terror.[4] As the cross mandates that we bear our own, especially in coordination with our demands for justice, Christians in the United States are rarely troubled to voluntarily sacrifice in a public way that makes biblical reflections on torture or war a topic of public discussion. They are unaware of the necessity of sacrifice as an avenue routed toward credibility. It seems the way that most Christians have dealt with the issues of war, economics, and even torture is to vote for the candidate of their choice and hope that government, or other Christians, come to their collective senses.[5]

3. Hauerwas and Willemon, *Resident Aliens*, 32. "We believe both the conservative and liberal church, the so-called private and public church, are basically accomodationist in their social ethic. Both assume wrongly that the American church's primary social task is to underwrite American democracy."

4. A personal anecdote come to mind. Around 2005, I saw a vehicle stopped ahead of me at a stoplight. It had an ICTHYS fish magnet on the left side of the bumper, and a sticker that identified the occupant of the vehicle as an officially licensed "Terrorist Hunter," such as one would be licensed for deer hunting or off-road recreational driving.

5. Hauerwas and Willemon, *Resident Aliens*, 26. The results of such behavior is that the church finds itself relegated to the margins of a discourse that can only deal in an "ends justify the means" vicious circle, or simply capitulates to an ethic that is deemed to be necessary to the success of democracy. For example, Hauerwas and Willemon write, "President Roosevelt issued an urgent appeal to all governments, at the beginning of World War II, saying 'the bombing of helpless and unprotected civilians is a strategy which has aroused the horror of all mankind. I recall with pride that the United States consistently has taken the lead in urging that this inhuman practice be prohibited'" (ibid.). Consider also Paul Ramsey, who criticizes Christian pacifism by citing Helmut Gollwitzer to paint a rather skewed portrait of non-violence by writing that pacifists

In a 2006 poll commissioned by Mercer University and the organization Faith in Public Life, 57 percent of those identifying themselves as evangelical Christians indicated that, in some cases, they felt torture of combatants or detainees might be justified.[6] Christian ethicist David Gushee, who describes himself as an evangelical, wrote in *Journal of the Society of Christian Ethics* that while 37 percent of those polled responded that torture was justified "sometimes," a 20 percent segment believe that it was justified "often."[7] It is a matter of observation that the George W. Bush administration was committed to placing evangelicals in very high positions and that the administration was also fully engaged in pursuing legal justifications for the use of torture as a legitimate interrogation tool.

The fact is that the same tradition that produced Dirk Willem and others like him, who practiced an undeniably biblical ethic in response to evil, now produces leaders who consider torture a legitimate and necessary activity. Since the era of Constantine, political power has had a substantial effect on the way in which Christians conceive of ethics. In the twenty-first century, Christian opposition to torture has been not only isolated, but has failed to address the issue in such a way that it will not return for consideration another day. There is moral failure on both accounts, if we agree that torture occurring within the context of Christian leadership is a topic of debate. That failure is not evident in the fact that torture occurred, but that the church has become an institution that would underwrite a government's claim to such a right, or remain quiet as it occurs.

American Christians have pursued political power and, as a result, may have ceased to be relevant as a confessing body, ceased to reflect an ethic that gives meaning to Jesus' life and death, and ceased to offer an alternative to the present moral compass of a nation that aligns true north with political victory. I suggest that the church must maintain an ethic that understands the nation-state may reserve the right to act outside of the boundaries of church ethics, and that, in order for the church to be the church, it must nevertheless speak out against such actions and sacrifice privileges in order to be wholly non-compliant. Yet, Christians must also offer comfort, solace, and alternatives to each and every person who falls victim to the ethics of domination—both victim and victimizer.

To begin, there must be some account of the evangelical defense of torture and a rejection of this account as being Christian in nature. Even after

"leave to non-Christians that very secular task which requires the greatest love and unselfishness, namely, the use of force . . ." Ramsey, "Is Vietnam a Just War?," 186.

6. Faith in Public Life, "Release of Poll on Southern Evangelicals," table 1, 2.

7. Gushee, "What the Torture Debate Reveals," 79–97.

the policy decisions driven by the events of 9/11, it was indeed difficult to find fully committed defenses of torture in Christian periodicals. It also proved difficult to find any authors who used the biblical text to support torture. However, Gushee identifies a commonality in those evangelical Christians who either supported torture or tacitly steered clear of the debate. As an engineer of a statement authored for the National Association of Evangelicals that condemned the United States policy related to torture of detainees, Gushee states that those organizations who refused to sign "An Evangelical Declaration against Torture" were political supporters of the Bush administration and the Republican Party in general.[8] Some of these organizations included Focus on the Family, American Family Association, Family Resource Council, and a lone dissenting organization, the Institute for Religion and Democracy.

No signers of the condemnation were representatives of the Southern Baptist Conference, according to Gushee.[9] "At a superficial political level, the split between those who signed [the statement against torture] and those who did not can be viewed upon political-ideological lines. The evangelical political right did not sign, the evangelical political center and left did."[10] Gushee has written a book that suggests "an emerging evangelical center is competing with the right for the hearts and minds of American evangelicals. The fracture between these parts of the evangelical community is obvious and may be irreparable."[11] As for biblical "support" of torture, Gushee found that political friends of the administration turned to Roman 13 as the most common, if not only, pericope to buoy their claims: God has chosen political leaders to use the sword against evil, thus, they deserve the support of Christians.

However, it is too easy to blame a right-wing political agenda for the church's relative silence on the issue. In fact, center-to-left commentators such as Gushee must accept some of the burden. He readily admits that a main objective of some evangelicals is to compete politically for adherents, thus legitimizing the negative discourse that occurs among those who claim to love their neighbors. It is saddening that both sides of the political aisle not only refuse to worship in the same congregations in most cases, but regularly compare the other side and its leadership to Hitler and the Nazi Party.[12]

Yet, Gushee writes credibly on the issue of torture and the manner in which the Bush administration, from the top down, supported the torture

8. Ibid., 86.

9. Ibid.

10. Ibid.

11. Gushee, *Future of Faith in American Politics.*

12. Gushee cites Tooley, "Evangelical Left's Nazi Obsession," para. 2, 4, 5. Republished with permission on the Institute on Religion and Democracy website.

of detainees. But he also admits that, when he first wrote in the popular evangelical magazine *Christianity Today*, though he felt it helped launch an "anti-torture" movement among evangelicals, that he had a regret.

> I regret a lack of significant christocentric argumentation. I ended the article with a reference to Jesus . . . but in an effort to speak to an evangelical community suspicious of 'sectarian' appeals to the model of Jesus and the radical demands of discipleship, and very much attracted to arguments based on government's mandate to use the sword to protect the innocent, I avoided grounding my argument in Jesus Christ in any thoroughgoing or explicit way.[13]

Gushee continues to believe, as stated in his post-*CT* journal article, that there were "good, tactical reasons for this approach." And, while he regrets not formally asserting a "rule of Christ" ethic in the article, he provides an important insight in his reassessment of that strategic decision. He wrote, "it is precisely our inadequate christocentrism and christomorphism that lie at the heart of our theological and ethical weakness as a religious community. Jesus Christ must be moved from the margins to the center of American evangelical ethics and public theology."[14]

My belief is that Gushee made a tactical decision to avoid turning to the gospel witness as the foundation for his "arguments" against torture for two reasons that are emblematic of the crisis of Christian ethics. First, as he has already admitted, the battle over torture was not a battle over the propriety of torture of enemies as much as it was presenting a problem indicative of a deeper evangelical commitment to political victory and the maintenance of political power. While Gushee and other center-to-left evangelicals may be adamant they are morally opposed to torture, they have chosen the political arena as the most appropriate venue for arguing Christian ethics, making it a political issue—and thus an issue of debate between reasonable people without bounding the discourse within a "rule of Christ." Second, the very opening of the issue to debate legitimizes a process that continuously makes it possible to consider torture as a response to evil. As an alternative to debating the ethics of torture, those who assert that torture is immoral must necessarily refuse to benefit from an apparatus that engages in such activity. The National Association of Evangelicals' "An Evangelical Declaration against Torture" did not explicitly invite Christians to do as much.

Though the final document undoubtedly illustrates why Christians should not affirm torture as a legitimate means of gathering information,

13. Gushee, "Five Reasons Why Torture Is Always Wrong," 33–37.
14. Ibid.

it fails to commend to readers any actions that might be interpreted as "cross-bearing" in response to the fact of torture. The lengthy statement organizes its argument in a manner that affirms such virtues as the sanctity of all human life, love for enemies, and even legal concerns, but nevertheless refuses to assert the necessity of embodying the gospel ethics that it cites as arguments against torture. There are no life-affirming activities that are recommended as examples of loving one's enemies or acting as peacemakers. There are no suggestions as to how members of the military might respond to orders concerning torture. There are no calls for the church to change the nature of its relationship with the government or the military outside of the call to end torture. There is no question of the legitimacy of the "war on terror," only the question of torture. It presents an entirely negative ethic supported by affirming verbiage. Was there a consideration that, if they were to use specific biblical arguments against torture, they might be led to consider the very nature of Christian participation in all wars, and not only the war in Iraq?

The idea that "cross-bearing" or voluntary sacrifice is a sectarian ethic has much to do with the problem of Christian ethics and the fact that an "evangelical" president could consider torture a legitimate act. Just as Gushee stated that he feared his anti-torture opinion might be marginalized as a "sectarian" ethic, there is reticence about any commendation of a Christian ethic that requires an act of self-emptying of privilege. While Christians will argue fairly strongly that war is often required to defend innocent people from suffering, it is rare that Christian ethicists or pastors will suggest that forgoing privilege and political or economic power is an appropriate action that will prevent war, or change the nature of the way the church thinks and speaks about war or its enemies.

It is primarily the ethic of power, or a critique of such ethics, that drives the rest of this essay. I suggest that while the Christian ethic embodied by Dirk Willems is representative of a biblical, Christ-centered ethic, such an ethic has not only been relegated to the place of individual witness, but also the very suggestion that it might be passed down as representative of a corporate Christian ethic would be viewed as a threat to the church's legitimacy in the world. At the present time, evangelicals and a vast majority of American Christendom will not only reject a call to give up political and economic privilege; they will insist that the church has a responsibility to maintain and fully engage the world from a position of political power. However, if the church maintains political power, it first legitimizes the policy arguments that raise the very possibility of torture, which then makes any attempt to articulate a biblical, Christ-centered ethic unintelligible due to prioritization of secular obligations and needs. The church will certainly cease to be Christian in such continuing circumstances, if it has not already.

Political power demands moral perspectives that privilege the responsibilities of power. The hermeneutical lenses through which the gospel is interpreted are colored by the responsibility of the state, monarch, or military as opposed to the nature of the cross. However, shouting that the reign of Constantine brought the church into a permanent state of apostasy does no one any good and limits the conversation to shrill assertions. At this point, I turn to a 2006 article written by Rabbi J. David Bleich in *Tradition* entitled "Torture and the Ticking Bomb." His article shows exactly how religious leaders can arrive at the conclusion that, in very specific circumstances, engaging in an immoral act may be legitimized when it is part of a process of saving lives, or may be excused by a jury of peers who understand the action was part of an obligation to protect innocents despite its categorization as immoral. Such is the nature of how Christians come to support war as a normative activity and, as an extension, will support torture as a potentially necessary act of faithfulness at some point in the future.

Bleich spends significant space ensuring the reader that torture is indeed immoral in nearly all circumstances. In fact, he agrees that torture is immoral in all but those moments deemed most critical, such as when information is needed in order to save a large portion of a populace from a bomb that is set to go off at any time. (Of course, television used just this scenario in episodes of the series dubbed *24*.) In his article, Bleich uses the Hebrew Bible and rabbinical commentators to show that if one can undoubtedly save the lives of many by torturing one person to get necessary information, one has, if not acted in a morally sound manner, at least earned protection from prosecution due to the individual's obligation to save lives.[15]

The fact that such a scenario is dubious from the beginning is not necessary to this argument; Bleich does a rather complete and convincing job of arguing that as long as we make policy that bans torture, an individual who tortures when motivated to save numerous lives at the last second can be forgiven *post facto*. He argues that in such a circumstance, while torture is an illegal act and even remains illegal despite the acquittal of the individual who uses torture:

> There is a striking precedent for such a moral stance in our contemporary judicial practice. For good reason, the various American jurisdictions have declined to legalize euthanasia. Yet in the few cases of mercy killing that have been brought to trial, by and large, juries have refused to convict or have found

15. Bleich, 107–9.

the defendant guilty of a lesser charge than homicide and, even when the defendant is found guilty, judges have mitigated the punishment. Thus the pristine moral value is preserved in theory while, when warranted, the harshness of its application is mitigated in practice.[16]

A Christian commentator might recognize Bleich's argument as being similar to that of civil disobedience. An individual does what he or she is directed by conscience to believe is the right thing to do despite its illegality, with a significant difference being that civil disobedience is intended to point out the oppressive or immoral nature of a law and is intended to facilitate the overturning of the law so that the activity is no longer considered illegal. Bleich intends for torture to always be illegal, and even prosecuted. Nevertheless, Bleich makes what is undoubtedly a *reasonable* argument on behalf of excusing a torturer from legal consequences if it can be shown that the action saved lives and was undertaken solely for that purpose rather than for what Bleich continues to condemn in his article: activity undertaken with an eye toward " 'punitive torture' and 'intimidative torture,'" which, in his mind, is "morally indefensible and repugnant in the extreme."[17]

Bleich's argumentation can presumably be used in the political realm, and while a purely secular argument might make use of his conclusions as an example of religion underwriting the possibility of justifiable torture, it stands on its own as a justification for such a possibility within the context of Jewish moral and religious tradition. One can see how, with the obligations of power and political responsibility being considered, a Christian could support such a claim. However, from a biblical, christocentric point of view, when one considers the overwhelming themes of self-emptying and voluntary sacrifice—of cross-bearing—the task is not to consider whether or when torture is an option, but rather, whether is it ever a Christian choice.[18]

16. Ibid., 95.

17. Ibid., 89.

18. This is an important consideration for establishing what I will later call the "messianic ethic." Utilitarianism and other choice- and decision-based situational ethics suggest that there might be a variety of options, one of which will serve the most people in the most palatable manner. Hauerwas writes that the Christian ethic, if it is to remain biblical and Christian, should not offer the opportunity to make choices between one ethical choice and another, but instead calls upon adherents to find creative ways to maintain a particular ethic. For instance, when reflecting upon the practice of abortion, he suggests that the major question is not whether Christians should support such a practice, but whether or not they create a community which provides the care necessary to make abortion unintelligible. "Morally the most important things about us are those matters about which we never have to make a 'decision'. Thus the nonviolent persons do not have to choose violence or nonviolence, but rather their being

Because of the nature of sin, torture is always a possibility when an individual or group finds themselves wielding power over another individual or group. Such is the case if one is to consider Bleich's defense of torture in the most specific cases. However, a community of interpretation will find it difficult to arrive at a place where the possibility of torture is realized if they read the Greek Scriptures in a manner that is every bit as reasonable as Bleich's exegetical methods, if not the methods approved by the Christian right and left. Such a hermeneutic community would first have to interpret relevant texts in a manner that allows for coercive political practices or militarism to be an option.

The story of Jesus and his acceptance of the cross as the indicator of the success of his ministry demonstrates a religious ethic that displays the following: Jesus assumed a leadership role that challenged injustice without committing any act of coercion or violence in response, despite the existence of circumstances that would justify the use of violence. Jesus ministered in his homeland, which suffered the status of an occupied territory. More specifically, he ministered in a land that his kin believed was promised by God to them as a fulfillment of divine promises to their ancestors. Not only was the promised land illegally occupied, but that occupation defied God's will. Finally, Jesus ministered in a religious environment that not only assumed that militarism was a means in which God would restore the glory of Israel, but read texts and shared stories of the Maccabean revolt against the Seleucids that served as a reminder of the potential for armed revolt to liberate the oppressed.

Jesus did not rally disciples around a central idea that Rome must be driven out of the occupied "promised land," but around an idea that they must embody a different ethic as an alternative to passively accepting the domination of Rome, or to continuously pursuing militarism against Rome in attempts to drive her out. In response to the evil of the Roman occupation and a corrupted Jerusalem religious hierarchy, Jesus practiced, and is remembered as calling for his disciples to practice, the eschewing of political, economic, and social power in favor of an ethic of community building and servanthood to both friend and foe. Jesus acted with knowledge that he

---

nonviolent means they must use their imaginations to form their whole way of life consistent with their convictions." Hauerwas, *Peaceable Kingdom*, 125. In another essay, Hauerwas insists that Christian pacifism has little to do with a kind of eschatological vision of a creating world without war, but instead states that "Christian pacifism, that is, a pacifism determined by the reality of Christ's cross, assumes we must be peaceful not because such peace holds out the hope of a work free from war but because as followers of Jesus we cannot be anything other than peaceful in a world inextricably at war." Hauerwas, "On Being a Church Capable of Addressing a World at War," 431.

would suffer a penalty of death as he continuously and publicly pointed out the injustices committed by those who had power and economic control.

The tradition of Jesus shows that when there was an opportunity or suggestion to use power or violence, he immediately rejected that option, though Jesus never failed to stand up against injustice and call for the powers to repent. Jesus not only operated from a position of socioeconomic and political weakness, he insisted upon rejecting the use of force as means to an end. In the second chapter of Philippians, Paul shows that this was not to be an ethic unique to Jesus, but a community ethic that was established by Jesus as the standard for Christian response to injustice and abusive power.

Such a distinction between the ethics of power and the ethics of servanthood is important in a culture that generally challenges individuals or communities with either/or situations. This either/or dichotomy, however, does not hold true when stated as a necessary condition of doing ethics. A Christian ethic, as concerns the issues of war, and even torture, places its adherents in a position where they refuse to participate in war and have no power to torture. There is of course some nuance that needs to be unpacked here, but the ethic is as follows: a Christian ethic based purely on the embodiment of the gospel record; living one's life as a member of community, and as an individual that engages in peacemaking; lovingly lifting the oppressor's burden; developing egalitarian communities that show no preference for wealth, gender, or race; and living with an aim toward emptying the self of any privilege that might serve to marginalize or embrace the victimization of another, or "the other." Loving God and neighbor, and loving even the enemy, become the normative day-to-day expression of both individual and community in a manner that makes it impossible to go to war, as one will already be negotiating for peace.

As for moral issues such as torture of enemies, the following is very important. Because the gospels, the New Testament corpus, and the manner in which we receive the gospels is of a corporate nature, it becomes the purpose and main activity of a congregation or gathering of disciples to read and then embody, or live out, those corporate interpretations. The question of what one is to do or how one is to act in a manner that reflects a gospel or Christ-centered ethic is a question that is addressed collectively by a body of interpreters. The concern for an overarching reading that advises all Christians in a unifying manner is not only not possible, but unfavorable, because such an overarching reading of any text will lead to a position of power, or the possibility of garnering power. Such power, and the attempt to acquire such power, is hard to reconcile with the text when a small group with limited power addresses the text through such a hermeneutic.

Does this mean that Christians will never torture? No, but since torture of enemies is hardly an ethic that is evident in the Christian text, a decision to engage in such an activity automatically supposes another, non-Christian ethic that an individual may voluntarily choose to abide by, even if his or her congregation or group rejects it as an appropriate expression of their moral vision. The Christian ethic is voluntary, so while an individual may eschew the Christ-centered interpretive activity of loving one's enemies by feeding them and providing drink, they may choose an alternative, secular, or military ethic by which to abide. *Such a decision automatically rejects the Christian path in favor of another.* A Christian may choose to torture, but in doing so may automatically render his claim to be a Christian moot. She may indeed find herself barred from participation in her congregation or group until she repents of her engagement with the world through adherence to the secular ethic.

Such is the nature of Matthew 18:15–22. This pericope not only suggests that a community of believers sets a standard for the behaviors or the ethics of its constituents, but mandates something far more important than establishing a standard of ethics. The verses mandate a standard of forgiveness, much like the secular finding of "not guilty" that Bleich demands above for the individual who tortures another as a matter of conscience. The significant difference is that the very practice of a Christian ethic with the biblical mandate to self-emptying and sociopolitical weakness would make it very hard for a Christian to be in a position to carry out any ethic other than that of peacemaking and lovingly changing the heart of the enemy or oppressor through the maintenance of personal and corporate dignity. We can see how this plays out in the sense of Dirk Willems; but what about another scenario—one that Bleich himself describes, which is reminiscent of the last episode of the television series *M.A.S.H.*[19]

Bleich writes in the aforementioned article that in order to save the lives of many, one life may have to be sacrificed. He uses the example of Jews in a secret hiding place, or any group of people in immanent threat of death that are in hiding, put in danger of having their presence or hiding place betrayed by a crying baby. It seems to Bleich (and others) that it may be necessary to stop the baby from crying by any means necessary in order to save the larger group from discovery and certain death. In other words, taking a life is immoral, but the sacrifice of just one in order to save many may still be a necessary task. Indeed, one might suffocate the child while attempting to keep it quiet so the cries will not betray others.[20]

---

19. Alda, "Goodbye, Farewell, and Amen."
20. Bleich, "Torture and the Ticking Bomb," 101.

In *M.A.S.H.*, the moral quandary portrayed includes a peasant woman faced with the decision to smother her crying baby to save the life of a bus broken down in enemy territory during the Korean War. Hidden in heavy bush while the enemy is marching by, a crying baby threatens to give away their presence. The effect of the infanticide is such that the show's major character, an American army surgeon named Pierce, breaks down emotionally to the point where he cannot bring himself to terms with the fact that a baby's life was ended to save his own among others. He is hospitalized due to the trauma, which he works through by constantly referring to the event as though it was a squawking chicken that was smothered. There are consequences to any decision, even or especially those undertaken under the auspices of a moral vision that prioritizes by necessity some lives over others, even if some of those lives sacrificed are innocent.

Like being in a position to torture, may God forbid human beings should ever be placed in such a situation. However, unlike the torture scenario brought to life by others, there have been instances of making heart-wrenching decisions about the lives of others such as the crying infant. The Christian narrative, which is also a Jewish narrative, makes sense of such a situation, as does the history of the church's early martyrs. Christians, at our core, should understand that voluntary sacrifice is sometimes necessary in order for others to live, even if it results in our own death. How heart-wrenching it is to make a decision to take a life of one on behalf of many. However, such a decision can be redeemed when that sacrifice is our own on behalf of others. One who reads Christian history will know that martyrs often took their children to martyrdom with them, as they knew of the vindication that would follow.[21] Early Christians sacrificed themselves and took their children with them because they had faith that their actions would be vindicated. Of course, the situation where a child might be sacrificed rarely ever occurs, but perhaps more likely than one in which it might be possible to acquire life-saving information from someone by torturing them. The question of what Jesus might do, however, should already be answered.

---

21. Evidence for this claim is largely legendary.

CHAPTER 5

Narrative

Enlightenment promises freedom from the overpowering forces of nature,
yet enslaves us to a second nature
(in the form of economic, technical, and bureaucratic necessity);
It provides us with power to fashion our world and our identities,
Yet reveals our impotence and self-arrogance.
Even though the economic apparatus
provides for the individual as never before,
the individual disappears before the apparatus that serves him.
Enlightenment . . . paradoxically brings
Both liberation and slavery, freedom and constraint,
Self-conscious transparency and ignorant opacity
about what it is we are doing to ourselves, to our world, and to others.[1]

The same environment that fueled intense demand for social and ecclesiastical change in Reformation Europe provided for scholars to intensify efforts to understand the canonical texts of Christianity through new interpretive lenses. Renaissance scholarship facilitated new ways of discerning both literal and historical meanings of the Bible, and this at first seemed a welcomed discipline by Reformation scholars.[2] Many scholars, though, used this opportunity to attack the veracity of much of the contents of the

1. Rocco, "Between Modernity and Postmodernity," 79.
2. Bird, "Authority of the Bible." Bird writes that many Reformers believed the original meaning of the texts would be recovered, and freed from bondage to "dogmatic interpretation and ecclesiastical control." On the other hand, many church leaders feared—and rightly so—that "free thinkers, as well as others, openly hostile to the Church . . . saw in the new criticisms a means to unmask religion and reject its supernatural claims by exposing the Bible's human character, crude expression, and fallibility" (54).

text. While it was not just the Bible and religious claims that came under attack during the Renaissance, Enlightenment thinkers of the seventeenth century no longer blindly accepted the Bible as a source by which reasoned truths could be established.

This new era asserted that humanity could somehow find a means to achieve its own measure of progress through the application of reason to any variety of perceived obstacles to public goods and personal happiness. This often meant that the traditionally held moral assumptions—assumptions that prioritized Christian beliefs and the biblical texts as the main informants of morality—were now considered suspect due to Enlightenment assumptions that religious tradition more often than not impeded the use of reason and logic.[3] Just as rationalists such as Spinoza challenged the realities of unexamined authority and the relationship between church and state, empiricists such as Hobbes studied the means by which words received meaning "to demonstrate that certain metaphysical doctrines are, quite literally, meaningless."[4] Traditional Christian assumptions were being overshadowed by a return to classical Greco-Roman philosophy. The standard religious statement of God's sovereignty—a God who acted observably in human history—was being discarded in favor of religious thinking characterized as deism.[5] Morally, this deviation from the belief that a God revealed

3. Mautner, "Enlightenment," 187. Self-reliance and individuality were the means to achieve such a standard, with persons bent on progress overcoming the baggage of "traditionalism, obscurantism, and authoritarianism. The Enlightenment project felt "a pressure to vindicate" traditional morality while establishing the move toward devising outcomes based upon individual desire and will; thus promoting strategies of "devising new teleology or . . . finding new categorical status" for these older values. MacIntyre describes the work of Jeremy Bentham as indicative of modernism's far-reaching concern that outcomes favoring individual happiness and generally-held social goods are victimized by religious morality fraught with superstition. Regarding traditional moral assumptions, MacIntyre believes Bentham held that "traditional morality was . . . pervaded by superstition." Bentham believed that "it is not until we understood that the only motives for human action are attraction to pleasure and aversion to pain that we can state the principles of an enlightened morality for which the prospect of the maximum pleasure and absence of pain provides a *telos*." MacIntyre, *After Virtue*, 62. He also states, "When the distinctively modern self was invented its invention required not only a largely new social setting, but one defined by a variety of not always coherent beliefs and concepts. What was then invented was the *individual* and to the question of what that invention amounted to and its part in creating our own emotivist culture" is a basic question of what has happened to the concern for biblical Christian ethics within a secularized and individualized culture. The Bible was not written with such a culture in mind, nor was such a culture possible or preferred to more communitarian understandings of the natural created world. MacIntyre does not provide a citation for his description of Bentham's work. Italics original.

4. Scruton, *From Descartes to Wittgenstein*, 84.

5. Ingraffia, *Postmodern Theory and Biblical Theology*, 3. He writes that Hume

divinely favored values was characterized by the belief that happiness and pleasure were the ideal moral guides, and that morals were dictated upon what actions produced the greatest experience of happiness and pleasure for the greatest number of people.

As for matters of faith, Feuerbach provides an example of a sort of culmination of Enlightenment thought concerning theological truth claims. Feuerbach submitted that the concept of God, or any religious claim in general, is nothing more than the imaginary projections of what are perceived to be the best of human qualities. "We cannot conceive God otherwise," he wrote, "than by attributing to him without limit all the real qualities which we find in ourselves."[6]

It did not take long to find the matter of Christian ethics being derived from the standpoint of maintaining intellect at all costs, even at the cost of rejecting many of the claims found in the Bible, regardless of intellectual prowess of the reader. Simple matters of faith were useless, if not obstacles to social progress, if they stretched the intellect too far. Concerned with absurdities ranging from miracles and resurrection to issues of particularity concerning the Christian faith, Schubert Ogden writes, "if the price for becoming a faithful follower of Jesus Christ is some form of self-destruction, whether of the body or mind—*sacrificium corporis, sacrificium intellectus*—then there is no alternative but that the price remain unpaid." Modernity has produced many persons who generally do not consider themselves open to the possibility of supernatural powers or deities who have influence over the day-to-day aspects of life, or over history in general. Such a person views him- or herself, according to Ogden, "as a unified being and attributes [such] experience, thought, and volition to [his or her] own agency, not to divine or demonic causes." [7]

I present here an antithesis to my project, adding to the thinking of the ecologist Nash in chapter 2. The question of ethics among contemporary

---

"worked to undermine belief in divine revelation and miracles, and consequently, both the authority and the content of the biblical gospels were attacked." The idea that history was the result of providence or divine guidance was rejected, and that the academic pursuit should include a search for the causes of events, not just the facts of them. Hobbes, in *Of Man, Being First Part of Leviathan*, called history the "register of knowledge of fact."

6. Feuerbach, *Essence of Christianity*, 38.

7. Ogden, *Christ Without Myth*, 130. Ogden is taking his cue from Rudolph Bultmann, who he believes insists that each human being must take responsibility for his or her own existence, or that "'Salvation' and all it implies will be meaningless." Robert Funk asserts that from such thinking it follows that "a history of salvation which attributes saving efficacy to certain historical events, whether miraculous or not, is not only incredible but irrelevant." Funk, *Language, Hermeneutic, and the Word of God*, 89.

empiricists and for much of the political and intellectual left-of-center has concerned itself not with how to a find rational means of incorporating religious experience into the formulation of "universals," but with the moral responsibility to shatter "provincial myths." Philip Kitcher states that "truth is not to be identified with what members of some specific community believe." He sees the role of scientific enquiry as one in which someone rejects "the conventional wisdom of the learned community, using procedures of inquiry to articulate some new truth." While the rejection of conventional wisdom is certainly necessary to biblical interpretation, is it doubtful that scientific inquiry will get any assembled community closer to truthfulness or its identity. Kitcher acknowledges that such empirically discovered truth "may not promote the happiness of the inquirer or of anyone else, [yet] judges the resulting state to be better than the starting point." Thus, for empiricists, the moral dilemma is not that there has to this point failed to be a universally held truth derived from reason, but that once a specific community's belief is somehow "discredited" by science, they will somehow be destined toward despair, but better for it nonetheless.[8]

Paul Van Buren, writing in 1963, may have been more kind toward the empiricist community's assumptions than others, but seems to have stated most appropriately what it has meant for much of the modern Western world. "The empiricist in us finds the heart of the difficulty not in what is said about God, but in the very talking about God at all. We do not know 'what' God is, and we cannot understand how the word 'God' is being used." Such spiritualizing practices suggest, writes Van Buren, that "secular humanity is not necessarily godless, but no longer knows how to express faith experiences in acceptable theistic terms."[9]

"Contrary to Enlightenment thinking," states Christopher Rocco, "the opposition between myth and enlightenment is not absolute." He believes the opposition is overcome when a commonly accepted mythology calls into question humanity's singular confidence "in the progress of reason and the superiority of modern cultural accomplishments."[10]

8. Kitcher, "Truth or Consequences," 50. Kitcher calls the process "painful enlightenment" (54).

9. Van Buren, *Secular Meaning*, 84.

10. Rocco, "Between Modernity and Postmodernity," 74. Also, "Reason, which once worked by thought and concepts, now refers to method alone. Indifferent to the qualitatively and individually unique, insensitive to multiplicity and particularity, impatient with tradition and history, as well as with religion, metaphysics and philosophy . . . the aim of the Enlightenment is the subsumption of all particulars under the general, the substitute of formula for concept, rule and probability for cause and motive" (80).

Rocco also views the Enlightenment perspective of history, as "the register of knowledge of fact," as being suspect. "Systems claim their concepts to be adequate to their subject. They claim to have identified it fully . . . But reality does not go into its concept without remainder."[11] Bernstein believes that what empiricists fail to observe is that science is not a practice in verifying or finalizing truth.[12] Facts require interpretation, and modernity denies an individual or community the very tools with which to interpret, by denying the value of the contributions of metaphysics.

Perhaps the greatest tragedy of the Enlightenment is that it isolates the narrative (or traditional/mythic) qualities of corporate life and renders them obscure—all the while developing insular theories of social behavior that are relevant only to other theorists. What is lacking in the practice of prioritizing reason to the *exclusion* of other ways of knowing is that "reason is calculative; it can assess truths of fact and nothing more," writes Alasdair MacIntyre. "In the realm of practice therefore it can only speak of means. About ends, it must be silent."[13]

Formal reason is not in any sense related to morality more than it is to those actions deemed immoral. There is no logical reasoning that unquestionably refutes, according to Rocco, the conclusion that murder, or genocide, or bombing civilian targets is immoral. The Enlightenment, given as it is to universals, gives occasion to modern political leaders such as Hitler and Stalin, whose regimes were propped up upon the totems of empirical claims. Enlightenment thinking also acts to justify such "reasonable" actions as the bombing of Dresden and the atrocities of Hiroshima and Nagasaki.[14] "The mathematics and physics men have their mythology," writes poet Robin Jeffers. "Their equations are false, but their things *work* . . . their equations bombed Hiroshima, the terrible things *worked*."[15]

---

11. Ibid., 83–84. "Systems inevitably enter into conflict with the 'objects' they purport to grasp. The multiplicity of qualities disappears in the system only to return to later contradict it. History defies systems . . . as the dialectic of Enlightenment attests. If history does have any unity, it is not given by any systematic construction but by suffering."

12. Bernstein, "Idols of Modern Science," 45. "Rather, science seeks consistency. One cannot claim more than that, for many things that are not scientific possess their own truth . . . They include the mystic knowledge of God, the universal comprehension of psychedelic experiences, or the wisdom of traditional understanding in supposed primitive cultures. Indeed . . . science even rule(s) out some phenomena-to science, they simply do not exist."

13. MacIntyre, *After Virtue*, 54.

14. Rocco, "Between Modernity and Postmodernity," 79.

15. Jeffers, *Beginning and the End*, cited in Bernstein, Bernstein, "Idols of Modern Science," 55. Also, Rocco cites the observations of Michael Foucault in writing that: "The

It often appears, upon inspection, that many of the facts that empiricism produces (rather than observed data) are in fact much more a creation of human desire than any formally grounded statement of empirically proven truths. MacIntyre addresses this in his discussion of human rights. He states that there is no concept of such rights in history prior to the fifteenth century, and that "it only follows that no one could have known what they were." As alluded to above concerning the realities of genocide and carpet-bombing, there is no more rational basis for suggesting that an established concept of human rights exists any more so than there is a rational claim undergirding one's beliefs in "witches and in unicorns."[16] It is not my intention (nor MacIntyre's) to assert that human rights ideals are not valuable assets to human existence and justice seeking. My intention is to suggest that without the human experience, a history of suffering, or a non-empirical realization that life has inherent worth, the Enlightenment notion that reason is the sole means of liberation is corrupt.

Inevitably, the institutional church could not escape the lure of "reason alone" and has limped through the recent past, paralleling the commitments and goals established by modernity. "Just as Western culture . . . sought an independent rational justification for morality, so also the Western Church has sought independent rational justification for the gospel," Jonathan Wilson writes. "Just as the Enlightenment project to justify morality was bound to fail, the Church's version of the Enlightenment project also had to fail."[17] A significant number of apologetic exercises over the last century are witness to this. Even Enlightenment heroes like Kant preceded such exercises by attempting to bound religion in the ties of rationality so they did not have to discard it. Theologians and Christian ethicists more recently have sought to justify Christian theological claims without reference to the gospel narratives. Yet, like MacIntyre's proposal that Enlightenment morality has used the language of a past moral structure to account for a morality that was contrived from a wholly other set of assumptions,[18] Wilson insists that the

---

enlightenment discourse of liberation—whether it is bound up with pseudo-scientific discourse of psychological, physical, or social therapies—simultaneously contains and conceals its opposite . . . The streamlined, functional, and efficient language of modern science—both natural and social . . . serves to exclude or silence the multifaceted, varied, and heterogeneous elements of experience that do not fit neatly into its explanatory schema." Rocco, "Between Modernity and Postmodernity," 79.

16. MacIntyre, *After Virtue*. He further states that "every attempt to give good reasons for believing that there *are* such rights has failed. The eighteenth-century philosophical defenders of natural rights sometimes suggest . . . [they] are self-evident truths; but we know that there are no self-evident truths" (69).

17. Wilson, *Living Faithfully in a Fragmented World*, 42.

18. MacIntyre, *After Virtue*, ch. 5.

Enlightenment church has been acting to justify Christian moral principles by shoehorning them into a schemata of rationality and reason. In the process, and as I have shown, the church has discontinued relying upon the gospel narratives as its primary, if not sole, source of ethics.[19]

Thus, while the Enlightenment critique of the following proposed narrative understanding of truthfulness will find it void of any rational basis (rejecting claims of salvation, resurrection, or divinely revealed morality as empirically unfounded), Enlightenment thought also fails to generate tangible evidence for any empirical source of human being, value, or goal. As history has shown, modernity has failed to produce any standardized or universally liberating alternatives to the reality of human suffering, let alone provide us with an account of truth. Additionally, the Enlightenment project has spawned criticisms from other philosophical voices, which have also proved to be suspicious of theological claims in particular. Postmodern thinking has sought to wrench humanity free from the supposed shackles of religion, and its stories as well.

The Failure of Philosophical Alternatives

Postmodernism simply offers to liberate us from dependency upon modernity. It details no other promises. Challenges to christocentric truth claims did not begin with the rise of empiricism, but philosophical thought over the past hundred years or more has been busy not only dismantling the truth claims of modernity, but also working to assail every metanarrative or foundational truth claim that comes before it as both contingent and oppressive.[20] The claim that there is a God who acts in history, or perhaps more particularly, that the actions attributed to a first-century Judean can somehow be *universally* authoritative, not only lacks credibility in most philosophical constructs, but has been rightly condemned by many as a useful tool used by elites to underwrite oppressive regimes, social hierarchies, and economies of various empires throughout history. The turn toward modernity not only viewed God "as a fiction or a projection of man [*sic*] . . . but the Christian God is rejected as *bad* fiction."[21] Indeed, Nietzsche likens claims to truth based on any empirical or metaphysical foundation to a "mobile army of metaphors."[22] For Nietzsche, God was dead not because of his own

19. Wilson, *Living Faithfully in a Fragmented World*, 44.

20. Lyotard identifies postmodern thinking as being defined by an "incredulity toward metanarratives." Lyotard, *Postmodern Condition*, xxiv.

21. Ingraffia, *Postmodern Theory and Biblical Theology*, 2.

22. Nietzsche, "On Truth and Lie in an Extra-Moral Sense," 46–47. "What then is

philosophical critiques of deity, but due to the very nature of unfaithfulness he observed in the behaviors of those persons calling themselves Christian.

An aspect that is often misrepresented or simply not understood about philosophical responses to modernist claims is the intellectual turn toward the "deconstruction" of propositions concerning not only varying metaphysical claims proposed by multiple cultures, but also against socio-economic and political truth claims made by empires (or nation-states) in competition for resources and political power. Lyotard noticed that modernity, in all of its forms and wherever it appeared, tended to shatter metaphysical beliefs and perpetrate the notions that specific realities apparently lacked substance in favor of empirically invented realities championed by the victors in history.[23] This is evident in the presently dominant metanarratives founded upon economic philosophies such as free-market capitalism (Locke, Adam Smith) and state-sponsored socialism (Marx), which have been oppressive tools of nation-states in securing power in the struggle for resources.[24] Marcus Raskin levels the charge of idolatry against these narratives of empire. He believes that virtuous characteristics have falsely been attributed to the practices of colonizing knowledge, capitalism, militarism, and social order.[25] It is just such assumptions that the biblical narrative stands firmly against. It is against such assumptions that Jesus preached. For Christians, the truth of the gospel exposes the truths claimed by capitalism or Marxism, or even the claims made regarding individual rights.

truth? A mobile army of metaphors, metonyms, and anthropomorphisms—in short, a sum of human relations, which have been enhanced, transposed, and embellished poetically and rhetorically, and which after long use seem firm . . . truths are illusions about which one has forgotten that this is what they are, metaphors which are worm out and without sensuous power; coins which have lost their pictures and now only matter as metal, no longer as coins." Also, Nietzsche, "AntiChrist," 647. "Nietzsche's disdain for God, or god, or any claim concerning deity is well known, and just as worn as the claims he attacks. He does not believe the Enlightenment project has done enough to dismantle theism with its "religion of reason" or tendencies toward deism. "That we find no god—either in history or in nature or behind nature is not what differentiates *us* [from the Enlightenment], but that we experience what has been revered as God, not as "godlike, but as miserable, as absurd, as harmful, not merely as an error but as a *crime against life*. We deny God as God."

23. Lyotard, *Postmodern Condition*, 77.

24. The narrative of Smith's pen, "It is not from the benevolence of the butcher, the brewer, or the baker that we expect our dinner, but from their regard to their own interest. We address ourselves, not to their humanity, but to their self-love, and never talk to them of our own necessities but of their advantages," is an example of an Enlightenment narrative that firmly contradicts Christ-centered praxis. Interestingly, even in its official atheism, the basic tenet of Marxism reflects a measure of the "Acts 2 church" in its maxim, "from each according to his ability, to each according to his needs."

25. Raskin, "Reconstruction and Its Knowledge Method," 23.

More positively stated, however, postmodern or deconstructionist criticisms "suggest that the search for ultimate or universal . . . conceptual strategies should be abandoned in favor of local, pragmatic justifications."[26] In other words, deconstructing the church is a matter of interpretation and embodiment that strips away centuries worth of manipulated, culturally and historically contingent meanings that have come to be accepted as creedal, dogmatic, or propositionally true, in order to give local understandings of the text the priority in congregational life and faith.

So, what do we make of attempts to speak with a religious sensibility in terms of expressing some sense of what is truthful? "When [empiricism] appeals solely to the truth of a [scientific] discourse to authorize it intellectually and socially, one represses reflection on its practical-moral meaning and its social consequences," writes Steven Seidman. "A discourse that justifies itself solely by epistemic appeals will not be compelled to defend its conceptual decisions on moral and political grounds."[27] Thus the need to embody the claims to make them credible enough to accept or reject as a contribution to grander conversation. For Christians, such behaviors must be embedded in a particularly Christ-centered discourse that rejects opportunities to act inclusively toward competing narratives, such as those of nationalism, economics, and utilitarian accounts of justice. There is also the challenge of succumbing to the ease of making claims without an eye toward competing with the apparently more sensible claims made by secular institutions and the sciences. Christians have tended to prioritize the normative realities that comprise wholly American culture and justice claims, without offering or embodying gospel claims that often state the contrary in order to be truthful regarding justice and faithfulness.

What would it mean for the church to maintain strict boundaries of discourse that limit our public witness to that of biblical language, unencumbered by the so-called realities of politics, militarism, and economics? In fact, secular agencies in particular have the means to control what sorts of ethics or moral vision are relative to a discussion of right and wrong, and have excluded those religious claims that run contrary to the utilitarian goals of the nation-state, especially democracies. Consider this: "Truth is whatever we can get our colleagues (our community) to agree to. If we can get them to use our language . . . our story is as true as any story will ever get."[28] Once we accept possibility that specific language is only useful

---

26. Seidman, "End of Sociological Theory," 134.

27. Ibid. 135.

28. Rorty, *Contingency, Irony, and Solidarity*, 6–7. Modern metanarratives are human constructs buoyed by particular language. Rorty writes: "The world does not speak. Only we do. The world can, once we have programmed ourselves with a language, cause

in certain situations, we allow that there is value and potential truthfulness to each story within its specific context. Unfortunately, pragmatism is a key component to navigating a postmodern world, according to Sire. Seidman believes that pragmatism has the advantage of diversifying and enlarging the number of voices participating as equals in social discussions.[29] The fact that the gospel refutes pragmatism as much as utilitarianism puts Christian ethics at odds with any argument, such that it must then be considered oppressive.

Languages are also a way in which persons attempt to grasp on to power, or to wrestle it away from another. The modern assumption that one epistemology or, in the postmodern sense, one story or language, is preferred over another leads to violence and oppression. As such, the postmodern thinker attributes oppressive inherencies to each and every epistemology or language. However, it is not just religious language that is deemed oppressive. Scientific discourse is equally demanding of acquiescence. Such are the assumptions of thinkers such as Michael Foucault, Edward Said, and others.[30] "The claim to truth," writes Seidman, "is inextricably an act of power—a will to form humanity . . . concealed in the will to truth is a will to power."[31]

It is necessary not only to refute the universal claims of Christendom and modernity, but also to respond to the assumed postmodern critiques of Christian ethics as I understand them. In doing so, I will draw heavily from some postmodern assumptions, but focus mainly on the possible truthfulness, or credibility, of narrative claims, and the value of localized narratives in communities where, when remembered, retold, and lived out in a *noncoercive* fashion, can become non-infringing truth claims embodied in a non-oppressive manner.

The Narrative Response

Human beings are, in actions and practices—and in fictions—storytellers. Through oral and written memories we become a people who tell stories that aspire to truth. "I can only answer the question, 'what am I to do'?"

---

us to hold beliefs. But it cannot propose a language for us to speak. Only other human beings can do that . . . Languages are made rather than found, and . . . truth is a property of linguistic entities, of sentences" (221).

29. Seidman, "End of Sociological Theory," 135.

30. Huebner, *Precarious Peace*, 103.

31. Seidman, "End of Sociological Theory," 135.

writes MacIntyre, "If I can answer the question, 'of what story or stories do I find myself apart of'?"[32]

Life experiences of every sort are lived out, remembered, and retold in narrative form. It is the stories we tell that underwrite an identity or worldview of an individual, a community, or an institution.[33] A grandparent or parent remembers and shares the story of their life with younger family members. A story of the storm on the night of the first-born's birth, or the sacrifices made by earlier generations during World War II, reveal the truth of lived experiences. Children ask over and again of their mothers and fathers, "Tell us how you met," while new couples share intimately with one another the stories and dreams of their lives. Churches, political parties, and community organizations all share stories of "the way things were" when they decided to pull together or take action to make dreams of a new community life a reality. Pivotal persons, events, and crisis or victories are all remembered in anecdotal stories that remind elders of their roots, and inform newcomers of the expectations and integrity of the community.[34]

The question remains: are narratives true (and can such claims be true regardless of facticity)? Statements of truth or moral vision that are reliant upon biblical narratives will almost always fail to meet the criteria that Enlightenment/modernity thought demands of truth claims. An enlightened Hume simply reflected upon the diversity of religious beliefs that existed in the world, as opposed to a universal expression of a divine being, as proof of the unreasonableness of faith. "Some nations have [been] discovered, who entertain no sentiments of religion," wrote Hume, "If travelers and historians may be credited, and no two nations, and scarce any two men, have ever agreed precisely in the same sentiments." Hume continues, "It would appear, therefore, that this preoccupation springs not from an original instinct

32. MacIntyre, *After Virtue*, 101.

33. Pambrun, "Hermeneutical Theology and Narrative," 283. "Narrative affirms a relationship to reality. Meaning is generated in the dialectical exchange between the story-like feature and the history-like feature of narrative."

34. Hauerwas, *Peaceable Kingdom*, 29. "First, narrative formally displays our existence and that of the world of creatures—as *contingent* beings. Narrative is required precisely because the world and events in the world do not exist by necessity. Any attempt to depict our world and ourselves non-narratively is doomed to failure insofar as it denies our contingent nature. Correlatively, narrative is epistemically fundamental for our knowledge of God and ourselves, since we come to know ourselves only in God's life. Second, narrative is the characteristic form of our awareness of ourselves as *historical* beings who must give an account of the purposive relation between temporally discrete realities. Indeed, the ability to provide such an account, to sustain its growth in a living tradition whose manifold storylines are meant to help individuals identify and navigate a path to the good. The self is subordinate to the community rather than vice-versa, for we discover the self through a community's narrated tradition."

or primary impression of nature."[35] Interestingly, much of Christendom has rejected narrative as the most intelligible theological language, let alone the preferred manner of formulating claims about the divine. Fundamentalists such as R. C. Sproul suggest that a rational, Bible-based theology surpasses the requirements of Enlightenment epistemology.[36]

In Sproul's mind, there is no reasonable way that the Bible can self-contradict or self-correct. Fundamentalists, in order to preserve their proposition that the Bible is a coherent revelation of an ultimately understandable God, reject any possibility of contradiction because contradiction stands opposed to the reasoning of an omniscient and omnipotent deity. Christian conservatives who are moved to find proofs of their biblical truth claims have attributed inerrant qualities to the text, calling apparent contradictions "paradoxes" or "mysteries."[37] Sproul suggests that the failure of Christendom to maintain spiritual (or otherwise) dominance in the Western world is very much due to the lack of rational thinking amongst those who have been bombarded by postmodern incredulity.

Nevertheless, postmodern reasoning leaves room not only for various truth claims to hold the *possibility* of being *considered* truthful, but such allowances are needed to avoid reliance on pragmatism to support its own "relative" veracity. One aspect of postmodern assumptions, rarely acknowledged, is that the very claims made by such thinkers are in fact dependent upon an understanding that there must be the *possibility* of a claim to be credible, if there is any credibility to their philosophical venture.

George Lindbeck writes that religious claims, like any other, must be allowed the possibility of making categorically true statements as well as those that are deemed symbolically true. He states, "We must also allow for its possible propositional truth."[38] Following Lindbeck's example, I will use the phrase *Christus est Dominus* (Christ is Lord) as a test of his thesis.

First, Lindbeck states a difference between "intrasystematic" truths and "ontological" truths. "The first test of truth is coherence," he writes. "The second that truth of correspondence to reality." Christian claims that "Christ is Lord" are true intersystematically as parts of a pattern. Thus, such

35. Hume, *Natural History of Religion*, 21.

36. Sproul, *Essential Truths of the Christian Faith*, xvii. "If we seek a coherent, logical, consistent, and rational understanding of the Bible, we are immediately accused of worshipping at the shrine of Aristotle. Because the philosophy of rationalism has often been hostile to Christianity, we flee from anything that remotely seems like rationalism . . . Christianity is not rationalism. But it is rational. It may have truth beyond what reason can fathom. But it is more rational, not less."

37. Ibid., xviii.

38. Lindbeck, *Nature of Doctrine*, 63.

a statement only has meaning in a holistic context of "speaking, thinking, feeling, and acting" according to their coherence with the overarching narrative that informs them. The statement is false, however, when used in a manner "inconsistent with the pattern as a whole that affirms" the overarching narrative's proposition. "The crusader's battle cry '*Christus est Dominus*,' for example, is false when used to authorize cleaving the skull of the infidel." Lindbeck believes such an action defeats the truth claims proposed in the context of Jesus as suffering servant. Thus, coherence is tested through the actions of the agent stating the proposition.[39]

Furthermore, such coherence is necessary to a theological truth in a manner comparable and contrasting with that of a mathematical statement. "A demonstration in Euclidean geometry which implies that parallel lines eventually meet must be false for formally the same reason that the crusader's cry must be false: the statements in both cases are intrasystematically inconsistent." As such, Lindbeck states that "the difference is that in the Christian case the system is constituted not in purely intellectual terms by axioms, definitions, and corollaries, but by a *set of stories used in specifiable ways to interpret and live in the world.*"[40]

While Lindbeck agrees that intersystematic truth is a necessary though insufficient condition for ontological truth, he states that intrasystematic claims are possibly true without necessitating ontological approval. Lindbeck writes that an intersystematic claim is meaningless "if it is part of a system that lacks concepts or categories to refer to relevant realities." However, "it is ontologically true if it is part of a system that is itself categorically true." Lindbeck turns to a literary example to make this point. "The statement 'Denmark is the land where Hamlet lived' is intersystematically true within the context of Shakespeare's play, but this implies nothing regarding ontological truth or falsity unless the play is taken as history." I understand this to mean that the statement "Christ is Lord" can only be viewed as ontologically true if it is in fact true that the historical person Jesus in fact lived the faithful life attributed to him by the gospels. As Lindbeck states in support of this, "A religious utterance, one might say, acquires the propositional truth of ontological correspondence only insofar as it is a performance, an act or deed, which helps create that correspondence."[41]

---

39. Ibid., 64.

40. Ibid. Italics added.

41. Ibid., 65. Religious utterances "acquire enough referential specificity to have first-order or ontological truth or falsity only in determinate settings." The statement "Christ is Lord" becomes a first-order proposition capable (so non-idealists would say) of making ontological truth claims only as used in the activities of adoration, proclamation, obedience, promise hearing, and promise keeping, which shape individuals and

Returning to the concept of narrative, it is important to tie the action based truth referred to by Lindbeck to the memory of Jesus' actions in the context of the covenant between Israel and its God, the actions of the earliest Jesus communities, and the actions of Jesus followers through history. My contention is that all of these actions are made intelligible only through the controlling narrative of the promises to Abraham, Israel, and David. However, it is the same actions of individuals or communities that give the narrative credibility.[42]

An agent's intentions are informed by an ongoing account of existence that incorporates aspects of both history and memory, and peripheral existence. Life is less intelligible if viewed simply as a series of unconnected events, though Enlightenment thinking has supposed humanity to be better served by the rejection of any tradition or history or personal past; anything that shapes one into something other than a *self-defined individual* free of such apparent constrains.[43] H. Richard Niebuhr believed there is no way to make oneself intelligible outside of the context of one's shared history with a community. Individualism deters communication.[44]

The actions of an agent based upon the intentions formed by narratives are designated by MacIntyre and Hauerwas, among others, as "practices" and "virtues." As mentioned elsewhere, I prefer "praxis." Practices embedded in communities are not only necessary to sustaining communication and relationships, but, according to MacIntyre, "Also in sustaining those traditions which provide both practices and individual lives with their necessary historical context . . . Living traditions, just because they continue a not-yet-completed narrative, confront a future whose determinate and determinable character, so far as it possesses any, derives from the past."[45]

communities into conformity to the mind of Christ.

42. Goldberg, *Theology and Narrative*, 34. Goldberg writes that "asking about the truth of a religious story involves no more than inquiring about the sincerity of the intention of the one who entertains such a story to follow some prescribed source of action."

43. MacIntyre, *After Virtue*, 204. "That particular actions derive their characters as parts of a larger whole is a point of view alien to our dominant ways of thinking and yet one which is necessary at least to consider if we are to begin to understand how a life may be more than a sequence of individual actions and episodes."

44. H. R. Niebuhr states, "Once more we discover that visions, numinous feelings, senses of reality, knowledge of duty and worth may be interpreted in many ways. We cannot speak of inner light at all, save in ejaculations signifying nothing to other(s) unless we define its character in social terms, that is, terms which come out of our history." H. R. Niebuhr, "Story of Our Life," 26.

45. MacIntyre, *After Virtue*, 220–21. "We all approach our circumstances as bearers of a particular social identity . . . As such, I inherit from the past of my family, my city, my tribe, my nation, a variety of debts, inheritances, rightful expectations and

As such, the concept of narrative theology first states that the story proposed is credible in its historical and modern context. Robert Roth states of narrative qualities of truthfulness that "reality is the dramatic action of the story itself."[46] Memory, writes Roth, is thus the key to reality, as opposed to how a thing is known. "If the story is the vehicle of reality, rather than either thought or sensation, then recognition, not cognition, is the way we grasp reality, or are grasped by it."[47] The reality of experiences can only be translated from one age to another through narrative, providing the story with the authority to credibly interpret events. "Theology is above all concerned with direct experience expressed in narrative language," writes Johann Metz. "This is clear throughout Scripture, from the beginning, the story of creation, to the end, where a vision of the new heaven and the new earth is revealed."[48]

---

obligations. These constitute the given of my life, my moral starting point. This is part of what gives my life its own particularity."

46. Roth, *Story and Reality*, 36.

47. Ibid., 52.

48. Metz, "Short Apology of Narrative," 252. "The propositions of myth provide a . . . kind of statement . . . marked by its credibility in the story by which a culture lives. Every culture, every age, has its worldview story by which it finds meaning in the mystery of life and the world. Credibility is the criterion for thesis statements, just as emotive statements are measured in terms of honesty, verbal statements . . . in terms of validity, and descriptive statements . . . in terms of facticity. Credibility means adequacy to meet the need of a faith by which to live in circumstances thrust upon a given age. The importance of meaning in such credibility statements may be seen in the fact that when myths are no longer believed, the culture disintegrates."

CHAPTER 6

Revelation and History Reconsidered

A rabbi might begin or end a spiritual message by interjecting the phrase "so says the Lord," just as the prophets of old did. A priest might finish a homily with reference to the majesty of God and the Vatican—a sort of "so sayeth the church." Last Sunday, there were Protestant pastors everywhere who, at some point during their sermons, stated, "Well, it seems to me . . ." Regardless of the manner in which the nature of the divine is organized to make sense to congregations, there is an important aspect of faith that accounts for much of reality that a reasoned consideration of history cannot. Robert Roth suggests that religious narratives allow for us, as reasoning creatures, to do what science cannot. "Stories," he wrote, "love the absurd, they feed upon it, because it too is a real part of our world. Philosophies cannot acknowledge the absurd."[1]

This next anecdote is helpful to set the tone for this chapter, which will focus on the theme of revelation, matters of history, and matters of "making sense of it all," so to speak. Roth provides levity with a story from Albert Camus's *The Myth of Sisyphus*.

> Camus tells the story of a man fishing in his bathtub. With a view to therapy, a doctor attempts to humor the man by asking "how are they biting"?
>
> "Why do you ask?" replies the insane man, "Can't you see this is a bathtub?" and then he goes on fishing.[2]

The concept of divine revelation often presents reasonable people with intellectual obstacles ranging from the conundrums of predestination vs. free human agency to the very real critique that the idea of divine revelation

1. Roth, *Story and Reality*, 23.
2. Ibid., 16–17.

is as absurd as both the madman fishing in a bathtub and the corrective of humoring the madman as a means of understanding the absurdity. There are no sufficient answers to the claims of revelation in a world where reason and scientific method are the dominant ways of "knowing." Often, the matter of making revelation relevant to conversations about history, knowing and understanding what is real, and interpreting life so as to navigate it with a semblance of success seems to center around a significant misrepresentation of what revelation is.

For many Christians, their concept of revelation, especially as it is believed or stated to have occurred through the Bible, does not simply bestow unquestionable authoritative status upon the canonical texts. Rather, some believers insist such authoritative status is universally valid and use an apparent logic of reason and scientific discourse to lure others into accepting biblical authority. No matter that reason and science consistently bruise and batter the claims made by Christians about the place of the Bible in public conversations about policy, morality, and truth.[3]

The present task may be to attempt a definition of revelation in the Christian tradition and go forward from there. Any such definition is nothing if not debatable, but an overview for the purposes of discussion contextualizes the concepts that will follow. The word itself follows the Greek ἀποκαλάπτω (apokalyptō) and means "to unveil," "to reveal," or "to disclose." Paul Tillich described revelation as "a special and extraordinary manifestation which removes the veil from something hidden in a special and extraordinary way."[4] The phenomenon of revelation, according to Tillich, is particular to the provision of meaning to events that appear to "disregard, for the time being, the question of the reality to which they refer."[5] However,

---

3. Perhaps an over-the-top yet relevant example is evident in the websites of entrepreneur Ken Hamm, founder of the Creation Museum in Petersburg, Kentucky. Hamm is a master of manipulating scientific language to reach unscientific "conclusions" about the veracity of biblical accounts of creation and other fundamentalist concerns. See https://answersingenesis.org.

4. Tillich, Systematic Theology, 108.

5. Ibid., 106, citing Husserl, Ideas. Tillich continues: "The significance of this methodological approach lies in its demand that the meaning of a notion must be clarified and circumscribed before its validity can be determined, before it can be approved or rejected." However, he immediately sees the consequences of leaving the concept of revelation to the logic of philosophers. I suggest that the phenomenology of the twentieth century was eager to allow for individuals to create meanings independent of science or sociological explanations, yet could not bear to allow for the particularity of religious understandings of meaning derived from the divine. For modernists and existentialists, the meaning derived from religion may have appeared to impinge on the universal consciousness that might be motivating individuals to allow reason to lead them to new frontiers of thought. For Tillich, the nature of the divine in revelation

we might take Tillich one step further and suggest that an ongoing characteristic of revelation is that it *consistently* questions the reality of the *zeitgeist*
in which it is received as well as the popular constructs of God or gods that
dominate contemporary spiritual sensibilities of the church and the culture.

An encyclopedia article from Carl Braaten finds value in phenomeno-
logical understandings of revelation. He believes that it provides for a method
of making revelation intelligible to a wider spectrum of understandings by
placing it within a context otherwise unfamiliar to most. Braaten writes that
the phenomenon of revelation is, ultimately, universally intelligible and also
universally relevant once understood in the context of the religion or community that provides it context for meaning.[6] From a point of view that could be
considered "progressive" on the spectrum of religious or Christian thought,
this move was made with a desire for universal understandings (which he does
not explicitly or implicitly state), motivated not so much by making Christian
revelation more accessible, but perhaps to make it more palatable so as to be
more relevant in terms of reasoning. This is one manner in which Christian
ethics or truth claims are often impeded—either by personal embarrassment
related to the contents of the biblical text, or the inability of the constituent to
make the biblical claims fit into universally reasoned truths that can be widely
accepted. Such contributions to public moral discourse are rarely relevant,
and rather easily rejected or benign attempts to engage in utilitarian discussions of morality and the common good.[7]

Aside from the Bible as particular revelation, the consideration of its
place as a means of historical revelation, with its stories of a supernatural
being acting in history alone or through the historical human person Jesus,
creates more problems for many Christians seeking to engage in moral discourse. Such an attempt within the boundaries of reasoned consideration of
events, or the ongoing discussions of utilitarian morality that feign reliance

supplies an important qualifier. "While phenomenology is competent in the realm of
logical meanings, which was the object of the original inquiries made by Husserl . . . it is
only partially competent in the realm of spiritual realities" (107). As I will show below,
however, Tillich stops far short of providing for a truly religious, or Christian, description of what might serve as a more fully and more particularly Christian experience or
understanding of divine revelation.

6. Braaten, "Revelation." It should be understood that the Braaten article is not
thought to be representative of the entirety of his thinking, but representative of what
I believe to be the error most common to contemporary Christian ethical thought as it
is related to revelation.

7. Consider two primary means of divine revelation, one being the canonical collection of ancient texts known as the Bible, and the other being the historical person
Jesus of Nazareth. Interestingly, Tillich has rather little to say about the Bible in his sec-
tion of *Systematic Theology* devoted to revelation. He has less to say about its authority,
or how the Bible is related to practical Christian meaning making.

on empiricism or scientific method as a means of resolving conflict or moral dilemmas, makes theological gymnastics necessary. But of course, theologians are flexible. It may be said, however, that while the Bible is varied in content and meaning, most theologians wishing to stay relevant have found Scripture to be less flexible than desired. It is the Bible and history that I will address presently, and how a Christian concern for ethics must be centered on the particularities of a Christ-centered understanding of both at the expense of universalizing the contents in hope of relevance. There is plenty of baggage to overcome.

Revelation as History

H. Richard Niebuhr talks about revelation in or through history, or the possibility of a God who acts in history to make new truths known to humankind, in a nuanced manner that recommends a specific way of interpreting history. He proposes that one must first refrain from "applying the value-judgment of true and false" and instead observe or interpret history by making "reference to differences in perspectives. There are true and false appeals to memory," Niebuhr writes, "as well as (to) external distinctions, but only uncritical dogma will affirm that truth is the prerogative of one of the points of view."[8]

Niebuhr finds that individuals and communities possess a dual sense of history—an external history of "things" and an internal history of "self." External history is comprised of a memory of impersonal events or data. This outward sense of history consists of "ideas, (and) movements among things . . . Jesus, from this point of view, becomes a complex of ideas about ethics and eschatology, of psychological and biological elements."[9] However, internal history is a sense of history in which Niebuhr believes divine revelation occurs. It is "personal in character." To illustrate the distinction, he refers to the nature of the "-eds" of externals as opposed to the "-ings" of internal experiences of historical events.

"Data are '-eds,' he writes, "what is believed, sensed, conceived; but [according to] the latter (internal history) what is given is always an '-ing,' a knowing, a willing, a believing, a feeling."[10] At this point, one might consider

8. H. R. Niebuhr, "Story of Our Life," 31.

9. Ibid., 32.

10. Ibid., 31–32. He continues, "Time is duration. What is past is not gone; it abides in our memory; what is future is not non-existent but present in us as potentiality. Time here is organic or it is social, so that past and future associate with each other in present" (34). Further, "Internal history is dramatic and its truth is dramatic truth, though

Niebuhr's distinctions to be somewhat forced, yet I believe he acknowledges the importance of reminding ourselves about the contrast between belief and faith as far as the matter of revelation through history is concerned. Claims of divine will being revealed through historical events—at least those claims intended to be understood as propositional and universally applicable truths—are often "inconsistent with faith."[11] Consider this in light of other "universal" truths claimed under the same conditions, primarily those claims that paint the popular notion of the Christian God as all-knowing, all-loving, and all-powerful enough to act in history and change the course of history by interfering in or redirecting it. "Historicizing revelation feeds the view of an arbitrary and capricious god of inequality," and accomplishes more to support the skeptical rejection of Christian claims than it does to make sense of the march of time.[12]

This is a concern related to the enterprise of systematizing human and political history through the assimilation of historical events into a singular religious narrative produced by Christendom. Creeds, dogmatics, and systematics tend to focus the minds of the faithful on those matters almost entirely unrelated to both faith and ethics. "Questions about predestination and freedom, eternity and time, progress and decline . . . assail the mind of the Christian. History seems always to lead to doubt rather than faith."[13]

One reason this sense of external history (which relies on a sense of universality as well as externally verifiable confirmations of what actually happened) is misleading in that it is used to build a case for divine revelation and unfairly burdens historical events as markers of such revelation. Such an attempt to attribute universal perspective to any event as revelatory will fail. Any understandings of an event as related to history, moral vision, or even interpretation of hard scientific fact are always contingent. For a historical event to have revelatory meaning, it must somehow be related to, or the event must occur entirely within, a context that can be related to an originating or ongoing history that is universally accepted. One must accept certain assumptions about what is real, how things are known, and most of all what role events play in an ongoing drama of life and being. An event can hardly be universally revelatory, or even consistently revelatory along a

drama in this case does not mean fiction" (35).

11. Ibid., 27.

12. Ibid. "The claims of evangelist of historical revelation seem wholly inconsistent with their faith. When they speak of a just God they point to a process so unequal that only those born is a special time and place receive faith while all those who lived before or in cultures with a different history are condemned to ignorance of what they ought to know for the sake of their soul's health and life."

13. Ibid., 28.

spectrum of understandings, if all revelation is contingent on understanding events through an experience or an inward historical understanding of a God who acts.

The biblical deity is unabashedly insistent, it appears, on being known through a very specific story regarding a very specific people and manner of revelation. More simply put, the God of Israel, according to most expressions of Christian faith, is known particularly through the history of Israel and in a historical event through which Jesus of Nazareth committed himself to a ministry that arbitrated the meaning of the history of Israel and its collective expectation in new and remarkably unorthodox ways. His life and ministry could only make sense within the context of a drama solely intelligible within the framework of how God and Israel worked through history, with Israel responding to world historical events in a manner that only made sense to them![14] We can only find this in the biblical canon, and even this demands a caveat.

A common error H. Richard Niebuhr attributes to Christians is the insistence by so many believers that the very aspects of revelation are themselves historical, such as miracles. This is representative of an attempt to justify events that only make sense upon the acceptance of specific but unverifiable claims (internal histories) by claiming them as external historical events, verified by their place in biblical literature. Niebuhr believes this is a history known from a non-participating point of view.[15] It is a passive belief to buoy support for truth claims, without accountability or responsibility for meaning making being a necessary aspect associated with the claim.

George Stroup introduces readers to some of this baggage in his argument toward a narrative understanding and statement of Christian faith. He begins with a familiar refrain—that revelation is, or at least originally was, a reference to "truths which were not accessible to reason." More broadly, he writes that contemporary understandings of revelation reference "the unveiling or disclosure of a reality that is not accessible to human discovery,

---

14. Frei, "Apologetics, Criticism, and the Loss of Narrative Interpretation," 47. Frei writes, "The religious meaningfulness of historical redemption or revelation, in contrast to factual reference or ostensive meaning of the gospel narratives, depends on there being an antecedent or concomitant religious context, independent of narrative, within which to interpret them" (48).

15. H. R. Niebuhr, "Story of Our Life," 36. "For the most part persons and communities do not have a single internal history because their faiths are various and the events of life cannot be related to one continuing and abiding god. They have 'too many selves to know the one,' too many histories, too many gods; alongside their published and professed history there are suppressed but true stories of inner life concentrated about gods of whom they are ashamed."

and which is of decisive significance for human destiny and well-being."[16] To follow, it should not make sense for communities of faith to expect revelation will underwrite their common understandings of God, historical understandings of God, or commonly accepted theological claims represented in long-standing dogma, creeds, or past systematic explanations of a biblically ordered world.

Stroup also states a concern for how Christians understand revelation, and what they fail to understand about themselves. Two of his four identified "attacks" on Christian claims regarding divine revelation are particularly important in my mind. I believe these negative claims have been assumed by many Christians as a standard of reasoning that then either infiltrates their faith and leads them to an embarrassment over religious claims that might be dismissed as magical thinking, or forces them into a problem that requires shoehorning claims of revelation into the same discourse that denies its veracity in the first place.

First, Stroup writes that "what is perceived as revelatory" by persons of faith is rejected by critics according to reason. Skeptics assert that Scripture as revelation "is in no way a divine incident of God's self-disclosure." The idea that Scripture is purely an article of revelation, ultimately unrelated to time and place (transcendent) or unlimited and timeless in its purview (non-contingent), is without support, save its place in spiritual tradition at best and magical thinking at worst. Furthermore, formal reasoning rejects claims of a God intervening in history, as critics argue that the total lack of evidence, empirical or otherwise, reveals only that "historical events are not indicative of a god acting in history to reveal divine will or truths," but solely a series of events awaiting interpretation and meaning based on verifiable facts and outcomes.[17]

This baggage is problematic for the assumption of a biblical ethic on two fronts, but in a different way than one might first think. "Liberal" religious or metaphysical constructs, and those persons who claim no religious or spiritual experience, will insist that there is no evidence of supernatural intervention in history, which renders all claims of unique divine revelation absurd. Secondly, conservatives overwhelmed with the epistemological demands of modernism and science reverse the skeptic's weapons of critique by demanding not only that a specific God does indeed act in history, but that this God reveals propositional truths and judges human activity through historical acts. There is a history of Christians apologists trying

---

16. Stroup, *Promise of Narrative Theology*, 41–42. I wonder if Stroup is cognizant of differences between phenomenological/existential understandings of revelation and historic Christian claims of similar regard.

17. Ibid., 52–53.

to use naturally occurring oddities combined with some sort of scientific method in attempts to somehow "prove" that a great fish could have swallowed up Jonah, or that the earth was created in six days with signs of age, or, indeed, that there could have been a literal virgin birth.[18]

Assertions of inerrancy and the rhetoric of *Sola Scriptura* have been detrimental to the way some persons of faith understand revelation. Christian ethics must begin from a starting point that is derived from faith, and from a refusal to coerce the implied veracity of particular claims onto those who are not Christians or who come to different understandings, thus providing different meanings to events. This is an important consideration often lost on the church as it preaches and teaches from the Bible. Many conservatives paint themselves into the lonely corner of an echo chamber, mistaking the repeated assertions of inerrancy for objective justification of their claims. This has a terribly negative effect on the possibility of a biblical ethic. "For all its homage to the authority of Scripture," writes Stroup, "conservative Christianity continues to confess the regional, parochial interests of the American middle-class with the promises, claims, and demands of Christian faith."[19] So, any reading of the Bible that attributes inerrancy to the Scripture itself, by intellectual neglect, reinforces the gravity of the culture and preferred socioeconomic realities that weigh heavily upon interpretations of so-called inerrancy as well.

Stroup is equally assertive in challenging progressive Christianity by demanding that it "offer a compelling description of what it means to live and understand one's self in the contemporary means of Christian faith."[20] The routine American experiences of wealth, social standing or mobility,

---

18. Again, see Hamm's answersingenesis.org. Also, naturally occurring anomalies tend to excite fundamentalists as potential proof that miracles of the Bible could be factual representations of historical fact. An example is found in a species of shark, living in captivity, that experienced a type of "virgin birth," better known in the scientific world as parthenogenesis. See Howard, "Shark Gives Rare 'Virgin Birth' to Three Pups," para. 5. For claims that science can provide proofs of virgin births unrelated to other species, see Olsen, "Scientific Proof of the Virgin Birth," in which the blogger engages in apologetics intending to scientifically defend the virtue of Mary the mother of Jesus.

19. Stroup, *Promise of Narrative Theology*, 23. Stroup believes the Bible has come to hold a "curious place" in Christianity. "The relationship between Scripture and the world has nothing to do with teaching children to memorize the Bible in order that they learn a proper morality . . ." Stroup recognizes "biblical illiteracy" as a "serious problem at all levels of the church's life." He laments a "hermeneutical gap" between the first and twenty-first centuries that has seemingly become "unbridgeable." He also believes that, on the other hand, there is such a drive to make the first century familiar and domesticated to our contemporary sensibilities that it is no more than a "mirror reflection of contemporary cultures and its values and worldviews" (24, 27).

20. Ibid.

and progress impact our considerations of the Bible. So too do they lead to that condition that Stroup identifies as a Christian "identity crisis." Because Christians avoid or ignore theological resources that would enhance their understanding of Scripture, if not provide for a recognition of how herme-neutics are important to our faith, Stroup believes we continue to clothe ourselves in an identity formed by culture rather than faith. "Their identi-ties—who they are, what kind of people they understand themselves to be—are shaped by other communities and other narratives."[21] If Stroup is correct in his assessment, the idea of revelation has lost its impact and also its ability to shape a biblically derived Christian ethic that is in fact Christ-centered.

Revelation might be the primary means of making known the plan of God, but there is something more important to this. Revelation is how persons of a specific faith make sense of the world within the boundaries of that specificity. The truths of revelation are contingent truths. Stroup challenges the common concern for universal meaning that marks con-temporary religious belief. "What one knows in revelation," he writes, "is not an idea or proposition that is universally true without reference to time and circumstances in which the event takes place . . . revelation cannot be separated from the event in which it makes itself known."[22] There is an im-portant matter that follows Stroup's statement. Revelation is not initiated by human activity. Created beings are not "so much the subject as the object of" revelatory events. God does not reveal the effect that sins have on us, but reveals that we are sinners and we must repent of sin as a witness to others and the ways we impact one another. Revelation is not the means through which humans will someday gain the basic knowledge about righting the ship, but a basic truth that we won't, and must be vigilant of the ways in which sin presents itself so that we can experience a deliverance from a state of simple acquiescence to such brokenness. "What one knows in a revela-tory event *is not something that could have been discovered given enough time and ingenuity.*"[23]

In summary, concerning the Bible, revelation, and historical events, I believe that Christianity has turned toward an erroneous tendency to in-terpret history in a manner that not only reflects, but codifies and coerces existing preferences by attributing to historical events a singular metaphysical

21. Ibid, 36.

22. Ibid., 42.

23. Ibid., 43. Italics added. I find this comment to undergird aspects of the gospel, if not most of the ethics I will claim below are biblical ethics, which contend that non-violence, voluntary sacrifice, and emptying of privilege are all revealed in the cross and the life and death of Jesus, yet are in no way indicative of timeless universal truths or "spiritually evolved" behaviors.

relevance and assimilates readings of both text and Western history to these events. This shows blatant disregard for what is stated above—that revelation, if it is divine, makes known things that were not only previously hidden, but also could not possibly make sense within the metaphysical or pluralist constructs that are common to the spectrum of humanity. It should be understood that, because the matter of revelation is a matter related to a specific deity (the God of Abraham), it can only make sense within long-standing understandings of that deity. Divine revelation by definition turns all such "universally understood" knowledge or understandings upside down.[24]

Presently, I will discuss points made by Stroup that round out the above discussion of revelation and history proper. He suggests that "because revelation is an event that takes place only by a means of God's grace it is a redemptive event for all those who participate in and respond to it." He contends that "revelation is not the solution to a problem but the unveiling of a mystery."[25]

I invite Christians to begin to understand revelation as a means of making what is perceived to be mystery less mysterious and more concretely intelligible to the world through the practice of particularly (or peculiarly) contingent behaviors. While the "problem" as we understand it may avoid scrutiny from the non-believing world, Christians know that the problem is sin, however that may be defined by various Christian communities. We might *not* solve the problem of sin. Yet, when radical sin emerges in apparently unprecedented ways, what is revealed is not a mystery, but an indicator that the church must find new ways of *responding* to radical evil or brokenness through understandings only available to the church of faith, through

24. H. R. Niebuhr, "Story of Our Life," 23. "Metaphysical systems have not been able to maintain the intellectual life of our community and abstract [or utilitarian] systems of morality have not conveyed the devotion and the power of obedience with their ideals and imperatives. Idealistic and realistic metaphysics, perfectionists and hedonistic ethics have been poor substitutes for the New Testament, and churches which feed on such nourishment seem subject to spiritual rickets." As American Christians continuously attempt to reestablish a civic or public mandate for articulating and/or legislating a universally relevant and controlling moral vision and code, the more a reliance on metaphysics as a civic spiritual vehicle becomes an attractive foundation for a return to the supremacy of Christendom. Metaphysics, as opposed to a specific and entirely contingent display of gospel ethics, is the only way in which any religious narrative can compete in a utilitarian and democratic society. The race to control the discourse and win the ongoing arguments of moral and ethical dilemmas in a world-wide or national conversation is doomed to fail, as stated above. Revelation, in this sense, will always be manipulated by attempts to rewrite history, reinterpret outcomes of the past, and control the possible outcome of the future in a way that makes it not revelatory, but most relevant to the conditions deemed necessary by those who wish to arbitrate truth to vindicate their own agendas, at the expense of a Christ-centered witness to God.

25. Stroup, *The Promise of Narrative*, 43–44.

the witness of both Scripture and Christ, which will not make sense to the rest of the world. The church can consider history an opportunity.

Such revelation can only occur—indeed, it is a mystery only to non-Christians—specifically to a community that has a distinctive and unique means of interpreting and reorganizing historical events in a manner that inaugurates a new manner of living. Christian ethics only begin to make sense when they are embodied in a manner that then reveals their value to those who voluntarily seek redemption from participation in radical sin. While revelation is certainly an act of grace, it is also undoubtedly an act undertaken by the church in tandem with a God who provides the church with the means to recognize new and subversive truths. Revelation is one of those means.

Now to flesh out some important points. First, I ask we consider for an instant that revelation is neither mystery nor paradox, but a call for the church to act in history with new understandings of brokenness. Moreover, I would like Christians and theologians to give up the philosophical concern for paradox when discussing revelation.[26] The concept of revelation invites a community of faith to witness to how God continues bestowing grace when hope otherwise seems lost or when violence seems to be the only credible reaction. Revelation is primarily a call to ministry, when the church must make a decision to respond not with belief, but rather with faith and healthy spiritual risk taking, despite its being most simply regarded as a statement of grace. I ask this: Why is there need for a doctrine of revelation when revelation just is? Is this a matter of well-stated belief versus faith? Or is

---

26. Engaging in apologetics to make sense of the problems posed by claims related to divine revelation so that secular entities might better understand or accept them as legitimate is a favorite pastime for some. Ultimately, however, apologetics relies on the acceptance of mystery and paradox to render the argument on behalf of God and Christian theology competitive. Christian ethics must consider revelation as an issue of understanding and meaning making and, as a spiritual call or invitation, a necessary theological task that helps more with identity and role formation than it has to do with witnessing to universal truths. Faith is a matter of highly contingent truth claims that rely on arguments of paradox or mystery only when an attempt is made to universalize such claims of truth in order to convince others of their veracity. A community of faith is not bound to accepting paradox or mystery as the final markers of credibility, nor is it bound to defend behavior grounded in faith despite its apparent absurdity. Rather, it embodies an ongoing christocentric response to the fact of sin in new ways that must be accessed for credibility according to the fruits they produce, more so even than any evidence for a God that ordains them. Consider Camus' "bathtub fisherman." There is no paradox or mystery evident in the insane man's actions. He is simply insane. Likewise, as Christians attempt to make sense of the absurdity of the world and realities of sin, there is no paradox evident in their actions, only the fact that the person speaking about divine revelation is in fact a Christian. If the man in the bathtub were a Christian, the doctor might ask, "How are they biting?" and the Christian would respond, "Can't you see this is a bathtub? I am practicing to be a fisher of men."

there a concern for protecting dogma—to protect universals in the face of "historical" evidence that God is calling the church to change?

This then is the primary and instructive means of the divine being revealed in Scripture. The Bible is witness to the presence and reality of radical sin in human history and human relationships. It is a narrative of much more than simply a history of sin, however. It is a narrative of how God has provided the means of responding to, and redeeming human relationships in light of, sin. The mystery is no more—but is revealed through the life of Jesus, as is the manner in which the people of God are called to respond to sin.

Revelation in Sum

Christians may define revelation as the interpretation of events through the maintenance and embodiment of the biblical narrative. This demands that the church or congregation who wishes to voluntarily identify as a people of the God of Israel and assume the messianic ethics of the New Testament must commit themselves to understanding and making sense of life, history, and the nature of the divine in continuity with the discourse of the text. This mandates a manner of thinking that accepts assumptions that otherwise fall outside of the present boundaries of scientific method, empiricism, and modern concerns toward scientific or reasoned universal understandings of what makes truth claims or assertions of truth credible. Human reasoning will always be successful in justifying means to a favored end.

However, reasoning according to the demands of modernity and much of Enlightenment epistemology cannot justify any morally acceptable ends, especially if a universal morally acceptable outcome is sought. It follows that revelation of divine will or the unveiling of new truths cannot be bound to history or to historical events. Revelation is only bound to the manner in which the church seeks to identify those events that occur in their due time, interpret them through the application of the biblical narrative, and then participate in history, acting out God's unfolding response to human activity so that alternatives may be offered to a broken and suffering humanity. When events that are significant in human or regional history occur, it is the church that is uniquely equipped to both observe and interpret these events. The church then begins to embody alternative ways of living faithfully according to the manner in which human sin and brokenness has been made evident. The unveiling is the making known of God's provision of yet another opportunity for humanity to understand and embody grace and mercy.

The church only knows of this mission because the nature of sin and the manner in which it plays a role in human history is a matter of biblical revelation. That it is the responsibility of the people of God to witness to God's willed response to sin is revealed biblically. There is no mystery—other than that sin has ruled human history, and God reveals a hopeful response to ever-evolving matters of sinfulness through the church. It is Christ and the messianic ethic of the New Testament that not only resolves the mystery, but allows for the continuing and consistently biblical response of the church to mediate and redeem the effects of historical events.

The Gospel of the Absurd

What must now be considered are the questions raised in the previous chapters. I have shown how difficult it has been to maintain a consistently biblical ethic. It is also evident that even the most conservative of churches, outside of those choosing the sectarian option, have found that the Constantinian trajectory toward combining power and secular rule in pursuit of moral outcomes fails to maintain a biblical, or messianic, character. In truth, those aspects of the messianic ethics of the New Testament are often rejected as absurd while concepts such as six-day creation and the virgin birth are defended and even used to manipulate public policy outcomes, if not elections. Just as progressives pick and choose those aspects of the gospel that tend to uphold non-violent and non-judgmental expressions of faith, conservatives will paint themselves into philosophical or unreasoned corners of discourse by demanding the veracity of miracle accounts, yet manipulating the economic and socially egalitarian aspects of the gospel. Yet, it is absurdity, or the turning of the world's manner of thinking and doing upside down, that is at the core of the Bible, from Genesis to Revelation. It is from this point that Christian biblical ethics must begin, and it is at this often embarrassing place that all messianic ethics must anchor their claims. Indeed, either the poor are blessed and the humble will inherit the earth or, for all intents and purposes, the cross is little more than a storied failure, a myth for the conquered and miserable to revel in as they await reward in the future but avoid the pursuit of justice and righteousness in the present.

Revelation, messianic ethics, and the kingdom of God are all matters of righteousness in the here and now. These themes have little to nothing to do with going to heaven after death. To understand such a proposition, we must now turn to matters of eschatology and apocalyptic thought. It is only when the gospel and the Bible are read through the twin lenses of end-of-age activity and a church born to witness and engage dramatically in the world that we can truly be a New Testament church with a messianic and biblical ethic. We now begin our journey into the absurd.

CHAPTER 7

Eschapocalyptic

A Gospel of the Absurd

A young man, age twenty-eight or so, stood in line to ask a question of John Spong. The bishop was speaking to a congregation that had invited him to deliver a workshop regarding the early church's claims of Jesus' resurrection. When the young man's turn came, he asked Spong to comment on the Revelation to John, the last book of the New Testament. What was most remarkable was not that this question was asked of Spong, who spends his life raking conservatives and fundamentalist Christianity over the coals (which often seems a necessary vice), but the pointedly negative tone of Spong's response. To boil down the overkill of this response to its bone, Spong basically stated that the Book of Revelation did not legitimately belong in the canonical text, and that it served no useful purpose. The bishop seemed to ridicule the questioner, going on to identify the text as dangerous, and representative of the kind of thinking among Christians that most represented a sort of corporate mental illness.[1]

1. I was in attendance at Spong's lecture with fellow theologian and former pastor Robert Webber in the spring of 2004. It was at this lecture that the Rev. Ian Lawton, a student of Spong, was introduced as the heir to Richard Rhem's pastoral position at Christ Community Church. While I assumed at the time that Spong's attack on both book and the questioning individual were not out of character, it took little time to produce a similar response to a similar question on an online Q&A site called *Christian Forums*, which bills itself as a site for liberal Christians. In fact, the question and answer posted on the online forum, if the response did indeed originate with Spong, were so similar to the question and answer at the lecture series that it might appear to some as though both question and answer are staged as a means of Spong matching an unfavorable eschatology with a preferred or new, well-intended universal eschatology. The following are excerpts from the letter that provide the gist of Spong's angst over the Revelation to John. The letter was in response to a question asking for explanation of the meanings behind the Apocalypse. "Dear Mr. & Mrs. Redel, I have never written about the Book of Revelation because I

There is another aspect of this story that provides important context. The church that held this workshop had hired a young, energetic Australian pastor to take over the lead from retiring Pastor Richard Rhem, who was known to introduce Spong as a "true prophet" whenever the opportunity presented itself. Reverend Ian Lawton had been hand-picked to take over for Rhem, and immediately led a willing congregation a step beyond what many progressives might have considered to be the boundaries of *Christian* identity. Two years after Lawton took the reins, Christ Community Church removed all of the crosses from the building, even the one that reached high from the steeple, in order to better reflect what the church had become, or was trying to be, in this conservative West Michigan community.

"Our community has been a really open-minded community for some years now," Lawton said. "We've had a number of Muslim people, Jewish people, Buddhists, atheists . . . We're catching up (to) ourselves."[2]

A local newspaper reported the events, where Lawton reflects on the purpose of the rather dramatic makeover of the church. He even invited the public at large to comment on or question the church's decision.

"C3Exchange will hold a public meeting to address questions about the changes at 7 p.m. Thursday at Grand Haven Community Center . . ."

"'Nothing's going to be expected of anyone who attends,' Lawton said. 'You don't have to sign up for anything. It should be a good, lively evening.'"

"Lawton said the church decided to change its name about a year ago and began taking ideas from members. He said the new name was chosen because the church is on Exchange Street, and our community is a place where people can come to exchange ideas." He said the church is considering painting a heart, a globe, and the word "exchange" on its exterior wall on the side where the cross stood, to symbolize "one love" for "all people."[3]

---

do not regard it as worthy of the kind of study that would be required to write about this book. I'm sorry it was included in the canon of the New Testament because it is so dated . . . I have no truck with those who read the Bible this way. Predictions about the end of the world, talk about the 'rapture' and 'no child left behind' are all so much literal nonsense to me . . . I have read the book of Revelation on several occasions. I studied it when I was in seminary, but in no great depth . . . Today I would rather spend my time on the gospels, Paul, or even the prophets, all of which have enriched my life greatly. I do not see such potential in the book of Revelation . . . When one tries to interpret the symbols as Mr. Redel does in his letter, he falls into the trap of assuming that there is some literal truth that needs to be discovered. That is not the case. If all the copies of the book of Revelation were lost tomorrow, I do not believe much of value would disappear. However, it does keep some religious fanatics busy so maybe that is its primary purpose." Spong, "Bishop Spong Q&A on Revelation," para. 4–6.

2. Hart, "Spring Lake's Christ Community Church Removes Cross," para. 3, 5, 9.

3. Ibid.

What so-called modern-day prophets such as Spong and Lawton may or may not have intended was happening at Christ Community, once a congregation of the Reformed Church of America. The gospel was being universalized, only this time it was not conservatives attempting to colonize non-believing communities into the Christian fold, but self-identified progressives either reaping the rewards of or, rather, coopting their faith in the historical-critical method. They followed their spirit guide in order to forge some sort of religious community out of the remnants of a faith destroyed by counter-literalism. Within two years or so, the new congregation, named C3Exchange, had to sell the building. What began as an attempt to make the Christian story a universally acceptable *moral* construct resembling the American "Melting Pot" *social* construct ended as a failed experiment in a congregation attempting to bury the embarrassing baggage of religion that did not suit its secular sensibilities.

A newspaper reporter wrote, "when the cross was removed, C3 Exchange had just changed its name and direction to become more inclusive to people of different religious and spiritual backgrounds. As a part of the church's transformation, it decided to remove the 40-foot steel cross that adorned the exterior of the church, located at 225 E. Exchange St. in Spring Lake, causing great controversy. C3 Exchange Executive Minister Lawton told the Chronicle at the time that the church was considering painting a heart, a globe and the word "exchange" on its exterior wall on the side where the cross stood 'to symbolize one love for all people.'"

"We honor the cross, but the cross is just one symbol of our community," Lawton said.

The reporter summarized the outcome of the congregation's decision to be one that could be identified as more inclusive. "C3 Exchange never installed its new, re-purposed display because it left the property in September 2011 after struggling to meet its mortgage payments and later began hosting its services at the Grand Haven Community Center."[4]

There is a lot more going on in the above anecdotes than might meet the eye of some, if not most of us. I suggest that, in the midst of the obvious contrast with, if not outright reaction to, conservative Christian ideas about eschatology and apocalyptic, we have in the above representations a fairly telling example of what happens when well-intentioned and, for the most part, well-reasoned folks react to their spiritual embarrassment, and project universal or transcendentalist renderings of hope onto the particular narrative of the gospel. Such universalism shames the past and buries the stories that allow for us to makes sense of the exodus and the cross. It allows

---

4. Anderson, "Spring Lake Church Plans to Reinstall Controversial Cross."

those embarrassed of claims of miracles and resurrection to marginalize the eschatological and apocalyptic nature of Abrahamic religions in favor of a spiritual or religious presentation that has *relevance to social, economic, and political realities* (or better yet, apparent necessities).

I propose that Christ Community Church of Spring Lake, Michigan, failed to recognize or value the primary peculiarity of Christian eschatology, which is, I believe, indicative of the present failure of the church catholic. This is a failure to identify the basic presupposition that Jesus, the cross, and his resurrection are at the heart of Christian eschatology, and as such, it is Christian eschatological and transformational *hope* that is the fuel of a Spirit-driven church, and not a cataclysmic end-of-the-world event that will punish the pagan and apostate alike in a scorching dragon-ignited lake of fire.

The eschatological hope of Christian faith is that the fact and nature of sin has been revealed, and is realized in ever-changing sociopolitical circumstances and physical phenomenon. In response, the church does not acquiesce to sin or evil, but recognizes the need to explore faith and text and embody a new manner of witness that not only challenges a growing acceptance of sin or emergence of latent evil, but also tests limitations that the secular world places upon what might constitute preferred subsequent outcomes. Thus, the church subverts both sin and the increasingly normative conditions that have allowed for newly transpiring evil to germinate and break through the darkness into a light of false legitimacy.

Again, at the very center of this cycle of ends and beginnings is the cross of Christ and resurrection narratives. The death of Christ on the cross is subverted by Christian claims of resurrection. The claims made by authority, or by those which would otherwise legitimize violence and domination as a means of pursuing justice, are subverted by the claim of the church that God will emerge as the arbiter of history and truth. Such arbitration occurs through Christ. God's justice is revealed through the witness of the church whenever injustice reaches the point of what secular institutions might regard as "critical mass." Despite the fact that the primary means of public Christian witness may result in impoverishment, incarceration, or execution, the biblical narratives indicate that there is rarely evidence of God's goodness or will exhibited outside of an often small band of faithful constituents that lives faithfully on the margins of the dominant culture.

God's response to human violence and sin subverts human insistence that violence and other power-and-control mechanisms are appropriate means to achieve favored ends. The cross subverts commonly accepted reasoning by insisting that hope and faithfulness are the only means of discovering and disseminating mercy and grace, let alone making it intelligible to the rest of creation. So, let's set to the task of unpacking all of this, as more than a little discussion must take place to counteract the literal readings of Christian eschatology and apocalyptic literature of both conservatives and progressives—readings that have tended to justify a hope for favored secular outcomes as opposed to a hope for the victory of the Lamb.

There is a lot to unpack. One of the more uncomfortable tasks might be that progressive Christian thinkers and laypersons need to be challenged every bit as much concerning eschatology and apocalyptic thought as those who have fallen victim to the "second-coming-end-of-the-world" theology that was never really part of the church tradition before or within memory of the disaster of Muenster.[5] Let it be stated presently that, in terms of the ethics under consideration in this book, eschatological understandings of past and present and concurrent apocalyptic risk taking are considered to be the heart of the gospel response to sin. The real challenge of messianic ethics and the embodiment of faith begins, ends, and begins again with faithful risk taking in the name of a God that has called the church, at its very core, to exhibit the same voluntary sacrifice, and endure the same sort of suffering, that is representative of Jesus' life as well as his death on a cross.

End Times and Armageddon Relieved of Baggage

Eschatology is a loaded term, and it has more than a few operative definitions. The Greek ἔσχατος (eschatos) is detailed primarily as "the farthest boundary of an area (the last place in the farthest corner)," as being the final item in a series, or holding status or being in a position that is furthest from the top of a hierarchy or an order. The Greek allows for one to take the expression toward a further extreme by using ἐσχάτως (eschatōs), meaning to be at "the point of death."

One might or might not be surprised to find that the use of the extreme form of the word is used just once in the New Testament canon, found at Mark 5:23. This might be of some importance to our understanding of how early Christians understood social and religious views of "the end." The author of Mark writes:

5. Rossing, *Apocalypse Exposed*. Rossing presents a thorough look into New Testament thought, early Christian understandings of apocalyptic literature, and the critical errors that undermine the quasi-fundamentalist readings of apocalyptic literature, understandings of the Parousia, and how the Darby/Scofield models of eschatological terror became so entrenched in certain Western religious groups. Surprisingly, Rossing does not write about the events of Muenster and the Anabaptist millennialist attempt to usher in an apocalyptic realization of the kingdom of God. For an entertaining lecture on Muenster in history, see Carlin, "Prophets of Doom."

He pleaded earnestly with him, "My little daughter is dying. Please come and put your hands on her so that she will be healed and live."

I suggest this literal use of the word is important not to expose the limits of literal end-of-the-world proof-texting, but to enhance our understanding of Christian hope. When the literal term is found—the word literally related to the final death or total and complete end of existence—it is used in the context of resurrection! For Christians, even in the earliest gospel texts, there is no acknowledgment of finality, but the hope of resurrection related to Jesus' ministry makes such finality absurd despite the obvious fact that everything does have an end.

Even in the context of the fall of the Northern Kingdom, then the Judean exile, the destruction of the temple (twice), and finally the very fact that the Romans were in charge of the world—and YHWH, in the minds of everyone but Jews and first-century messianics, was not—Jews and early Christians of the ancient Near East had continuing hope. In fact, Jews and Christians *knew* for a fact that God would vindicate the faithful and turn the world upside down according to its conventional knowledge. Then it would become evident to all that YHWH was indeed and always had been in charge. How did communities of faith know this? Because God had worked in history before on behalf of Israel.

An example of particularly Jewish eschatological hope is found in the ancient central prayer of Judaism, the *Amidah, Tefilat HaAmidah*, or, most simply and familiarly to many Christians, *Shmoneh Esreh*: the Eighteen Benedictions. This daily prayer reflects the nature of the eschatological hope that has always been and still is present in Judaic faith and practice. Especially reflective of this, and important to our understanding of the messianic hopes around the time of the ministry of Jesus, is the expectation of the restoration of both Jerusalem and the Davidic monarchy to a place of political and economic significance. The middle of the liturgy petitions YHWH for action on behalf of Israel: knowledge, repentance, forgiveness, redemption, health, and economic prosperity. Then follows six specifically eschatological pleas: the ingathering of the exiled (and gathering of the diaspora), the restoration of justice, the destruction of sects and heretics and of Israel's enemies, the vindication of the righteous, the return to glory for Jerusalem, and the coming of the God's anointed in the line of David.[6]

6. Dunn, *Jesus Remembered*, 393–96. Dunn presents an outline of first-century Jewish eschatological thought with a fourteen-point delineation of kingdom of God premises. He believes that evidence points to the hope for a unified and restored Israel and the return of YHWH to dwell in the temple. Jews believed that this eschatological kingdom would mean economic prosperity and physical health for every Jew. There

As stated, much of the hope we find in the Benedictions were said to be realized through God's work in Jesus. First-century Jewish messianics sang songs of triumph in Christ despite the fact that they were regularly being forced out of synagogues and disowned by their families[7]—songs that were fully immersed in Jewish understanding of the end times. When messianic Jews sang, "every knee will bow and every tongue confess that Jesus Christ is Lord," the end times they had in mind were not indicative of an anticipated end of the world. Rather, Christian and Jewish expectation anticipated an end to Roman rule and an end to the apparent rule of sin. The end times were an indicator that a new age was dawning, not that everything was hurtling toward its ultimate demise.[8]

This Jewish hope was indicated not only according to the firm insistence that Israel and Jerusalem would be restored to a state of glory that would be evident to all other nations, but that there would be a general resurrection of the dead so that those who suffered in faithfulness and died will be vindicated in this glory. This hope of resurrection is primary in the Benedictions, and in both Jewish and Christian apocalyptic literature. Indeed, the mighty premise of Christian eschatology is that the resurrection of Jesus is the indicator of God's plan to be faithful when the time is full, and all will be made righteous in a future age.[9] Until that age, Jews and Christians alike are called to live a faithful life of witness. Christians have a blueprint for such faithfulness, that being the life and ministry of Jesus, which must be embodied if the nations are to know what salvation might look like.

---

was a consistent use of great banquet imagery, a renewal of covenant, full repentance, an outpouring of the Spirit as foretold by Joel, Zion as the center of the universe as opposed to Rome, the expansion of the promised land to status of an unboundaried empire, a time of tribulation and suffering or desolation, a catastrophe that affected Israel and the rest of the world, a final destruction of evil, the glory of Jerusalem and YHWH restored, resurrection, judgments, and vindication or finality for the unjust in the fires of Gehenna. Dunn's list nearly mirrors the contents of the Benedictions.

7. John 15 provides an example of how first-century messianic Jews were making sense of their marginalized status with post-temple rabbinical communities.

8. Wright, New Testament, 331. "The eschatological expectation of most Jews of this period was for renewal, and not abandonment, of the space-time order as a whole, and themselves within it. Since this was based on justice and mercy of the creator god . . . it was inconceivable that those who had died in the struggle to bring in the new world should be left out of the blessing when it eventually brake upon the nations and thence on the world."

9. Ibid., 332. "Resurrection and the renewal of creation go hand in hand. If the space-time world were to disappear, resurrection would not make sense . . . Resurrection would be, in one and the same moment, the reaffirmation of the covenant and the reaffirmation of creation."

So, if the hope is for restoration and that "every knee will bow" before YHWH, how can we make sense of this end-of-the-world narrative that has become so popular with the culture? In fact, outside of some sociological understandings of Western industrialization, market economics, and a fear of social sciences, we cannot. The end times is not a biblical concept, but a modern one. To repeat, the end of the world was not a Jewish or Christian hope.[10] The hope of YHWH is the end of the world as they, and we, understand it to be regarding our contemporary eon. The future remains a continuing fact of the cosmos, and the earth.

To understand eschatology and apocalyptic, if we are to have an understanding of these themes in the present and undo the more recent interpretations of modernity, we must recognize the narrative consistency of these two themes throughout biblically recorded "history." From Exodus through the books of Judges, Ruth, Kings, and Chronicles, the whole of the Hebrew Bible is filled with the story of how YHWH acts in the interests of Israel—for or against, but always working with the seasons of history to accomplish anticipated outcomes. The suggestion or exhortation that Jesus is Christ makes no sense without Jewish apocalyptic and eschatology.

Early followers of Jesus gleaned through Scriptures to muster texts that made sense of Jesus' ministry, death, and resurrection in terms specific to the ongoing story of God and Israel. They pointed to apocalyptic and prophetic literature so that their claims of fulfillment would make sense. It would be impossible to claim that anything actually occurred in Christ if it were not for the Jewish expectations of God acting in history in just such a manner. The expectation of a Christ is representative of Jewish eschatology. Christ's non-violent ethic, his inclusion of Gentiles under the umbrella of God's grace, and his reorganizing often maladapted understandings of Torah is representative of the apocalyptic claim that messianic expectations and the covenant promises of God to Israel were fulfilled in Jesus of Nazareth. God revealed the divine will through Jesus in new ways that, though understood entirely within the context of Judaism, were as entirely subversive in their content and projected outcomes as they were intelligible within the context of the past.[11]

10. Ibid., 333. Wright contends, along with a large spectrum of scholarship, that "*there is virtually no evidence that Jews were expecting the end of the space-time universe* . . . There is abundant evidence that they, like Jeremiah before them, knew a good metaphor when they saw one and used cosmic imagery to bring full theological significance to cataclysmic socio-political events." Italics original.

11. Bratten, "Last Things," 1174. "Eschatology was a constitutive part of the story of salvation . . . The prophets announced the day of YHWH, the coming of the messiah, and the New Jerusalem, looking forward to a new and different *future in history* . . . In apocalyptic writings we find visions of a wholly new *future of history*, a new age above and beyond this one." Italics original.

Let's also recognize that the eschatological narrative is seasonal, however, and not linear in the manner we understand most narratives to play out. Eschatology has little or nothing to do with the concept of progress or a civilized march toward a universal morality and truth.[12] While eschatology is about hope, it is quite possibly more of a statement about the past—one that identifies epic change in a manner that only makes sense when placed into the perspective of how a God has consistently worked to change the way creation understands sin through the seasonal perspective of this God's creation and creatures.

The prophets of Israel "were not so much driven by a vision of the future as by confidence in the past, the past that had antecedently shaped their present and would continue to influence its forthcoming course."[13] Think about that for a moment. If eschatology represents how we witness to hope for our salvation in a future that is based entirely upon what God has accomplished toward salvation in the past, apocalyptic is the claim that we can only respond to new understandings of sin by revealing the new ways in which the church embodies the old stories of the cross. Voluntary sacrifice as a means of responding to such sin is, again and again, the only Christ-centered witness against sin in the present.

The legitimacy of revealing God's desire within the boundaries of an ancient narrative that should be understood *prima facie* as intending to subvert reason can only be assessed as credible or incredible against the manner in which the claim of Jesus' own execution and resurrection, and the history of the church, are the measure of revealing how God's grace, mercy, redemption, and reconciliation have a revelatory effect on the nature of new ways in which the world has mistaken sin for progress or justice.

12. Science and progress are not vehicles for moral visions to be realized, nor do they buoy the veracity of moral truth claims. Dunn describes the Western view of time as linear in nature. He points to John Ballie's *The Belief in Progress* as a book that first illustrated the implications of this on Christian faith. "We see some affirmation of this basic worldview in the irreversible forward steps . . . of the modern period—the development of printing, of aviation, of radio, and television, and the revolution in information technology." Dunn warns that "we do not mistake . . . scientific progress must lead to moral progress." Dunn, "He Will Come Again."

13. Malina, "Exegetical Eschatology." Malina suggests that the attitude of first-century Greco-Roman and Palestinian thinkers was markedly "present-oriented." An event that was about to happen was forthcoming, a sort of expanded present rooted in a process launched in the present. If some "end" were coming soon, it would not have been so much a future expectation any more than it was, most simply, a part of the what was always underway in the present rather than a cataclysmic expectation of an ἔσχατος.

The Eschapocalyptic Train is off the Tracks

For many reasons, however, much of Western civic religion and the attending neoconservative readings of Christian apocalyptic verse have instead insisted on reading the parts of the gospels and the Revelation to John as literary records of what will occur, literally, when the God of Abraham and Sarah decides to end the world and history in a final sweeping away of evil. Why this literal reading of apocalyptic imagery and the end-of-the-world scenarios are so popularly accepted, or even how they are understandable, fails to explain why so many Christians refuse to discuss the potential for metaphor to be the primary lens through which to understand apocalyptic writing and eschatological thought. James Dunn wrote:

> We are all accustomed to picturing the biblical visions of hell in terms of a fire that burns without being quenched. The imagery was in part drawn from the fires of *Gehenna*, the constantly smoldering rubbish dump outside the wall of Jerusalem . . . Are we to take that image literally? What then of Dante's portrait of the deepest circle of hell as a deep frozen lake in which souls . . . are forever trapped? Or C.S. Lewis's portrayal of hell as a depressingly gloomy, smoggy city? Are these alternative images rendered false by the predominant canonical one? Were Dante and Lewis wrong to depart from the biblical one? The more appropriate answer is to say that all three are attempts to portray and unimaginable human future in terms drawn from the most horrific experiences in human life. Here once again language falls far short of what we are trying to say.[14]

As I intended to illustrate in the opening anecdote regarding a West Michigan congregation's own experience of *reaction against* literal interpretations of end times theologies of "prophecy," progressive Christians

---

14. Dunn, "He Will Come Again." Also, Bratten wrote, "There are three unsatisfactory approaches to 'last things.' 1) to construct . . . a literal timetable of events that will happen soon or in the distant future; 2) to interpret the images as metaphorical expressions of religious experiences and inner states of mind *unrelated to real history and the future*; 3) to read apocalyptic literature as social commentary or subversive rhetoric of an oppressed community in times of persecution." Bratten, "Last Things," 1174. Italics added. While others such as Wright have successfully challenged Bratten's third claim, the other two are important to consider, and even the third should be taken seriously, as not all apocalyptic literature is the product of an oppressed community, but rather a prophetic or messianic community that may or may not be experiencing oppression during authorship. Bratten indicates that the overarching theme of Christian apocalyptic is not the fact of oppression or suffering, but instead is the repeated exposition of the gospel and keeping Jesus at the center to control the nature of eschatological theology through history. He adds, "the central motif of Jesus's message was the Kingdom of God" (ibid.).

must not make the mistake of fighting maladapted literal eschatological and apocalyptic constructs by insisting in *equally literal terms* that such constructs are impossible and irrelevant, as John Spong has done. To do so is to marginalize the text in the manner that the bishop hopes to. Congregations and communities of Christ must come to an understanding that our role is not to predict the future, or to warn of the end of the world, or to get people to heaven so they can avoid the coming wrath of God and a one-way ticket to hell. However, we should recognize that apocalyptic texts do indeed call us to action on behalf of faith.

We begin by understanding that Christian eschatology and apocalyptic faith demands that we participate in the biblical narrative as active constituents. As discussed above, our understanding of history is necessarily one that interprets events specifically through the lenses of a creator God who is revealed variously in Scripture, the gospel, and the body of Christ. We must also avoid the error of spiritualizing history and the apocalyptic texts to the point of confusing our ethics with the heavenly realm or supposed transcendent truths as opposed to here-and-now moral embodiment.[15]

To avoid the theological errors, and the very real and dangerous social tensions produced by literal readings of apocalyptic literature, we must be honest about the impossibility of leaping across the chasm of centuries of meaning to arrive at modern understandings of apocalyptic thought. Just as importantly, we must not be stuck in the common assumption that first-century Jews were intellectually blinded by superstition and lack of what we believe to be scientific understanding. While they did not have access to the amount of information we currently possess at our fingertips, this does not mean that first-century folk were uninspired thinkers or incapable of logic.

Also, one should recognize the errors inherent in dismissing the very important role such language and imagery played in the way the early church understood its call to witness to the world. While we cannot be concerned to take such imagery literally, we must understand the nature of how imagery in any text carries with it layers of meaning that would have been easily decoded within the context in which it is written and disseminated. Do not scorn first-century Christians as folks who believed that dragons

---

15. Malina, "Exegetical Eschatology," 53. "The definition" of apocalyptic and eschatology "must be stripped of its etic features. For example, the following categories were non-existent in antiquity. 'Otherworldly;' 'transcendent reality;' 'eschatological salvation;' 'another, supernatural world;' and 'the future' were not considerations for first century Jews. If such terms are used" in our discussions of ancient themes of salvation, "they must be defined in some comparative perspective. If they are left to stand, they imply and ethnocentric as well as anachronistic perspective."

and angels and a Whore of Babylon would be observed in cosmic combat at cloud level during their lives or in any future age.

In light of our understanding of eschatology and apocalyptic to this point, I suggest that we think in terms of apocalyptic and the role such thought played in *defining* the New Testament church, rather than simply being a component of it. Again, the life, death, and resurrection of Jesus is apocalyptic, and the same are all part of eschatological theological concerns that set the agenda for a truly messianic ethic. The way to share such narratives in times of uncertainty or in the presence of the enemy calls for the use of symbolic language to share truths in special ways with those who have ears to hear.

Metaphors are not to be considered as "merely decorative ways of saying something that could be said literally," suggests Dunn. "Rather, metaphors are a way of saying that which cannot be said literally or which literal description would be inadequate to describe."[16] In religious language, metaphors can be described, according to Janet Martin Saskice, as "reality depicting without pretending to be directly descriptive."[17] There is no indication that texts such as Daniel or the Revelation to John predict future cosmic realities that have no grounding in the perceived reality of either past or present. Nevertheless, we can identify literary or artistic strokes that are intended to communicate something extraordinary. While eschatology provides us with the tools that facilitate hope for the present and future according to the manner in which God transitions the people of God to a new age of understanding, apocalyptic provides the tools for the church to act accordingly.[18] While metaphor allows for us to understand more about the texts of the early church and ancient Judaisms, more must be done to state how important themes of eschatology and apocalyptic are in the present, and how the metaphors of ancient apocalyptic literature have very little to do with the contemporary witness and mission of the church.

Breaking the Chains of Modernity

Presently we begin to consider what eschatology and apocalyptic means for the church and what should be considered to be a time of necessary church reformation and renewal. Christendom is decaying and must be allowed to die. However slowly its demise may be, in light of what we know of God's activity in the past and of what is continuously revealed in light of the cross

16 Dunn, *Jesus Remembered*, 403.

17. Ibid., citing Saskice, *Metaphor and Religious Language*, 145.

18. Shakespeare, *Derrida and Theology*, 151–52.

of Christ, we can only understand the end of the church as we know it with the assurance that the church will indeed continue on. This renewal must occur in a manner that subverts not only old understandings of the role the church is to play in a liberal democracy and a postmodern world, but all of our understandings of what and who the church is, and how worship should reflect the historically subversive work of the Spirit. For decades, the church has rejected its identity as an apocalyptic witness to the world, instead choosing to maintain a comfortable order of progress and power.

Remember, the manner in which we are to be the church in this age of renewal and reformation will seem absurd to all who cannot place faith in the resurrection story. The gospel moral vision of non-violence, egalitarian community order, and the subversion of the authority of empire and political entities can only be made credible when the church, or particular actors within the church community, live out an ethic that makes such moral claims credible. It is difficult to claim faith in Jesus as Prince of Peace when one relies on the military to stabilize access to resources and world markets. The church is called to respond to such corporate secular assumptions of truth, which is in fact latent corporate sin. The subversion of such insidious sin demands that normative considerations of social order and concerns for a universal good be reidentified as sin disguised in attractive yet necessary compromises that in fact reject the desire of God for the church. To make such a theological maneuver, and to state spiritually that those things which have been readily consumed by the culture as "the common good" are instead a rejection of the gospel order, progressives especially must learn to feel comfortable speaking enthusiastically in christocentric terms. Particularly Christian claims must be at the center of what is to be revealed by the church as an answer to the question of redeeming a broken world if we are to answer as a church, and not as constituents of a more widely palatable universalism.[19]

The very thing that a majority of American Christians seem unwilling to do is assess corporate or national sin in a manner that confronts the power of the nation-state and its economic and military priorities. This accommodation of state power indicts the church as a compliant contributor to such sinfulness. The conservative idea that abortion or unbiblical sexual behavior is responsible for "apocalyptic" events such as natural disasters and failing economies is adversely responsible for hiding the truth of corporate

---

19. Harink, *Paul Among the Postliberals*, 73. "Post-Christian, postmodern, third millennium North America" is "in the habit of believing something is profoundly wrong about staking religious claims in terms of conflicting worlds, life and death, truth and falsehood. In this context, those terms are reserved for such matters as national survival [whether political or economic], the institutions of democracy and free markets, and inalienable rights and freedom of choice."

national sin from the populace, for such judgment redirects our concern for sin away from ourselves and onto minorities and marginalized persons who cannot defend themselves from such scapegoating.

Ellen Charry writes that "New Testament writers anticipated, or perhaps provoked, Christian clashes with the empire." She suggests that contemporary Christians "struggle," in the context of liberal democracy and as members in good standing of the sociopolitical power apparatus, "to remain uncomfortable in a comfortable culture, which compels them to conform."[20]

For Charry, this is very much a matter of "clarity" in which the church has become such a socially and politically complicit member of the culture that it is perhaps unable to see the curtain, let alone the men standing behind it and wielding power. She believes that biblical eschatological hope prescribes an "apocalyptic clarity [which] pits the pure church against the evil empire" in a relationship between the two entities that is set within a "complex frame." The church is called to recognize through the course of biblical revelation, the gospel, and the early church that a primary concern for the church is revealing alternatives to the actions of those who claim authority that supposedly surpasses the moral vision of the church. The mission of the church, in light of the exodus and the cross, it to expose the "false gods of Rome" and be "ambassadors for Christ." The credibility of the gospel "now relies on" the church.[21]

It is through the church's identity as the main entity through which God's truth is revealed, thus "it not only gives hope of God's power to rescue, it also interprets how things were, are, and ought to be. Its purposes are to inform and influence human life by means of the values and insights expressed within the symbolic and narrative form."[22]

However, there is a side of eschatology apart from fiery metaphor that not only makes progressive Christians like Spong more than a little uncomfortable, but there is little doubt that apocalyptic leaves less room for gray area than is appreciated by progressive concerns for universalism and/ or overarching truths (even if they are "hidden" from human discernment,

20. Charry, "Sharp Two-Edged Sword."

21. Charry writes about apocalyptic literature in a rather romantic way, yet it is compelling reading. Concerning clarity, she writes that it "seems to be a constant feature of apocalyptic . . . wherever there is perceived to be a cosmic struggle between goodness and evil . . . wherever there is a longing for a future era of peace and righteousness in which God will wipe away every tear, there peeps the eschaton, the fullness of time [births] the vindication of the Righteous." Ibid., 164.

22. Ibid. Charry also identifies another important aspect of eschatological hope and apocalyptic literature. She writes "It is, or can be, an instrument of spiritual nurture." As we will see below, it is also a component of spiritual authority that can be utilized in calling churches to be stronger in the faith."

progressives seem not to realize that their insistence on universal truths actually work against the fact of diversity in spiritual thought and religious discourse). Apocalyptic literature strives to be clear on a division between what is good and what is evil, and is most often interpreted by communities with an apocalyptic vision as being indicative of their own righteousness in light of vulnerability to attacks from evil. Apocalyptic communities tend to believe that "goodness is readily distinguishable from evil, and that they are on the right side of the cosmic divide. Even if it looks like the forces of evil have the upper hand in the struggle there is no real acceptance of evil's eventual triumph." Zealotry, at least apparently, is always a troublesome by-product of apocalyptic.[23]

In a setting such as the United States, however, where the church has for so long received favored status in the seats of power, and been a source of strength for the government if not an outright resource for government to utilize in achieving its goals, this clarity can be confusing for many believers. Christians in the United States rarely consider their government or nation as an instrument of blatant sin. In fact, what seems often overlooked or rejected by American Christendom is the manner in which apocalyptic literature denies the place of the nation-state as an arbiter of justice. More often, such apocalyptic language facilitates confusion and will blur the supposed clarity of revelation for patriotic or nationalistic theologies to a point where biblical apocalyptic assumptions are subverted.

Also confusing for many within the context of liberal democracies is how national entities often act in opposition to the gospel, or the revealed will of God, yet just as often in a unsuspecting manner. Empires and governments are often identified in Scripture as the very instruments of wrath through which the divine plan is accomplished. Empire is a constant fact of scriptural context, and it is through empire and human authority that God's true power is thought to be, or interpreted to be, revealed. Whether in the plagues against Pharaoh or through the destruction of the two kingdoms by Assyria and Babylon, judgment is often carried out through the enterprises of military might, unjust empires, and outright persecution of the righteous. Even in non-apocalyptic literature, judgment of God's own people comes at the hands of the unjust, the mockers of God, the powers and principalities of this world.

Charry regards this as a "source of anxiety reflected in the apocalyptic expectations of conflict and suffering built into the gospel itself." She finds that the belief that God will punish God's own people through the use of malevolent entities such as Babylon or Rome is a tension that often frustrates

23. Ibid., 165.

attempts to make sense of the apocalyptic lack of middle ground. However, this is more of an indicator that it is only in apocalyptic community that alternative responses to historic crisis is found. This is true in spite of the order that has been maintained by empire, which is revealed to be sinful and in opposition to kingdom ethics. What we find in Christian apocalyptic, and in books like Daniel, is that the people of God must serve as good citizens, but are always called to be kingdom citizens first and foremost. It is in God's faithful assemblies that the true nature of empire and secular authorities is revealed as sinful, idolatrous, and founded upon the violence that is antithetical to the salvation that emerges from the cross. Like Daniel before it, the Revelation to John is in fact a "counter-cultural subversion of both Roman and Judaic claims of truth and power," which not only reveals that Christ is king, but that any claims made to the contrary are anti-Christ and therefore a threat to God's truth being fully revealed and grasped.[24]

According to apocalyptic, even, if not especially, those churches that claim Jesus is Lord are also at risk of judgment if they fail to recognize the that eschaton is at hand. Apocalyptic calls the church to *repentance* as much as it calls the church to *reveal* new responses to sin. The tone of Revelation shows that all congregations are not the same, nor is their witness, nor are their understandings of the gospel. Most often, contemporary congregations cannot be categorized as apocalyptic or otherwise, and may often feel targeted by apocalyptic witness. This places people of faith in often difficult positions, if not in outright opposition to apocalyptic claims of an eschaton.[25] The Revelation to John provides evidence that, even within seventy years of the resurrection, "worshipping the Beast was something many of John's Christian readers were tempted to do, or were actually doing."[26]

This identification of the religious community at large as complicit in evil is an early aspect of the Christian gospel. "Jesus predicted that judgment would fall on the nation in general and on Jerusalem in particular. That is

24. Ibid., 166.

25. Charry writes that "according to the Apocalypse, Christ desires a militant church that will absorb suffering rather than accommodate the powers that be. Indeed, to preach Christ by employing the same tactics as the Beast would give Rome the victory." John confronts his audience, especially Laodicea, about what is lacking in their witness to the cosmic victory that Jesus claims over Rome. John cites that complacency, or perhaps even complicity is the result of their failure to confront the evil that Jesus reveals is inherent in the Roman empire. Some Christians were surrounded by Pagans and lost their grip on the gospel's demand to be radically separate from the culture at hand. Other Christians seemed bound to the economic security and stability offered by maintaining ties to Roman authority, and seemed reticent to reject Rome as an evil entity. "In light of Philippians 2:10–11, we can see that confessing the name of Jesus intended to provoke the state. Jesus Christ was the proper threat to all counterclaims against divine authority." Ibid., 166.

26. Bauckham, *Theology of the Book of Revelation*, 15.

to say, he reinterprets standard Jewish belief in terms of a coming judgment that would fall on impenitent Israel. The great prophets had done the same." Jesus, however, was not simply a second-temple prophet that reignited the flames of judgment inaugurated by the prophets of old. He was in fact following the lead of his contemporary, John the Baptist.[27]

The very roots of Christian faith are not only found in eschatological hope and an apocalyptic overturning of both sociopolitical and religious standard truth claims; they are found to originate in the very roots of Israelite hope and faith. There is to be revealed not only that sin can be crouching at our very door, but that the history of God promises that new ways of identifying and overcoming sin are to be revealed. Because this God has always acted to save creation, we are assured this God will do so again. Our hope lays in our past, yet the manner in which we make sense of both past and present must be revealed consistently and in new ways. Jesus of Nazareth is the standard through which Christians consistently reveal the truth, which is by non-violent truth telling, even as we risk suffering.

What Is to Be Revealed . . .

If there is to be a paradox that can be identified (which I deny earlier), one might consider it at this point. History was a concern for the discussion of revelation, and so it is true for our discussion of eschatology, and the meaning of apocalyptic beyond metaphor. Apocalyptic is not only an understanding of truth, but it occurs only within a specific range of meaning if it is to be Christian. Moreover, there is the matter of how truth claims are to be revealed. Presently, I wish to turn to an exciting piece written by John P. Manoussakis entitled "The Anarchic Principle of Christian Eschatology in the Eucharistic Tradition of the Eastern Church." Manoussakis speaks to the matter of the role facts play in our identity formation, which can consist of both of those elements proposed by Tillich and Stroup above. Just as I state that God demands some sort of recognition that salvation is realized only in maintenance of faith despite the apparent absurdity of the gospel claims, Manoussakis believes that "nothing undermines our freedom more than a predetermined and given nature; our fixed facticity."[28] As such, our present

---

27. Wright, *Jesus and the Victory of God*, 323. He writes, "Jesus seems to have adopted the theme" of the need for the national repentance of Israel" from John, who predicted 'the wrath to come' saying that membership in physical Israel was no guarantee of a share in the age to come."

28. Manoussakis, "Anarchic Principle of Christian Eschatology," 30. He writes, "Most of us understand ourselves as who we have been—our identity is like a record in which every action, every deed and thought, transcripts, professional résumés and

is actually defined as much by our future as our faith is a practice in trust that God's truth and desire is revealed in the biblical past.

How might the gospel redefine our realities? It is not only in the eschatological nature of our understandings of time, but in our understanding of Jesus as the fully revealed nature of God that we are liberated from the "predetermined facticity" that allow secular authorities to hold sway over what is possible and what is not. Various data is used by secular enterprises to define what is good and what is not, and what might be reasonable truth and what is to be construed as absurd. Yet, for Christians it is through the gospel and the experiences similar to those of the earliest church leaders like Paul that we claim newness in Christ. We are freed from the manner in which our past defines us, and instead come to be defined by what God has in store for our future—not so much by how salvation rewrites our past, but rather how it authors new chapters for us, opening a new sort of future for us along with a new reality. "We are not who we have been," argues Manoussakis, "but who we will be." This is indeed an exciting reality of the apocalyptic nature of the gospel and our understanding of how the church works once individuals are liberated from secular claims and born again in the Holy Spirit. "The church," he writes, "offer[s] a new logic—the logic of the new."[29]

This logic contrasts with conventional wisdom about how the past informs what we know to be true. While Christians claim that the nature of God and creation, as well as the nature of sin and "salvation" from the effects of sin, are revealed in our common claims about how God has worked in the past, our understandings of history and knowledge based upon experiences are significantly different from Enlightenment understandings of how we

---

medical files. In all these cases, and for the various institutions they represent—the police, the academy, the marketplace, and the medical establishment—we simply *are* our past."

29. Ibid., 30. This coincides with the claim that we have hope for the future because we know from the past that God works toward salvation. The credibility of our claims comes from the continuous understandings of God and God's work that are made known by the Bible, through Jesus, and in the church. The past underwrites the truth of our claims about the present and for the future, just as resurrection underwrites our faith that if we act faithfully ourselves, we will receive the inheritance of God's favor just as Jesus has. Faith is not only our trust that in grace and mercy God will vindicate our faithfulness, but is the awareness that Jesus was resurrected because of his faithfulness. We can trust that the weakness and absurdity of the gospel is the only manner in which God's desire is revealed only if we trust that we will be similarly vindicated. Society is obsessed with the past for different reasons, and the culture is obsessed with a far different understanding of the past than that which is represented by Scripture. Manoussakis states that secular knowledge is an "entirely protological" epistemology. He cites Kant and writes, "knowledge is based by necessity on experience, and experience is always the experience of that which has been and come down to pass, that which, in other words, can be measured, observed and written down in files such as those mentioned earlier."

know what is. Enlightenment thinking and its heir, modernism, will indicate that it is the past that determines the present as well as the end. There is a beginning, or cause, to any event.

Theology is different. While the Christian will also argue that we know what is true and what will be true because of our understandings of the past, we interpret the present and the hope for a better future because our past is one of salvation history and the activity of the people of a creator God. We have an understanding of history revealed in a specific manner that places all of human activity and subsequent history in the categories of creation, incarnation, crucifixion, and resurrection.[30] In other words, we understand truth through the event in which God revealed truth through Jesus and the cross. Yet, we can only understand this past from the promises of the future that we glean from the resurrection of Jesus. Our past determines our understanding of history only through our understanding of what is anticipated in the future. Stated simply, we can have faith in non-violence and voluntary sacrifice of privilege as an answer to sin only because we understanding that we will be vindicated in a manner similar to Jesus. God reveals the true promise of what the future holds for creation—not death or violence, but life and rebirth. Secular history may show that power and control and domination of others might produce favored outcomes, but the church identifies with a God who prefers far different outcomes achieved through the application of a far different ethic than one that requires the domination of others.[31] Life is lived not for the purposes of history, but in light of a final restoration of relationship that has been long foreseen by the creator.

This is a definite turn away from the literal end-of-the-world eschatology of fundamentalists and many conservative churches, but it differs just as significantly from the outright rejection of apocalyptic that is represented by John Spong, or the universalism of progressive Christian thinking that focuses more on peace and rights-oriented justice than the peculiarly

---

30. Ibid., 31. He continues, "What would be, for example the "cause" of the crucifixion? Does the cross make any sense at all if seen by itself, that is, as the effect of that which has preceded in the life of Jesus? We would argue that the cross becomes the cross only one it is seen from the future, that is, from the point of view that follows it."

31. Ibid., 31–32. "'It is not at the beginning of that man is truly himself [sic].' For as Heidegger would say, the beginning determines humanity and history only insofar as it 'remains and advent.' Lacoste writes 'Meaning come at the end.' In this respect, eschatology is *anarchic* through and through, for it alone can effect such radical subversion of the ἀρχή of principles and beginnings." Manoussakis continues: "Eschatology . . . reverses naturalistic, essentialist, and historic models by making the seemingly improbable claim that I am not who I am, let alone who I was and have been, but rather . . . I am who I will be" (ibid.). Citing Heidegger, "Hölderlin's Earth and Heaven," 195; Lacoste, *Experience and the Absolute*, 137; Ziziouslas, "Toward and Eschatological Ontology."

Christian call for the rejection of privilege and an assumption of suffering servanthood by those same privileged. Manoussakis states that in order to have a proper Christian eschatology, a biblical eschatology, we must "turn away from the narrations and cataclysms and catastrophes." He writes that Christian eschatology is *not* "the end of history" but instead it "*is* the incarnation, and it is the incarnation as it unfolds in history . . ."[32] Manoussakis believes these three points act as a "refutation of a rather dominant tendency in Christian theology of assigning eschatology to a semi-utopian time at the end of history" that might or might not come at the end of our lifetime. "By relegating eschatology to a realm beyond experience, we have come up with the perfect alibi for getting all too comfortable with the world in its current state." He then suggests that this tendency to consider eschatology as a catastrophic end of time mocks the biblical presuppositions of what happened in the incarnation, and what "wonderfully subversive" claims were specifically made through the incarnate Christ and the early church concerning our future "and the reversals" claimed in Christ "might bring."[33]

To sum, with the help of Manoussakis's fine article, the eschaton is not the end that is claimed or even hoped for by conservatives. Yet, it is not really even an "end" in the realm of *telos*, or a goal recognition or achievement, nor is it a completion in the sense of process. "The ἔσχατον can be found on either side of the end of history, or on both sides, before it and after it, but it should never be identified with the end itself." We have no knowledge of when the kingdom will be fully realized, at what point in salvation history we are at in our present, or even of the true nature of the eschaton to which we are called to witness. We can only witness to the fact of sin, and new ways of responding to sin in a manner consistent with Christ as we understand him through the Holy Spirit. The eschaton is in fact an opportunity. "The kingdom of God does not coincide with the culmination of history," writes Manoussakis, "but it signals a breach in the body of history, a rupture occasioned by the encounter with the other."[34] It is both in the church and in "the other" that we must always recognize Christ. Such is the nature of apocalyptic, and such is the nature of the Christ.

32. Manoussakis, "Anarchic Principle of Christian Eschatology," 33. Importantly, one should identify a difference in the direction of Manoussakis's article and my use of his article toward the purposes of this book. While Manoussakis rightly attributes an unfolding recognition of eschatological truths through the continuing celebration of the Eucharist, I rather identify this ongoing recognition of the incarnation as occurring through public witness and the display of Christ-centered ethics as informed by understandings of ongoing eschatological seasons and the church's call to both recognize and respond to such eschatons.

33. Ibid.

34. Ibid., 34.

CHAPTER 8

Seismic Shifts and Acts of Philip

I will share two times among many that I was put in a position to "put my money where my ethical utterances come from." The first came during a family visit with friends who lived in a community that provided homeless folks with a room and helped them meet other needs. My family lived in this community for three years, and I also worked at the local gospel mission in town during that time. I knew a lot of the folks around the neighborhood, and I also knew some of their stories. Their stories, in fact, were often similar to my own.

During the end of my drinking years, I had bottomed out enough to seek treatment through the local community mental health organization. One of the young social workers assigned to my case had just earned his bachelor's degree after working through his own addiction problems. He had personal knowledge of the kind of struggles I had, and was empathetic with my situation. This young social worker was one of scores that saw no progress in my life while they worked with me. Nevertheless, together they had a big impact over time.

Soon after my last drink I entered the social work program at a local Bible college, and I was able to start work at a gospel mission. One night during my second year working there, I was directing men toward their beds and this young social worker walked in to get a cot for the night. He did not recognize me, or he feigned unfamiliarity. But I knew him. He was high, and had been using long enough to have become homeless. A few nights later a group of coworkers of the man came looking to help him. He must have known they were looking, because he disappeared for a few nights until they stopped coming around.

I only saw this young man a few times before my family left the state for me to attend seminary. I met him one last time at the community I mentioned above. He had come into the house to find the crack pipe he had left behind in the bathroom. He was asking to get it back, and since I was very familiar with the item he was describing, I would not let him retrieve it. I walked into the bathroom and found the stem right where he said he left it. I acted according to my first thought—one that my life experience and work with other addicts had prepared me for. As a person of faith and a man in recovery, I could not give it to him.

He became distraught and agitated, and threatened me with violence if I did not give him the crack pipe. I replied that I could not in good faith give it to him, because it was killing him, and I would not participate. I suggested alternatives. He could sit down with me and the head of the community and we could work out a mutually favorable ending; he could walk away without the pipe; or he could follow through with his threat of violence. I would not fight back or defend myself, as Jesus forbids it. The man came toward me, launched a few punches that did no real damage, and pulled the tool out of my hand. He turned and ran out the door.

My five-year-old son witnessed this struggle. During our discussion of what had occurred, I explained that my actions were related to my faith in Jesus and my hope for the well-being of the young man. I could do nothing that I felt would bring harm to him, and both fighting back and giving up the pipe would have done such harm. My son said I took a punch for Jesus. My hope was that he had learned something about my faith, and that he might even understand it.

About two or three years later, we had another incident calling us to practice non-violence, and it seems that the prior lesson, while impactful, did not suffice in the way I had hoped. Two men had escaped from a prison up north and had been breaking into homes in our area. A few local schools were closed during an afternoon because there had been a break in; weapons were stolen and the armed criminals were still at large. When I learned that we were advised by the sheriff's department to lock our doors and watch for suspicious activities, I talked with my wife about what we might do.

The first thing I did was take our hunting weapons to our neighbor's house so neither I nor the men on the run would be able to use them against another human being. I then went to the store and bought food to share on the very slim chance they would happen by our house. They never did come by, and as far as I know we were never in any danger. But when I came home the next day, I learned an interesting lesson about Christian ethics—it needs to be practiced more than every three years in which the opportunity presents itself.

I learned that handing down a non-violent ethic to the next generation, and anticipating that it will be accepted without repeated opportunities to practice it nor a wider community to reinforce it, is not something that can be handed down like holiday traditions. When I returned home from work the next day, my three children were all playing happily among a junkyard-quality mess of iron skillets, toy golf clubs, and baseball bats.

I asked about the mess in the living room and got a quick reply. "We know you won't fight, Dad, but we didn't think we had the same chances as you do, so we were gonna fight the prisoners." As I look back on this, I have considered a number of reasons why my children, at that time ages fourteen, nine, and five, were preparing to fight instead of offer a shared meal with escaped prisoners. Naturally, their age had a lot to do with it, and while they would all say they are Quakers, non-violence was not something they themselves had put into practice in any concrete manner. It was an idea to them, and having heard stories of their father being attacked with knives at the mission, or seeing him punched and not fighting back, equated non-violence with physical danger and potentially painful outcomes. It is difficult to ask children to consider accepting such a burden without some very deep thinking on their part. And some questioning.

But there is something more to the decision they made, which was probably more about preparedness in the face of anxiety than actually having to fight against what they heard were potentially dangerous persons. It may be that the children saw their father's religious behavior as unique to their dad yet unrealistic for children who had not experienced inner-city Detroit violence or physical attacks at the mission, and did not stand at six feet and weight three hundred pounds. In fact, there may have been no options that seemed reasonable to my children in the face of perceived danger. The iron skillets and baseball bats may have been so much bravado intended to cover anxiety. I doubt the kids were going to fight at all. In fact, they had not been trained in any response, because the danger they perceived to be near that day was simply not a common experience in their lives.

One might question why perhaps-scared children were left alone for a few hours. Simple: we had to perform necessary tasks outside of the home. Like any children living in a violent neighborhood or war zone, children are left alone with a teenaged caretaker because economic realities demand it. My wife and I did not have the privilege of making sure one parent was always at home, and the kids remained under the care of our oldest daughter for four hours. There was no indication of anxiety in their behavior when I left the house, and had it not been for the articles of war that littered the living room that afternoon, I would not have known that anxiety had existed at all. It may be that the cooking utensils did the trick, and they felt stable enough in their environment to simply carry on. It never came up again.

I have come to believe that intentional non-violent responses to specific situations are not normative for Christians, not because they are too
difficult an ethic to maintain, but because we do not live in communities
that seek out opportunities to embody such faith on a larger scale. If there
were Christian assemblies where the whole congregation and assembly of
saints practice non-violence, and train their children in the daily practice of
non-violence, the children of that community learn different ways of deal-
ing with anxiety related to crisis. There is still anxiety—indeed, it may often
be related to the threat of violence—but it is not just mother and father
practicing faithful pacifism. Rather, non-violence as a matter of living faith
is evidenced in every aspect of every life by which they are surrounded.
Such children know no other alternatives than to love their enemies.

Apocalyptic Ethics in the Early Church:
Where the Church Went Wrong

So out of the ordinary were the behaviors of Christians during the first three
centuries of the Common Era that their adversaries mocked them as a "third
race." By this it was meant that the early church was not a religious sect
that fit into definitive categories of Barbarian or Greek in social or religious
practice.[1] One of the reasons for such distinction was the manner in which
Christian social practices were thought to be outside of intelligible behavior
was the "communal" and care-taking nature of the churches.[2]

Wayne Meeks refers to the narrative of the early church as an "insider's
story," a story line we have identified above as an ongoing Hebrew/Israel-
ite story of how a specific God, YHWH, engages in covenant relationship
with creation. The ministry of Jesus does not indicate any transition to a
new narrative, but a new chapter in an ongoing story. This new Christian
chapter extends and expands understandings of this history in which a
specific people known in the personages of Abraham and Sarah, Moses,
Ruth, David, and so many biblical characters respond to events through
which YHWH has changed the world. Thereafter, the ministry of Jesus, his

---

1. Meeks, *Origins of Christian Morality*, 9. For Christian converts "who would come
to accept their stigmatization as a 'third race,' neither Jew nor Greek, could sometimes
say that their *politeuma* was in heaven, not on earth." Meeks identifies the Greek term
as "revealing" in the sense that is was a term often utilized by organized groups of
immigrants—"resident alien"—for example Jews in a Greek city (13).

2. Ibid. Meeks writes, "Christian groups most effectively distinguished themselves
from other cult-associated or philosophical schools . . . [by] their practice of communal
admonition and discipline, the organization of aid for widows, orphans, prisoners, and
other weaker members of the movement" (213).

subsequent execution, and vindicating story of bodily resurrection from a publicly humiliating and heinous death are given meaning by the church through the manner in which the church continuously lives the story out.

If we take seriously the countercultural, counterintuitive, and sacrificial nature of the gospels, we must absolutely recognize the following: once injected with eschatological and apocalyptic understandings of sin and the role of the church in addressing brokenness, a Christian moral vision necessitates an extraordinary ethic that can only be deemed credible if it is embodied by a community of faith. More than a few critics of Christendom have recognized the church's failure to establish a consistent biblical ethic, let alone practices that embrace the kind of eschatological thinking and apocalyptic outlooks defined above.[3] McClendon writes that a Christian moral vision cannot leave behind the context and motivation of the gospels when acting in the present. "More generally," he writes, "the vision should show how a people's identity is construed via narratives that are historically set in another time and place but display the redemptive power of the here and now."[4]

How can we get ourselves in touch with an ancient moral vision and practices while keeping mind the warnings of Ricouer and others above regarding our desire to relive or "mimic" the Christian communities of the first century? For instance, regarding the Sermon on the Mount, we are left with a sketch of kingdom ethics, as opposed to a rule. Meeks states that the standards expressed by Jesus are simply descriptive of "the will of the Father in heaven." "Yet," Meeks writes, "the 'will of the Father' is not an abstract perfection."[5]

Jesus does not lay out a blueprint of behaviors that indicate the nature of godliness; rather he identifies concrete situations in day-to-day life in which God desires human beings to repent of normative human brokenness and exhibit specific behaviors that will lead to redemptive relationship. Jesus illustrates moral instructions that "belong to the realm of the everyday:

3. Cahill, "Kingdom and Cross," 159. Cahill describes the church as being historically reticent about the embrace of a truly Christlike ethic. She writes, "Christians are supposed to act with compassion and forgiveness, especially to those in need. What constitutes basic moral goodness from a Christian standpoint has never been all that mysterious. Yet interpreters of the New Testament down the ages have evaded its moral message with ingenious rationalizations, and personal exceptions."

4. McClendon, *Ethics*, 34. McClendon suggests the following directives of moral vision. First, he calls for an awareness of the biblical story (also, see Stroup above), and secondly, missionary outreach with responsibility for costly witness. He identifies discipleship as a directive, with faith practices as indicative of life transformed by faith in Christ. Fourth, McClendon calls for community, a corporate expression of daily sharing in the moral vision. Ibid., 38.

5. Meeks, *Origins of Christian Morality*, 200.

marriage, truth-telling, facing foreign soldiers and other enemies, giving alms, praying, forgiving people and fasting."[6] These are not indicative of religious ritual or a mystical seeking of enhanced relationship with the divine. The Sermon on the Mount illustrates how Christians are to live every day in order to realize the moral vision that encompasses the kingdom of heaven. Yet, for any of the sermon to make sense, or for any of Jesus' kingdom vision to be realized, his teachings were contextualized by editors and leadership to fit the needs and anxieties of each church.

These were not relativized ethics tailored to fit a non-Christian moral vision. Each community interpreted certain of Jesus' moral exhortations in a manner that described how they were to live in a Christlike manner within their specific context, yet in constant tension with the moral concerns of the Greco-Roman world. The gospels of Mark, Matthew, and Luke show how specific teachings were interpreted and then performed as a witness that was both true to the memory of Jesus and practical as witness to this truth of the gospels in unique ways that were apparently often nonsensical to the world around them.

Constantinian Dilemma: The Briefest of Overviews

As stated above, the fourth-century state legitimization of the church had a significant effect on the ethics of the church.[7] Ever since, interpretations of

6. Ibid., 200–201. "There is no clear line between the secular and the sacred. On the other hand . . . (there is no) code of behavior. Although Jesus directs that new disciples must be taught to observe 'all I have commanded you' we have here no system of commandments. The rules are exemplary, not comprehensive, pointers to the kind of life expected in the community." Meeks writes that Christians are "left with the puzzle that . . . his teachings recorded here do not add up to an ethical system." In other words, if Christians "are to 'achieve all righteousness,' the members of a community need to know much more than Jesus' collected teachings." They knew the narratives of the Hebrew Bible, the narratives of Mark, the order to an assembly to bind and loose according to the institutional memory of Israel for continuity, and to go forward in faithfulness according to the Spirit. As such, the new assemblies needed to contextualize the teachings of Jesus that were handed down in order to address their specific circumstances and witness to the gospel accordingly.

7. Frend, *Rise of Christianity*, "From Pagan to Christian Society, 330–60; "New Perspectives in West and East," 554–91; 616–50. See also González, *Story of Christianity*, 151–57. González writes, "Obviously, the most immediate consequence of Constantine's conversion was the cessation of persecution," but that "One of the results of the new situation was the development of what may be called an official theology. Overwhelmed by the favor that the emperor was pouring on them, many Christians sought to show that Constantine was chose by God to bring the history of both Church and Empire to its culmination, where both were joined . . . Others took the opposite tack. For them, the fact that the emperors declared themselves Christian, and that for

Scripture have tended toward accommodating the realities of empire (and later, democracy), and the needs that such political structures have to use coercive force, litigate outcomes respective of individual rights, and regularly engage in deception and use morally questionable power and control mechanisms. The United States proves no exception, despite the commonly held view of the church that America is itself a vehicle to express corporate faithfulness. In order to ensure outcomes that are favorable to political order or wealth, but not nearly favorable to the moral vision described here, the church has come to support morality and ethics that do more to marginalize "the other" than to seek relationship with them.[8]

I have suggested that to begin a return to being a church that reflects faithfulness, a starting point is not to suspend reason, but rather to prioritize faithfulness to God and the divine desire for human relationships as evidenced in the life of Jesus. We must also revisit the history of the early church to identify not only what the witness of the church looked like before Constantine, but what social and political factors facilitated the radical changes I believe occurred during that era that skewed the manner in which Christians viewed the role of the church in the world. Consider examples of testimony from early Christian leadership for an introductory perusal of early normative Christian moral vision and ethics. The following literary evidence presents an ethic of non-participation before the church accepted Rome's invitation to advocate for the thrones of Rome and heaven to sit akin to one another. The ethic is overwhelmingly non-violent in nature. It

---

this reason people were flocking to the church, was not a blessing, but a great apostasy." Some of these left the corporate church and went to the desert to live as hermits. González writes that this choice was due to the newly realized lack of opportunity for martyrdom. Others became reformers, and "simply declared the church at large had been corrupted, and that they were the true church." These radicals tended to attack the church in North Africa (circa 340) by singling out bishops whom they accused of "yielding their faith," during persecutions, "but had been restored to communion." Some critics of these bishops were led by Donatus, a newly elected bishop of Carthage who believed Rome could be convinced to see the error of their favoritism of elites. While Donatists were the largest group attempting to purge the church of perceived unfaithful, many existed throughout the empire. Donatists were also politically interested in excluding these certain bishops, who had won regional social and economic power during the reign of Constantine. González states that those church leaders were thought to be a "latinized class of landowners, merchants, and military officers." He identifies the Donatists, and other groups, however, not so much as anti-empire, but "opposed the world—although for them many practices of the empire were worldly."

8. McClendon, *Ethics*, 17. "The church's story will not interpret the world to the world's satisfaction. Hence there is a *temptation* (no weaker word will do) for the church to deny her 'counter, original, spare, strange, starting point in Abraham and Jesus and to give instead a self-account or theology that will seem true to the world on the world's own present terms."

is also countercultural, and demanding of personal emptying of power and privilege. Finally, it is an ethic of faith over Greco-Roman reasoning.

In his second *Apology*, Justin Martyr remarked on the meaning of repentance, and what his baptism meant as he turned away from the reasoned philosophy of Athens to the faith of Jesus Christ. Justin was born to pagan parents and considered himself a Gentile. Born in Samaria, he was doubly disregarded by Jewish opponents as indicative of all that was wrong with those who claimed Jesus of Nazareth is the Christ.[9] His thinking represents much of Christian thought in the second century.

He wrote that the philosophers of the world elaborated on reason according to partial understandings of truth, or what he declared to be "contemplating some part of the (w)ord [logos] . . . but did not know the whole of the Word, which is Christ, and they often contradicted themselves."[10] As for moral vision, Martyr states clearly that turning away from old ways of behaving according to the standards of happiness in the world in favor of Christian behavior has little to do with reason and everything to do with witnessing to the truth of Christ. He writes about celibacy as a practice, abstaining from "magic," and eschewing the valuing and acquisition of "wealth and possession" in favor of sharing all wealth in a common purse in which church leadership shares with church members in need.[11] He adds, "we who hated and destroyed one another on account of their different manners would not live with men of a different tribe . . . since the coming of Christ, live familiarly with them, and pray for our enemies, and endeavor to persuade those who hate us unjustly to live comfortably . . . to the end that they may become partakers of the same joyful hope of a reward from God the ruler of all."[12]

While such lists of behaviors or practices were common in Greek thought, and lists delineating the good from the bad are commonplace in the Bible, it is telling that for nearly three hundred years the Christian literary witness focused on a canon of ethics that very clearly illustrated what the marks of Christian behavior were, over and above ritualized aspects of worship.

Rarely is an example of formal ritualized worship found in Scripture or other early Christian texts. The focus of Christian identity centered mainly upon practices that observably separated the faithful from persons and social norms considered to be virtuous or acceptable in Greco-Roman society. The most visible behavioral antitheses of Roman social practices were prescribed

9. See his *Dialogue with Trypho* as a record of ongoing debates between Jewish scholars and philosophers and Christian converts.

10. Justin Martyr, *Second Apology*, 193.

11. Justin Martyr, *First Apology*, 167.

12. Ibid. Justin Martyr then warns his readers that Christ "was no sophist, but his word was the power of God."

actions that stemmed from a moral vision founded upon love of neighbors and enemies, non-violence, service to the poor, and egalitarian relationships.[13]

John Driver reports that in the third century, Hippolytus of Rome wrote a rule that recognized how military service might affect new converts, and he provided guidance for Christian participation in the activities of both military and government. This rule, written circa 200 CE, provides an example of how Christian ethics assertively countered Roman social and military ethics. Hippolytus actually instructed soldiers not to fight, and indicated that baptized Christians who wanted to join the military be excommunicated "because they have despised God."[14] It seems as though, during the reign of Constantine and his decision to legalize and favor Christianity, more persuasive literature was necessary to reinforce the importance the non-violent ethic.

Apocalyptic Ethics: A Case Study of Sorts

That non-violence and love of enemies was still important to the ethics of the early church is evidenced by extra-canonical tales such as the *Acts of Philip*. Not to be confused with the *Gospel of Philip* of the mid-third century,

13. Driver, *How Christians Made Peace with War*, 23–28. Driver cites numerous examples of Christian ethical admonitions against violence. Beginning with writings of Ignatius, Clement, and Polycarp in 95 through 110 CE, he also cites Athengoras, writing in 185 in *Plea for Christians* as employing arguments against abortion, or the "seeing a man put to death, even justly." He cites Justin as writing against violence in 165. Irenus on Lyons is cited as arguing that Christians have "beaten their swords into pruning hooks" near 190, and Turtullian wrote against Christian participation in war during the same time. In the early third century, Cyprian of North Africa wrote that "God willed iron to be used for the cultivation of the earth, but not on account that murders be committed." Origen of Egypt argued that "we no longer take up sword against any nation, nor do we learn war anymore, having become children of peace, for the sake of Jesus, who is our leader." See also the first-century document known as the *Didache*. This text is a kind of rule that reinforces the commands of the Decalogue, but prioritizes the teachings of Jesus, emphasizing non-violence, love of neighbor and enemy, and even goes beyond the canonical lists by formally forbidding abortion and infanticide, and, pederasty. *Didache*, para. 1–10.

14. Driver, *How Christians Made Peace with War*, 47. Citing three articles from "The Apostolic Tradition of Hippolytus," Helgeland et al., *Christians in the Military*, 37. The Traditions of Hippolytus include three articles concerning military service: "17) A soldier who is of inferior rank shall not kill anyone. If ordered to, he shall not carry out the order, nor shall he take the oath. If he does not accept this, let him be dismissed. 18) Anyone who has the power of the sword or the magistrate of a city who wears purple, let him give it up or be dismissed. 19) The catechumen or believers who wish to become soldiers shall be dismissed because they have despised God." The reference to wearing purple is an indicator of symbolism pertaining to politicians, rulers, judges, and others with civic power and authority. Christians were not to serve in such a capacity, so as "not to lord it over others."

the *Acts* attributed to the apostle is dated by Bovon to have originated in the mid-fourth century. I mention this to show that love of enemies was an integral witness of some communities even after the Constantinian power-shift occurred.[15] This mostly forgotten document regarding ministry attributed to Philip has all the markings of apocalyptic literature. There are animals that speak, dragons, idolatrous representations of serpents, and abusive and controlling tyrants. In the case of Philip, a ruling authority is presented as a particularly abusive husband who drags his wife around by her hair following her conversion to faith in Christ. The local magistrates are brought to judge Philip and his ministry partners, Bartholomew and Miriam (yes, a woman minister). In true apocalyptic form, the proconsul "gnashed his teeth, saying: torture these deceivers that have deceived many women, young men, and girls . . ."[16]

The three missionaries were whipped, dragged through the streets in front of assembled crowds, and put on display for execution. According to the story, the torture only succeeded in adding new members to the ranks of the faithful. The text declares "scarcely anyone stayed home," but came to watch the trio being thrown into a pit of temple vipers, then be sentenced to death. Nevertheless, "many in the crowd believed in the grace of Christ, and were added to the apostle Philip and those with him, having renounced the idol of the viper, and were confirmed in faith, being magnified by the endurance of the saints."

Of course (this *is* apocalyptic, after all), Philip and his team survive the viper pit only to receive worse treatment. Philip is hung on a tree upside down. Then, this apocalyptic tale takes a literary turn that is anticipated, yet still must be so entirely shocking that it would cause gasps from those who heard it read. The Christians who were confronted with this twist would be more than convicted; they might have been left incredulous. The tale turns to the absurd as it points to the will of Jesus and the importance of the ethics of non-violence in the early church, perhaps as a response to the perceived manner in which state sponsorship was affecting the church.

Remember that in the discussion of apocalyptic it is not just unbelievers who face judgment, but those persons of faith who fail to submit the full range of Christian sacrificial expectation. In the *Acts of Philip*, the apostle is reprimanded for failing to embody the full extent of Christ's own faithfulness. According to a full measure of absurdity, packed down and overflowing, Jesus disciplines Philip *while Philip is being crucified upside down!*

15. Bovon and Matthews, *Acts of Philip*, 12.

16. *Acts of Philip*, 500.

The narrative of ethical instruction describes the Apostle John coming ahead of Jesus to the spiritual aid of Bartholomew and Philip. Miriam has already been relieved of any suffering, having been transfigured. John enters the city, greets the martyrs, and casts public judgment upon the citizens and ruling class for torturing the people who warned them of the dangers of worshipping the serpent gods, and for their reverence of idols. The citizens attempt to abduct John in order to torture him along with the others, but cannot grasp hold of him as he is protected by a sort of spiritual barrier.

Still upside down, Philip loses his patience and cries out to the heavens to avenge his suffering by burning the city and its inhabitants in revenge. This is decidedly unchristian.

"And John and Bartholomew and Miriam restrained him, saying, 'Our master was beaten and scourged, was extended on the cross . . . and said 'father forgive them, for they know not what they do." Yet Philip is angry, and would not listen to the counsel of his friends. They remind him that Jesus himself was lowly and meek, and beg him to show patience for those who crucified him. Philip declares, "go away and do not mollify me; for I will not bear that I have been hanged with head down, and they pierced my ankles and heels with irons. And you John . . . how much have you reasoned with them and they have not listened." Philip then curses his tormentors in Hebrew. And it works. The earth opens and swallows the entire city into a fiery abyss.

While in torment, however, the whole town repents while experiencing the convincing terror of the fires of Philip's hell. So, Jesus appears and reverses the cosmic punishment delivered on behalf of Philip, restoring everyone to a state in which they can serve God, because they in fact have repented of their idolatry. The citizenry glorifies the Lord and comes to faith. Meanwhile, Philip is still hanging upside down, and he remains angry.

Now comes the apocalyptic kicker—the Jesus punch line. Jesus says to Philip. "Did you not hear,[17] thou shall not render evil for evil? And why have you inflicted this destruction?" Jesus then basically tells Philip to take the log out of his own eye; that he is not in a position to cast a death penalty upon anyone in light of his own sin.

Philip is incredulous! He responds angrily to Jesus! He asks how in the world Jesus can be angry with him for sharing the gospel, overwhelming false gods, and cursing the persecutors of the church to fitting damnation. "In thy name I have persecuted all the error of the idols . . . and all the dragons," cries Philip. "And these men did not receive your light, therefore I cursed them to Hades alive."

---

17. *Acts of Philip*, 501.

Jesus rebukes Philip for disobeying the most important aspects of his commandments, and what the authors or the community that devised this literary ethics lesson must have thought to be in jeopardy as far as their Christian identity was concerned. That being love of neighbors, even when those neighbors are enemies bent on persecuting the church.

"Since thou hast disobeyed me, and hast requited evil for evil, and hast not kept my commandment," Jesus says to Philip as he is suspended from the tree, "thou shalt finish thy course gloriously indeed, and shall be led by the hand of my holy angels, and come with them into the paradise of delight."

This doesn't sound bad at all. Philip must be getting impatient to be turned upside right, and perhaps be free of the pain of crucifixion, but Jesus is not finished. Not finished at all. "But, I will order thee shut out of paradise for forty days, in terror under the flaming sword, and thou shalt groan because thou hast done evil to those who have done evil to thee." Jesus justifies both Miriam and Bartholomew, then says, "But I, O Philip, will not endure thee because thou hast swallowed up men into the abyss; but behold, my spirit is in them, and I shall bring them up from the dead, and thus they, seeing thee, shall believe in the glory of him that sent thee."[18]

The story indicates that not only is non-violence and suffering reflective of God's will for human relationships, and the manner in which God wants the church to represent faithfulness, but those who must be saved will find salvation in the manner in which God metes out justice—even those who declare him righteous from the start. It is through patient suffering that the gospel promotes repentance in others. If the *Acts of Philip* represents at least one response to the Constantinian shift of the fourth century, what does a messianic gospel look like today? What kind of witness does the church commit itself to? How are we countercultural? How do we challenge the assumptions and truths of empire? In what ways are we called to sacrifice? And finally, in what ways do we witness to the absurdity of the gospel that is indeed the truth of God? This is a large interpretive order, to say the least.

18. Ibid.

CHAPTER 9

After Virtue Ethics

A Messianic Care Ethic

I now aim to provide a means for readers to consider a way of doing Christian ethics that best makes sense in a congregational or denominational context. The existing systematic arguments that intend to maintain specific dogmatic or creedal propositions have sold Jesus short. My aim is to promote a manner of "doing ethics" that prioritizes community making and identity and meaning making as primary illustrations of what I perceive to be a peculiarly messianic ethic. As I surmised in the stories regarding my children's ambivalence toward non-violence as a way of responding to potential threats of violence, it stands that while many individuals have found ways of consistently embodying the gospel through non-violent action, the task becomes burdensome when attempts to establish normativity around the actions of one or two contemporaries are thrust upon others who have compartmentalized their faith entirely within the construct of our American culture.

The faithful actions of such individuals are often relegated to the realm of prophetic witness, acts of perceived self-righteousness, or acts that require a kind of courage known by individuals who are simply battle-tested enough in their own lives to be examples of what the church should, but cannot, be. I do believe such ethics are in evidence too often restricted, however, to those communities that maintain a sectarian identity. Individualism relativizes and subverts Christian ethics.[1] However, commitment to

1. MacIntyre, *After Virtue*, 195. "For liberal individualism a community is simply an arena in which individuals each pursue their own self-chosen concept of the good life, and political institutions exist to provide that degree of order which makes such self-determined activity possible." This describes the antithesis of what I believe to be representative of Christian community. It illustrates the tension that I believe *should*

a communal expression of ethics not only allows for a context that makes acts of faith more intelligible to both individuals and outsiders, but provides the support that is absolutely necessary to live with faith as the primary informant of future expectation.

Reading Scripture as Story, Literary Not Literal

We find in the stories of Scripture those many ancient characters who provide examples of the very faith and practice—and brokenness—that we experience as a church. Some are obvious heroes, yet all are broken. These are the stock characters of the Bible, those sinful yet faithful persons who engage in apparently destructive acts or patently dishonest behaviors when all seems lost. From Abraham to Joseph, from Moses to Rahab and Joshua, from Ruth to David to Esther to Daniel, individuals have the strength and fortitude to carry on when all is evidently lost.[2] Above all, these characters address issues of faith and faithfulness.

Consider how Kierkegaard's character known as Johannes in *Fear and Trembling* works through the differences between acting on faith and acting

---

exist between a community that voluntarily accepts the challenge of sectarianism over the not necessarily dichotic alternative of pure secularism. The sectarian response to Constantinianism is rather the insistence upon being Christian and nothing else, though we may engage in relationships with those honoring differing social constructs. Hauerwas writes in *A Community of Character*, "When Christians turn from . . . being Christian," to engage in the discussion of doing ethics in the secular society, "the substantive claims they make about Jesus no longer seem operative. Or, their appeals to support various social strategies appear accidental in that the social strategy has been or can be justified on different grounds" (37).

2. Evans, "Introduction," xvii. "Johannes goes to some pains to distinguish Abraham's faith from 'worldly wisdom,' the calculations of human probability . . . Faith is not merely a vague hope that this or that could possibly happen if something else happens. For example, Johannes distinguishes faith from one of its 'caricatures,' which he describes as 'paltry hope' that says 'One can't know what will happen, it still might be possible.'" Evans further describes Johannes' struggles with faith and reasonable behavior be continuing to distinguish between "paltry hope" and "our sense of what is probable and what is possible" as related to human experience. "Faith . . . has an entirely different ground. Johannes is enigmatic in describing faith's ground; perhaps since he lacks faith himself he does not fully understand what this ground is . . . He says that faith holds to various possibilities 'by virtue of the absurd,' and he is clear that someone who looks at things from this viewpoint has completely rejected human calculative reasoning. On the contrary, faith requires a clear-headed understanding that from the perspective of human experience the situation appears impossible." Johannes himself describes this as such: Abraham "believed . . . that God would not demand Isaac of him, while he still was willing to sacrifice him if it was demanded. He believed, by virtue of the absurd, for human calculation was out of the question" (30).

out potential insanity. The acts of biblical heroes are not acts of persons refusing to see reason or having lost their sense of reality. They reasonably see that the end of what will be one chapter has come, and another, new chapter is to be written. Their faith is that the story continues toward an outcome that vindicates their faith and practice regardless of immediate or intermediary outcomes.

Christian faith and practice occurs in a similar context. Regardless of the obvious facts and reasonable assessments of events in the field, Christians act not in accordance with a moral vision that seeks to accommodate sin when their lives are threatened, or when all is lost, or even to prevent potentially stark consequences. Rather, faith drives us to act in accordance with God's will, which must be reflected at great cost in order that truth will be promoted as an alternative when the next chapter is inscribed onto the parchment of history. Faith suggests to us that when God's time has come, all will be set right and the people of God will be vindicated, as will their acts of judgment, mercy, and faithfulness. This faith is not changed by the fact that events may not be deemed favorable to the faithful. Think of Daniel, Shadrach, Meshach, and Abednego. They remained steadfastly faithful despite being thrown first into exile and then into furnaces and a den of lions.[3]

The resurrection is key to what I believe to be the narrative conjunction of claims to power and authority variously made by empire(s) and the historical counterclaims made by Israel and the early church. Christians claimed that the changes in the world that God had wrought are evidenced in God's own embodiment of the very sorts of righteousness displayed by the heroes of the Hebrew Testament, lived out tangibly in Jesus as the Christ. "God became a human person," Jesus' followers believed, "in order that humanity should become as God had always willed."[4] It is in Jesus' life, early Christians claimed, that God had fully revealed the divine will for how humanity was to engage in every kind of relationship. As Jesus' preaching and teaching focused on the inauguration of the kingdom of God, so did the church develop a moral vision and specific practices that reflected this kingdom vision. The consequence and ever-present risk, when and wherever the kingdom was preached, was the fact of the cross, which loomed over Jesus, and over the early church. It was the faith in resurrection, and in a full

---

3. "Shadrach, Meshach, and Abednego answered the king, 'O king we have no need to present a defense to you in this matter. If our God who we serve is able to deliver us from the furnace of blazing furnace and out of your hand . . . let him deliver us. But if not, be it known to you O king, that we will not serve your gods and we will not worship at the golden statue that you have set up.'" Dan 3:16–18 (NRSV).

4. Meeks, *First Urban Christians*, 1.

restoration of the faithful to right-relationship with God and one another, that made continuing discipleship attractive, or at least possible.

Moral Vision, Ethics, Practices, and Virtues

To provide a framework for messianic ethics, I propose a definition of Christian moral vision as follows.[5] First, a community may choose to identify the inherent goodness in God's creation, and the power that sin has to interfere with this goodness and create an environment of human brokenness. Evidence of brokenness is observed and experienced in the suffering, violence, and distrust that marks both historical and contemporary human relationships. This brokenness itself is the definition of sin—a break in relationships with the Creator and with creation itself.

Second, a Christian moral vision is contingent upon God's revealing the nature of sin to those who believe, and God's desire that human beings commit themselves to redeeming relationships with creation, Creator, and one another. God's definitive statement of human wholeness and righteousness is demonstrated in the life of Jesus. Thus, the church is called to witness to the truth of God's redemptive activity by incorporating the teachings of Jesus into our everyday life. This is the embodiment of faith, and salvation.

The church is that faithful assembly of Christian disciples called to teach and facilitate the embodying of Jesus' faithfulness. Such practice mandates corporate interpreting and acting out of Jesus' teachings in a manner that makes God's response to evil observable to a critical world. Congregations thus establish a form of gospel order, a social ethic through which this moral vision may be implemented publicly. The church and this social ethic is a conduit for witness both to God's own righteousness, and the invitation for created order to respond to such righteousness through the raising up and maintaining of an active, reflective, faith community.

It stands that if we are to restore faithfulness to the church, or at least identify a means by which we may facilitate corporate rebirth and repentance experiences, we might need to reread, reinterpret, and, most importantly, renew our commitment to Scripture. We must also trust ourselves to explore faith in a manner that is not bound by the limits of what is believable or reasonable.

---

5. Compare with ibid., 4. "Morality . . . names a dimensions of life, a pervasive and, often, only partly conscious set of value-laden dispositions, inclinations, attitudes, and habits." He offers an example of morality as a vision contingent upon context. To say to a child "behave yourself . . . presupposes that the child has learned what behavior is required: some stage of morality has been internalized."

However, there must be a recognition among many Americans that a Christian ethic is necessarily different from the ethics of patriotism, governance, medicine, or general behaviors that constitute what may purportedly be best for society as a whole—at least if the ethic is to be decisively Christian or biblical. This reality has been lost on much of the Christian world.[6] Because the church has enjoyed so much economic and political relevance and power, it has consciously engaged in activities that promote the filters of culture and political reality while trying to make the gospel a legitimate contributor, if not the main informant of secular American morality. It might be said that the ethical decisions of American Christians are reflective of their political hopes far more than their faith in God.

It is an individual or organization's intentions, says MacIntyre, that provide insight into their moral character.[7] If moral agents suggest their behaviors reflect the moral vision of the kingdom of God, yet the intention of their behaviors is to manipulate secular political outcomes and establish Christianized social norms in secular milieus, the outcomes confuse two distinctly different paradigms.

Christian behaviors are intended to produce a kingdom of God that stands in tension with secular society. Attempts to overcome secular power regimes with Christian ethics become non-Christian once they are introduced through secular institutions. They simply make no sense outside of church communities, because secular governments have different obligations, and different motivations toward different outcomes, than does the church.

Characters, Character, and Characteristics in Interpretation

It is important for interpretive communities to find value in identifying Abraham and Sarah; Isaac and Rebekah; and Jacob, Leah, and Rachel as literary characters every bit as much as they might or might not be historical.

6. Hauerwas, *Peaceable Kingdom*, 52. In Europe and the Americas, "Protestants could only assume that Christian ethics was little different from the consensus of whatever culture they found themselves apart. This is most strikingly illustrated by Protestantism's inability to be more than national churches."

7. MacIntyre, *After Virtue*, 190. "We cannot . . . characterize behavior independent of intentions, and we cannot characterize intentions independently of those settings which make those intentions intelligible both to agents themselves and others." To suggest that one's behavior is Christian when it is intended to promote the legitimacy of non-Christian outcomes, or produce Christian outcomes in secular setting, promotes either conflation of moral dichotomies or confusion, manipulation, and a coerced implementation of outcomes that end up being illegitimate within the boundaries of each distinct narrative.

Allowing one's self to identify the literary importance, or type, allows for certain themes to develop that are otherwise missed from a purely literal-historical perspective. Alter suggests "it may often be more precise to describe what happens in biblical narrative as fictionalized history," and rest assured that "history is far more intimately related to fiction than what we have been accustomed to assume."[8]

Beginning with the multivarious Genesis stories, it is easy to identify how specific characters and repeated situations allow for a theme to be developed. This theme uses readily identified social agents and situations to establish not only a familiar setting for the audience, but a vehicle for revealing how God acts independently of human assumptions and usurps our expectations. For example, it is an ancient practice still recognizably practiced in contemporary cultures that the eldest son is generally favored in one manner or another, especially as related to inheritance, patriarchal obligations, and care for elder parents. Yet, in Genesis and elsewhere, it is most always the youngest son that receives some sort of favor, either through illegitimate or dishonest means or miraculous intervention on God's part.

"The firstborn," writes Alter, "very often seem to be losers in Genesis by the very condition of their birth."[9] Patriarchs and birth order have very important meanings not only in socially and historically known ways, but also as representations of how God manages the narrative of salvation within a human context. What is important to recognize in these literary *qua* historical narratives is that stock characters and situations are used to show how God often acts contrarily to both human expectation and rigidly maintained social structures. Genesis uses characters that are representative of historically known circumstances as well as vehicles for revealing how God turns such social standards on their head.[10]

8. Alter, *Art of Biblical Narrative*, 24–25. One important fact is that the Hebrew Bible, while consisting of ancient oral and scribal narratives, is edited from the perspective of a people in exile. The themes of the Hebrew Testament are chosen and woven together by scribes and editors who develop the stories to serve a specific, historical reality, as well as the need to curate narratives that allowed for the maintenance and preservation of national identity, religious integrity, and hope.

9. Ibid., 6.

10. MacIntyre, *After Virtue*, 28. "Such characters partially define the possibilities of plot and action. To understand them is to be provided a means of interpreting the behavior of the actors who play them, just because a similar understanding informs the intentions of the actors themselves . . . precisely because of the way [characters] link dramatic and moral understandings." MacIntyre suggests that stock literary characters help limit the manner in which actions are interpreted within a story by a culture that has a corporate understanding of how such characters portray real-life social roles and responsibilities. What's more, the use of such characters, who can only be narrowly understood, limits the possibilities of misinterpreting what is happening—especially

The stock characters and settings that make the Bible such an illustrative collection of texts are not representatives of universal behaviors, moral codes, or even the social priorities of past. What characters do for us is to prompt expectations of what should happen considering the culturally mandated roles each character or social agent is bound by, and limit the way in which we might interpret or understand exactly what might be happening in a story.

Let us return to the struggle of Kierkegaard's Johannes, who must come to terms with the fact that Abraham was truly going to sacrifice his son, all the while having faith that YHWH would intervene despite the order. Of course, we understand that Abraham is faithful, but there is far more to the story than perhaps even Johannes knew when he attempted to make sense of it. What would early Hebrews have made of such a story? What would be expected of Abraham by early Hebrews and other ancient Near Eastern peoples who heard the story?

Consider what was expected of a patriarch such as Abraham. Of course, we know that Abraham was concerned to have a son, the heir promised by YHWH. It is difficult to be a patriarch when your wife is barren. In Genesis 15, we know that Abraham was already having some questions regarding these promises. It is in chapter 15 that YHWH makes formal covenant with Abraham—one that the Chaldean chooses not to participate in.[11] In this covenant, YHWH reiterates the promise of a son, a nation of descendants, and a land promised to those descendants.

---

if social convention is being turned upside down. But there is more to it. "Characters are the masks," he writes, "worn by moral philosophies," to perform the tasks of lending intelligibility to even the simplest actions taking place within a specific context. Furthermore, stock characters impact the way we evaluate ourselves, and the behaviors of those around us in regard to their moral agency. "A character is an object of regard by members of the culture generally or by some significant segment of them. He furnishes them with some sort of moral ideal" (29).

11. Gen 15:8–18. In this narrative, verse 2 provides an indicator that Abraham is starting to perhaps doubt the promises of YHWH. In verse 8, he asks how he will know that his promised heir will possess the promised land. The next few verses make little sense to most readers. Abraham retrieves some animals and cuts them into halves, making a sort of walkway. Ancient audiences would have immediately understood this as a standard means of covenant making. Both contracted parties must walk between the halved carcasses. The blood of the animals that collects in the walkway ends up on the feet of the two parties, establishing a contractual obligation enforced by the threat of death for breaking the covenant. This was not an unusual covenant. What ancient audiences would have noticed is that, in fact, Abraham never walked between the carcasses. Only YHWH, represented by a smoking oven and flaming torch, passes between them. The intended audience realizes that even when Abraham cannot accept the consequences of breaking covenant, YHWH explicitly accepts the consequences on Abraham's behalf!

Abraham does have a son born to him, but it is the product of relationship with Hagar, the Egyptian slave of Sarah. This son is illegitimate in the eyes of anyone hearing this story, and would seem to interrupt the flow of the narrative significantly. There will be competition for the promised inheritance. Or not, as Sarah is unable to have children. Nevertheless, YHWH stands at Abraham's tent in Mamre and promises one more time that it is Sarah who will produce the legitimate heir.

Naturally, this is to be understood as drama. Ears would be tingling and thoughts running wild as to what will happen between the two sons concerning the inheritance. At least it might seem. But the problem of the oldest son being born of a slave woman might not be considered as a real obstacle to Isaac's rise to patriarch status. Yet other obstacles always seem to be introduced. Oddly enough, the biggest obstacle to YHWH's promises being fulfilled is introduced by the divine self. Hagar and her son are turned away after Sarah becomes jealous. The fact that Hagar and Ishmael were driven from their home would have been understood by the audience as a sacrifice of sorts. Like the ancient scapegoat, where an animal was sent away to its death in the wild to atone for sins, leaving Hagar and Ishmael to die in the wilderness has similar connotations. It eliminated any competition for any piece of inheritance, thus clearly identifying Isaac as the beginning of covenant fulfilment by YHWH. The eldest son, illegitimate or not, was scapegoated and sacrificed. Only YHWH's intervention saved the lives of the mother and child, and this was unknown to Abraham.

It may or may not be important to consider the sending away of Hagar and Ishmael a sacrifice, but for interpretation's sake, it might be important as related to the way in which God turns Abraham's expectations upside down. It has already been stated clearly by the text that Abraham is a faithful person. It is also shown by the text that Abraham is up to the task of negotiating or asserting himself while in the presence of the deity. Considering everything that has happened, including the sending out of his son Ishmael to die in the wilderness, another obstacle puts the audience on edge.

God calls to the Chaldean. "Here I am," replies Abraham. God has decided to "test" Abraham, per the Scripture. "Take now your son, your only son, whom you love, Isaac, and go to the land of Moriah, and offer him there as a burnt offering on one of the mountains which I will tell you."

Everyone in the ancient audience is a little puzzled now. But, it is not because God ordered a sacrifice of the firstborn. In fact, in the ancient Near East, during the age of the patriarchs and during much of the time the Bible was being edited, it was not uncommon for firstborn sons to be sacrificed to a deity. The demand to sacrifice Isaac, however, was peculiar to the audience's ears for a few reasons. Had not Ishmael already been sacrificed?

And had not God saved Hagar and Ishmael? Had Ishmael been rejected as a sacrifice? Will God also save Isaac? What son will take Isaac's place, for Abraham and Sarah are incredibly old at this point. The command to sacrifice Isaac is not extraordinary to the audience, but the incredible number of contingencies regarding the fulfillment of YHWH's promises to Abraham are ever increasing.

Kierkegaard's Johannes tries to make sense of what Abraham does. He has no idea that child sacrifices were common during the period of the patriarchs, or simply cannot attribute such evil to YHWH. But Johannes knows that Abraham could attribute such demands to YHWH, thus necessitating interpretation of the story. Johannes finally regards the actions of Abraham as being in line with what I believe to be true for apocalyptic and eschatological ethics. Johannes believes that Abraham believes the sacrifice is inevitable. Then, we also know that, despite the fact that all is lost, Abraham still acts in faith that, for whatever reason, God may intervene to save Isaac's life. And, if God does not intervene, so be it. God will set things right when God is ready to do so.

In fact, the stock characters in this story turn out to be the narrative means through which an exciting truth is revealed about the way God responds to our own sin and need. Remember that Abraham, even though considered the pinnacle of faithfulness, was reticent to enter covenant as an implied equal with YHWH. It was YHWH who promised to uphold both ends of the contract, which was ratified in blood. While the stock character Abraham might surprise us with his obvious capacity to stand up to or question God, be it ever so humbly, he is faithful to the core even when he sees that his faith competes with obvious reason. How can Abraham raise an heir when he continuously is called upon to sacrifice them like other patriarchs of his age, despite the obstacles he experienced in witnessing their births in the first place?

It turns out that the stories are not, for the most part, really about Abraham. What the audience finds is that, instead of demanding sacrifice, YHWH rejects the sacrifice of human life by those communities or individuals in search of divine favor. What is revealed is that God rejects sacrifice in favor of showing grace, mercy, and faithfulness to those whom God makes covenant with.[12] This turns the accepted standards of the era upside down.

12. Yoder, *Politics of Jesus*, 78 n3. "The modern reader sees this as an instance of God breaking God's own rules," especially as related to the narratives of Kings and Chronicles where child sacrifice is a scourge of Israel. King Manasseh was guilty of making his children "walk through the fire" as a sacrifice to Molech. For the reader or audience of this era, Yoder believes Abraham's action "was no more ethically scandalous or viscerally disturbing than the killing of the villain in a western film is to most

What we learn from our stock characters, especially in the ancient stories of Genesis, the Judges and Samuel, from the prophets and from the kings of Israel and Judah, is how the nature of sin, and how our acts of faithfulness, set the tone for an audience to have an idea of what it means to participate in this ongoing covenant with a creator God. While we may find a number of ways to relate, both positively and negatively, with the characters of the Hebrew Bible or the New Testament, ultimately we learn from them the nature of acting in faith when all seems lost. Either because of our own sin or sin against us, whether due to the mandates of nation-states or majority-rule legal obstacles, we act in faithfulness regardless of the characters we identify with. We can do this because, while the stories may not be historical or empirically true, we agree with others to understand them to be truthful representations of how God will act or how history and truth will be arbitrated in the future. As our characters show throughout the text, this has little to do with what we believe. What may be true is that sin has all the apparent power, and violence will apparently prevail. The Christian response is that God may indeed demand my suffering now, but I have faith that God will set things right and I will be vindicated. In resurrection, death and violence have been defeated.

There are other important elements regarding the manner in which biblical characters, and reoccurring settings or situations, provide a foundation for ethics. If we look to these characters and circumstances for guidance, we might be able to tease apart those elements of activity and moral consideration that provide for the development of specific behaviors related to social roles within the church, as well as the culture at large. For instance, we find various representations of faithfulness and similarly diverse representations of sin in biblical characters that indicate to us aspects of the moral vision of the kingdom of God. Then, we see these characteristics represented in the New Testament in view of the way in which God has satisfied the covenant between Israel and YHWH in the life of Jesus. And this is the key to a narrative understanding of ethics. We begin to know and relate to the God of Abraham and Sarah through Scripture. The nature of sin as defined by God is revealed through Scripture. And finally, the nature of how God wants a community of faithful persons to respond to this sin as

watchers today." Yoder believes the test of Abraham was to sacrifice Isaac at the expense of his future as promised by YHWH. However, YHWH has always been faithful to Abraham, so any miracles necessary to fulfilment of promises were presumed by the audience. What is revealed in the stories of Ishmael, and the intended sacrifice of Isaac, is the nature of YHWH. Little is revealed about Abraham other than his faithfulness is to be considered a stock characteristic of Christian faithfulness. We as Christians can act in faith beyond belief, as Abraham did, because of what is revealed in these stories about the nature of God.

a means of establishing a path toward redemption is revealed in Scripture, and, even more so in the life and voluntary sacrifice of Jesus.

Embodiment of Covenant Fulfillment: Practices and Virtues

Faith or faithfulness, then, is at the very core of Christian biblical ethics. Because Christians believe that YHWH exhibited full righteousness incarnationally through acts of faithfulness of Jesus of Nazareth, the Christian narrative is that the messianic hope of Israel was fulfilled in Jesus' ministry, and it is widely accepted that the death of Jesus was sacrificial in a sense that it erased anything that would stand between a righteous God and creation. Gentiles were now welcomed as heirs to the covenant promises made to Abraham.

Without engaging in lengthy discussion of πιστις Χριστου (*pistis Christou*)—"faith in Christ" versus "faithfulness of Christ"—theology, I want to stress something important to messianic ethics. The gospel accounts and the rest of the Greek Testament are heavily invested in the sort of behavior that Christians are to exhibit to the world.[13] While much of Protestant theology has focused on the tenets of *sola scriptura* and *sola fide/sola gratia* per the rather troubling conscience of Martin Luther, it has failed to give account to the fact of the importance of ethics in Scripture. It is evident upon reading Scripture that one's faith or measure of faith is indicated by the nature of one's actions, the ability to confess and repent, an ability to serve others, and behaving consistently regarding the commands of Christ as priorities of faith. The fact that we often fail is less important; rather, failure is confessed, forgiveness and grace delivered, and repentance restores one to faithfulness. As such, much of the New Testament suggests that Christians are called to embody the ethic of Christ—to exhibit the faithfulness of Jesus Christ—as markers of our faith, through behaviors that make our claims about Christ not only observable to the world, but potentially credible and attractive to the world. This is disciple making.

Christian ethics is disciple making, and disciple making absolutely must be done in community. Disciple making is training others in practices such as non-violence, feeding the poor, and visiting the prisoner because there is a specific meaning when such acts are undertaken in the name of Christ. Moreover, such activities can only make sense when connected by the individual to a story that supports the community commitment to such actions. One only understands why it is "good" to feed the poor or refuse

13. Miller, "*Pistous Iesous Christous*," 3–6.

the military option when one has been taught why, and furthermore, how to engage in such practices.[14]

I will briefly mention Aristotle to initiate a turn to virtue, and then to care-based ethics as examples of Christian messianic performance. I limit my time with Aristotle for one reason in particular. Though he is often viewed as the "father of virtue ethics," he limited the scope of ethical and free moral agents to privileged males. He argued that women were less than human and he wrote in favor of maintaining the health of a socially superior classes of social and political elites. Not only has such thinking been properly stocked in the basements of philosophy, there is the unfortunate reality that such assumptions are still wedged into some religious and theological thinking across the spectrum. I acknowledge Aristotle because he does mark the beginning a type of ethics that are found in womanist and feminist thinking that I will discuss later.[15]

Meeks states that "Aristotle did not think one could persuade people to do good by rational argument; a person becomes virtuous by training, by forming good habits." Furthermore, Aristotle taught that in order "to develop a character that was virtuous, then a child had to grow up within a moral and educative community."[16] I believe this agrees with the position by MacIntyre that "pure" reasoning and the principles of philosophical modernity is not producing what it has promised. Training in virtues was suggested to produce a morally superior agent to reasoning. Aristotle made certain distinctions, regarding some moral agents as "continent" or "self-controlled . . . and [others] fully virtuous." The continent person knows what she should do and does it contrary to her desire. To be fully virtuous, this agent chooses the "good" over "desire" with a sense of joy. Virtuosity

14. MacIntyre, *After Virtue*, 258. "If the conception of good has to be expounded in terms of notions as those of a practice of the narrative unity of human life and of a moral tradition, then good, and with them the only grounds for authority of laws and virtues can be only discovered by entering into those relationships which constitute communities whose central bond is a shared vision and understanding of goods. To cut one's self off from shared activity in which one has initially to learn as an apprentice, to isolate one's self from the communities in which point and purpose of doctrines, will be to debar one's self from finding any good outside of one's self."

15. Berges, *Feminist Perspective on Virtue Ethics*, 45. Berges tackles this issue, suggesting that moral perspectives that rest upon the embodiment of virtues can easily overcome the obstacle of Aristotle's misogyny. Aristotle is an agent in the history of philosophy—we cannot start from scratch despite the fact that history has baggage. However, there is a history of virtue ethics "outside Aristotle" to find "later in history . . . women who are writing within a virtue ethics perspective. While still related to or informed by Aristotle, they remain feminine in perspective and provide a new authoritative voice to the tradition."

16. Meeks, *Early Christian Morality*, 7.

is regarded as a morally superior state to self-control due to the agent's embodiment of her beliefs with a sense of joy related to doing what is good rather than desired.[17]

There is another important aspect of Aristotelian thought that stands in firm contrast to what I believe is the development of ethics in early Christian communities. Aristotle is known to state that the ultimate human "good" or *eudaimonia* was made manifest in the practices of benevolence and justice. His *Nicomachean Ethics* illustrates those virtues he believed allowed for the ordering of a political society that served to achieve what was best for humankind, ultimately identifying what is good for humanity and training others in the practice of those virtues so that this state of social happiness could be maintained.[18] When church scholars later "rediscovered" Aristotle, they were quick to Christianize his concern for "happiness and fulfillment." Thomas Aquinas is identified as one of the first to restate Aristotelian virtue ethics by claiming that the ultimate Christian goods (contingent virtue ethics) were the achievement of "union with God through the virtues of *xaritas*; charity of self-sacrificial love."[19]

It is important not only to mention the discrepancies between justice in Aristotelian thought and in biblical ethics, but for the purposes of this project, to briefly touch on the distance between Christian or messianic ethics and the modern articulations of justice that have much influence on Christian ethicists and libertarian thinkers. MacIntyre chooses two secular theorists of justice to draw the distinctions between virtue ethics and the utilitarianism of modernity we find in Rawls and Nozick. For both Nozick and Rawls, and I believe the entirety of modernist thought, "society is

17. Lawler and Salazar, "Virtue Ethics: Natural and Christian," 452. These authors qualify Aristotle's assumptions about virtue by suggesting that the same sort of argument contrasting self-control and virtue is in place when agents act in accordance with moral vision despite the presence of crisis, such as people in poverty finding money and returning it. "The harder it is to act virtuously, the more it is against our personal and emotional desire, the more virtue is required to act virtuously." Therefore, the ability to deal with conflicting emotions and still act virtuously is in fact evidence that the virtuous behavior has indeed become normative behavior for the moral agent.

18. Aristotle, *Nicomachean Ethics*, 203.

19. Lawler and Salazar, "Virtue Ethics: Natural and Christian," 445. We might ask what Aristotle would have believed about carrying one's cross as an expression of eschewing desire to do the "right thing" with joy. It may be insightful for Christians to understand the word *Nicomachus* not only served as the name of Aristotle's son, but is the Greek word used to describe courage in battle—the highest form of courage identified by Aristotle. Three centuries after Aristotle, Christians would believe martyrdom to be the highest form of courage. Moreover, there is the issue of justice, or Christian righteousness, which would not escape the critical eye or scorn of pre-Christian Greeks.

composed of individuals, each with his or her own interest, who come to formulate common rules of life."[20]

Nozick, a libertarian anarchist, states that there are basic sets of rights that should be enjoyed by individuals that should not be violable by a state, or other individuals or groups of individuals.[21] I find personally that Nozick provides us with a useful tool to discuss conservatism within a context that can properly be critiqued from a Christian non-conformist or countercultural perspective. Rawls' theory of justice and his social contract perspective is perhaps most indicative of the type of liberalism that would appeal to Christian thinkers hoping to follow in the footsteps of the Social Gospel movement led by Rauschenbusch.[22]

There are two basic considerations for Rawls' theory of justice. The first is that "each person is to have an equal right to the most extensive basic liberty compatible with a similar liberty for others." The second consideration of Rawls is twofold: justice should aim to be of the greatest benefit to the least-advantaged members of society, and institutional and political offices and positions must be open to all under conditions of equal opportunity.[23]

In fact, I believe that Nozick and Rawls provide excellent secular starting points to discuss the reform of social and political institutions. The most glaring problem Christians face in such discussion, however, is that both

---

20. MacIntyre, *After Virtue*, 250.

21. Nozick, *Anarchy, the State, and Utopia*, 31–35. "There is no justified sacrifice of some of us for others," writes Nozick. "This root idea, namely, that there are different individuals with separate lives and so no one may be sacrificed for others, underlies the existence of moral side constraints, but it also, I suggest, leads to a libertarian side constraint that prohibits aggression against one another." Nozick sees non-aggression (which may or may not be interpreted as a commitment to non-violence) as the best way to ensure that individuals do not become viewed as "little more than resources, or, a means to a political or economic end." I raise awareness of Nozick, in accordance with MacIntyre, because the anti-empire and much-evidenced anti-authoritarian nature of Jesus' ministry and the early church might be interpreted by some who find resonance with Nozick's rather conservative libertarianism as exemplary for the church. In fact, the gospels, read through the lens of Nozick's vision of anarchy, would read similarly to the manner in which they are read by American conservatives and liberals, with a primary focus on individual and human rights rather than kingdom justice. Certainly, Nozick might agree that self-sacrifice on behalf of others is the right of the individual. To promote such sacrifice as a matter of God's justice over one's potential to benefit from individual free moral agency is to attempt to bridge an attractive chasm that cannot be successfully spanned. Such an outcome is not Nozick's intent, but political conservatives will find his individualism in the context of rights-based societies can be shoehorned into an ethics that does not demand sacrifice of individual prosperity and liberty as a matter of Christian obedience.

22. Rawls, *Theory of Justice*, 55. Nozick's 1974 work cited above is a response to Rawls' social contract theory.

23. Ibid., 60, 302.

philosophies are incompatible with messianic and biblical ethics because they ignore the base biblical truth that claims sin as a *fact* of human existence—one that can only be overcome through the preaching and practice of the gospel of Jesus as Christ. Also, there is no biblical way to relate rights to the themes of justice when sin is viewed as more indicative of what is truthful than the utopian concerns for an agreement to prioritize individual liberties or provide fair equity to those who lack. While the Bible has absolutely nothing to say on the individualism of Nozick's anarchy, it has even less to say about the sort of "all things being fair" construct by Rawls, or the proposal that individual agents can voluntarily refute their privilege or quest for advantage in developing an ethics of justice, or fairness. The Bible has nothing to say of either fairness or individualism. It has much to say of obedience.

Christian obedience has form and is shaped by prescribed behaviors. It is the practice of such behaviors over time that teaches prescribed ethics of discipleship and makes the behaviors intelligible and credible. One important qualifier to biblical ethics is that the practices and virtues deemed "Christian" are not, as Aristotle demands, a pursuit of or journey toward *eudemonia*. Happiness is not a matter of justice, nor is it a concern delineated within the biblical text (though joy certainly is). Ethical practices "involve standards of excellence and obedience to rules as well as the achievement of goods," writes MacIntyre. Such standards are not a matter of individual rights, at least, not if our concern is biblical ethics. The concern of Christian community is rather the concern of the authority of that community in detailing what behaviors reflect the kingdom of God and make the claims about this kingdom truthful. When an individual submits to a biblical ethic, they formally submit their behaviors and public performances to the judgment of the community. Obedience is indeed a primary activity of Christian community, a practice by which one will subject their own "attitudes, choices, preferences and tastes to the standards which . . . define the practice."[24] Faithfulness is a practice, just as prayers for those who persecute a community is a virtue that can only be enacted in faith, and in obedience to a community that commends itself to such activity.

Community is necessary to the accomplishment of the social good that is anticipated by specific practices because "goods can only be achieved by subordinating ourselves in our relationship to other practitioners (Romans

24. MacIntyre, *After Virtue*, 190. He defines practice as behaviors that lead to virtuous behavior, or "any coherent and complex form of socially established human activity through which goods internal to that form of activity are realized in the course of trying to achieve those standards of excellence which are appropriate to, and partially definitive of, that form of activity, with the result that human powers to achieve excellence, and human conceptions of the ends and goods involved, are systematically extended" (187).

12 and John 15 provide the obvious examples of this expectation). "We have to learn to recognize what is due to whom; we have to be prepared to take whatever self-endangering risks are demanded along the way; and we have to listen carefully to what we are told about our own inadequacies and reply with the same carefulness for facts."[25] It follows, then, that the practice of obedience as a marker of Christian community must produce virtues such as acting with courage and honesty. Such practices and virtues enable communities and individuals to engage their social roles and test social boundaries and expectations[26] to the limits in the pursuit of the biblical outcome of justice. Obedience produces the virtuous behaviors that allow for Christian disciples to embody God's justice.

Biblical, messianic, Christian ethics endorse practices that are obedient to the standards of a community that reads and interprets the text together. This community then develops and tests specific standards by engaging in and teaching social practices that reflect the text, the moral vision gleaned from the text, and the commandments and practices of Jesus and the early church. Through the continuous practice of behaviors that reflect the moral vision of the kingdom of God, individuals develop virtues necessary to making the practices intelligible to the rest of the world, and lend credibility to the beliefs that underwrite the practices. It is the continuous practice of such virtues that provide individuals with the courage and truth to act on behalf of God's justice and righteousness no matter what limits may be placed upon them socially by the outside world. In the realm of virtue ethics, the moral vision of Christian community is made possible by the continuous practice of behaviors that embody the salvation that comes through Jesus.

25. Ibid., 191.

26. This may clarify the importance of identifying the literary importance of biblical interpretation to the practices of Christian ethics. We all have roles in our communities, whether they are the roles of parents, presidents, poverty victims, persecutors or persecuted, sons, daughters, mates, prostitutes, or "johns." The fact of social roles, when viewed in light of the Bible, does not limit us, but rather define the possibilities of how social practices or virtues may be the primary means of overturning the unjust nature of so much role-delineated boundaries in the world. The practices and virtues of the kingdom of God allow for the negative components and stereotypes of social roles to be overthrown, or tuned upside down in favor of justice.

Beyond Virtue: Messianic Care Ethics

"Virtue ethics . . . offers an answer to the question, who am I to become?"[27] The biblical text provides a narrative that invites its interpreters into authorship of the stories that follow. We are reminded that authorship includes the call to live out the teachings of Jesus. We are invited "to become and be like Jesus, and because we are like him, to do as he did," write Lawler and Salazar. As such, "the controlling principle of Christian virtue ethics is *imitation Christi*: first, be like Jesus, then do as he did."[28]

I propose that the primary messianic behaviors embodied by Jesus, thus prototypical of Christian biblical ethics, might be as follows. First, obedience to the God of Abraham and Sarah, whose desire for faithfulness is made known through Jesus. Jesus reflects the divine will through his own love, and his command to disciples to love both God and neighbor (and even our enemy). This love is made tangible through practices of various sorts, and in surprising ways. The parable of the Good Samaritan is perhaps the clearest example of how such an ethic is taught. While I do not intend to exegete the parable of the Good Samaritan at great length, it is the most useful example to use in transition to those steps messianic ethics calls us to take over and beyond mere virtue ethics. Practices embedded in this parable include spending time and income on behalf of "the other," caring for one who is injured or ill, and violating social rules or taboos on behalf of someone else's life or well-being. The virtues that might be derived from such practices as caring for one's neighbor might be identified as compassion, courage, emptying of privilege or self-interest, mercy, grace, and forgiveness. It must be noted that the Christian expectation is that such care is undertaken with joy, despite the attending expectation of suffering. I find the concept of "care ethics" as presented by many women both within and outside of the Christian church community as being truly discerning in what it means to be more Christlike, more biblical in our perspective, and more present in our work for God's justice.

First, the briefest of introductions to feminist and womanist virtue ethics. Berges states that care ethics are set apart from virtue ethics by two particulars: "it's focus on women's experience of morality" rather than the entrenched focus of ethical thought on the "independent male making decisions for himself . . . it focuses less on the relationships that make up moral experiences than on actual practice."[29] I believe that womanist thought helps

27. Lawler and Salazar, "Virtue Ethics: Natural and Christian," 465.

28. Ibid.

29. Berges, 109–10. Also, see Botti, "Feminine Virtues or Feminist Virtues," 109. She writes, "rather than being primarily concerned with care ethics as being grounded

expose the importance of identifying with Jesus, especially for Americans of European descent, through the blackness of Jesus—a blackness that can only be recognized through the suffering of blacks, and black women, at the hands of institutional racism and white supremacy.[30]

Before considering womanist thought as a primary prism through which to view Jesus and his ministry, as well as Christian ethics, I want to take Carol Gilligan into account. Her work is important in the founding and development of care ethics. In her study of differences in the moral process between boys and girls, Gilligan developed an important response to the well-received moral development theory of Lawrence Kohlberg. She brought a feminist hermeneutic to the verbatim of Kohlberg's research interviews, and perceived boys to be more "rights" and "justice" centered in their moral reasoning, and girls to be more centered on outcomes related to "responsible care."[31]

Botti believes Gilligan's subsequently termed "care ethics" "emerge as a moral model which puts at its center the agent's capacity to be attentive, caring, and responsive in relation to the needs of others . . . and which defines moral responsibility in terms of the development and practice of these capacities."[32] While ethicists will certainly identify the differences in Gilligan's model from Kohlberg's more widely referenced moral developmental stages, subsequent feminist thought, and most ethics constructs of the past century, I suggest that, just as Aquinas is thought to have led the church back to Aristotle, Gilligan and other feminists (womanists even more so) have exposed a long-buried truth of Christian ethics: that caring and caretaking—and as McClendon believes, "presence"—are the primary messianic virtues.[33]

Gilligan's *In a Different Voice* provides insights gleaned from interviews with children concerning their moral development. She highlights the manner in which Kohlberg's interviewers perceived differences in reasoning.

particularly in 'feminist virtues,'" an alternative exists, which is to consider care ethics as "an account of ethics that is able to deal with the particularity, difference, and concreteness of all human beings." This is one of the themes feminist elaborate in order to give an adequate account of ethics for all.

30. Womanist theory and theological thought is described in Alice Walker's *In Search of our Mother's Gardens*, xi–xii, in a move toward expanding feminist thinking beyond the concerns of privileged women of European descent. The term is said to be derived from the notion of "acting womanish," which was said to African-American girls who acted serious, courageous, and grown-up rather than like children. For an in-depth and informative critique of early feminism, read hooks, *Feminist Theory*.

31. Botti, "Feminine Virtues or Feminist Virtues," 110.

32. Ibid., 112–13.

33. McClendon, *Ethics*, 108. "Presence is one of the profound forms of Christian witness. There is a Catholic religious order whose members live inside South American prisons and jails in order to be present to and for prisoners."

Sixth-graders "Jake and Amy" were asked a question of moral reasoning derived from the dilemma commonly known as the "Heinz Dilemma."[34] The moral concern in this narrative is whether it could be morally acceptable or not to steal a drug for the healing of a man's wife, because he cannot afford the price and the druggist who patented the medicine will not lower the price. Kohlberg used this dilemma in his study of moral development, and was not concerned for a right or wrong answer, but rather sought to categorize stages of moral development across the human lifespan.[35]

Gilligan perceived something different than did Kohlberg when studying the verbatim of "Jake and Amy" regarding Heinz.[36] While she believes that males tend toward justice-and-rights-oriented moral reasoning, she also states that men are more "I" focused and right-versus-wrong centered in their reasoning, while women, in her estimation, were identified more by relationships and caring than pursuit of justice. According to Kohlberg's assumptions and research method, the moral judgments of "Jake and Amy" "seemed to initially confirm familiar notions about the differences between the sexes, suggesting that the edge girls have on boys in life-stage

34. Kohlberg, *Essays on Moral Development.* "A woman was near death. There was one drug that the doctors thought might save her. It was a form of radium that a druggist in the same town had recently discovered. The drug was expensive to make, but the druggist was charging ten times what the drug cost him to produce. He paid $200 for the radium and charged $2,000 for a small dose of the drug. The sick woman's husband, Heinz, went to everyone he knew to borrow the money, but he could only get together about $1,000 which is half of what it cost. He told the druggist that his wife was dying and asked him to sell it cheaper or let him pay later. But the druggist said: 'No, I discovered the drug and I'm going to make money from it.' So Heinz got desperate and broke into the man's laboratory to steal the drug for his wife. Should Heinz have broken into the laboratory to steal the drug for his wife? Why or why not?"

35. Ibid. "Stage one (obedience): Heinz should not steal the medicine, because he will be put in jail." "Stage two (self-interest): Heinz should steal the medicine, because he will be much happier if he saves his wife, even if he will have to serve a prison sentence. Stage three (conformity): Heinz should steal the medicine, because his wife expects it. Stage four (law-and-order): Heinz should not steal the medicine, because the law prohibits stealing. Stage five (human rights): Heinz should steal the medicine, because everyone has a right to live, regardless of the law. Or: Heinz should not steal the medicine, because the scientist has a right to fair compensation. Stage six (universal human ethics): Heinz should steal the medicine, because saving a human life is a more fundamental value than the property rights of another person. OR: Heinz should not steal the medicine, because that violates the golden rule of honesty and respect. OR: (transcendental morality) Heinz should choose to spend more time with his wife in their remaining days, both acknowledging the cycle of life-and-death which is a part of the human condition."

36. Gilligan, *In a Different Voice,* 24–35.

development during the early school years gives way at puberty with the ascendance of formal logical though in boys."[37]

Yet, Gilligan found that the interviewers, perhaps particularly in the case of "Jake and Amy," were so firmly grounded in Kohlberg's concept of morality and moral development that they were confusing the subjects and turning the interviews into an interrogation-like experience. Gilligan sees this as the point of breakdown in the process of moral discernment. Girls were consistently reported to stagnate in moral development and reasoning skills after puberty. From a feminist perspective, however, Gilligan finds that girls, with the "Amy" of the interview as a prime example, were often being or feeling bullied by interviewers who thought the girls could not reason through the logic of the moral dilemmas, when in fact the professionals were unable to identify the different ways in which girls were contextualizing the dilemmas.[38]

Reasoning and logic as approaches to ethics have long been established as the means of resolving conflict, beginning with the Enlightenment and taking control of cultural assumptions since modernity. Gilligan, however, writes that in the case of Kohlberg and "Jake and Amy," "seeing in the dilemma not a math problem with humans (instead of signs or numerals) but a narrative of relationships that extends over time" is the difference between Kohlberg's assumptions and an ethic of caring. "Amy envisions the wife's continuing need for her husband and the husband's continuing concern for his wife, and seeks to respond to the druggist's need in a way that would sustain rather than sever connection." It appears that while "Jake" is concerned for justice that considers and weighs justice to produce a legal outcome that will correctly prioritize life while considering property rights, "Amy" is as much concerned for the druggist's place in community as she is for Heinz and his wife.[39]

37. Ibid., 25.

38. Ibid., 29. "Amy" was feeling interrogated by a professional who could not contextualize or make sense of her answers. It begins to appear that the interviewer uses power and manipulates the direction of the interview to fit Kohlberg's assumptions. When Gilligan reads the verbatim text through feminist lenses, there is a "shift in the conception of the interview. It immediately becomes clear that the interviewer's problem in understanding Amy's response stems from the fact that Amy is answering a different question from the one the interviewer thought had been posed."

39. Ibid., 26. "Jake considers the law to 'have mistakes,'" which can be corrected by judicial authority, or perhaps with light sentencing regarding the details that led to Heinz stealing the medicine. "Amy sees this drama as a mistake, believing the world should just share things more and then people wouldn't have to steal." Both children recognize the need for agreement, but see it as mediated in different ways—"he impersonally through systems of law and logic, she personally through communication in relationship" (27).

Gilligan unpacks the differences between "Jake and Amy" with the attention to "Amy's" thinking, which had been apparently ignored by Kohlberg, or at least found unacceptable to the interviewer. She writes that "Amy's" world is:

> A world of relationship and psychological truths where an aware-ness of the connection between people gives rise to a recognition of responsibility for another . . . of the need for response. Seen in this light, her understanding of morality as arising from the recognition of relationship, her belief in communication as the mode of conflict resolution, and her conviction that the solution to the dilemma will follow from its compelling representation seem far from naïve or immature.[40]

The concern for care ethics is not "*whether Heinz* should act in this situation (*should* Heinz steal the medicine) but rather *how* Heinz should act . . . (should Heinz *steal* the drug)." Gilligan writes that in Heinz dilemma these two children see "two very different moral problems—'Jake' sees the conflict as occurring in the realm between life and property that can be solve by logical deduction, 'Amy' a fractur(ing) of human relationships that must be mended with its own thread."[41] Gilligan cites a basic understanding that care ethics allows for prioritizing love for others as you love yourself. This challenges the moral development model—changes it entirely. According to Gilligan, the rights and justice authoritarian model (mediated criminal justice) demands "*not doing* what [one] wants because [one] is thinking of the welfare of others." The care ethic model instead commands "*doing* what others are counting on regardless of what you yourself want to

---

40. Ibid., 28. "Amy's judgments contain the insights central to an ethic of care . . . Her awareness of the 'method of truth' as the central tenant of nonviolent conflict reso-lution and her belief in the restorative activity of care, lead her to see the actors in the dilemma arrayed not as opponents in a contest of rights, but as members of a network of relationships."

41. Ibid. "Rights and justice authority-dependent models present a focus on "win-ning and losing and the potential for violence" and stand in firm opposition to a man-ner in which care provides a way to resolve the dilemma with attention given to "the web of relationships" within the conflict "that is sustained by a process of communica-tion. With this shift, the moral problem changes from one of unfair domination, the imposition of property over life, to one of unnecessary exclusion, the failure of the druggist to respond to the wife" (29). Furthermore, Gilligan finds "most striking . . . the imagery of violence in the boy's response, depicting a world of dangerous confrontation and explosive connection, where she sees a world of care and protection, a life lived with others whom 'you may love so much or even more than you love yourself" (33).

do . . . Responsibility signifies response, an extension rather than a limitation of action. Thus it connotes an act of care rather than the restraint of aggression."[42]

What makes Gilligan's work so important to me is not necessarily that it is thought to be representative of feminist ethics.[43] More important is that it seems so grounded in the same sort of practices as those represented by Jesus and the early church. It is easy to read as much in the gospel stories of healing, bringing "the other" back into community, feeding militants, and truth telling at risk to self. As Gilligan notes in her representation of care ethics, Jesus commands his followers. It is more than a "do unto others" practice; it is "love others as you love yourself," and act accordingly at risk of the recognition of your own rights or own access to avenues of authoritarian justice. The challenge for you, the reader, is now to read the gospels with Gilligan's care ethics in mind. Further on, I will refer to womanist ethics and ask that we all read the gospels together again in our effort to find the foundational practices that are most reflective of Jesus' ministry.

The suggestion of care ethics is that care as a practice of ethics should come prior to commendable and preferable outcomes regarding justice because "care is necessary to human life, whereas justice isn't: no one can survive without care, no infant can live if it is not cared for, but plenty of life has gone on without justice. Care is universal and formative: there can be care without justice."[44] Jesus in no way dismissed the importance of justice. Justice in fact can occur in the absence of care. This seems not to be the

42. Ibid., 33. See also Jesus' reference to *Lex Talionis*. In Matthew 5:38 Jesus is remembered to say, "You have heard it said, an eye for an eye, a tooth for a tooth." This is an example of an ethic that limits the response of one seeking justice. One cannot seek justice beyond the measure of the violation. The exemplary care ethic is found in Jesus' command in verses 39–48 that teaches a subversive yet nonviolent and caring way of retaining dignity in the face of injustice while working to lovingly change the nature of the oppressor's behavior. For more on Jesus' ethics in Matthew 5:38–48 see Wink, *Engaging the Powers*, 175–84.

43. Botti, "Feminine Virtues or Feminist Virtues," 111. Gilligan resisted the "idea of a female minority and proposed that girls' moral reasoning was not a deficient reasoning of a novel minority understanding of moral circumstances." Rather, Gilligan was developing a "fully different human voice." The premise of a novel or minority moral vision is identified through a proposal "that certain factors limit the moral capacity of women . . ." For instance, the belief that women "naturally default to 'their care for and sensitivity to the needs of others' or the 'emphasis on connections rather than separations'" should instead be presented in ethical discourse in positive terms and not deficiencies of reasoning. Such a deficiency is also falsely assumed to be embedded in females genetically. Care for the needs of others as a practical ethical foundation is "not a woman's perspective, but rather a more accurate view of morality and human relationships."

44. Berges, *Feminist Perspective on Virtue Ethics*, 118–19.

method of the early church, however. Berges suggests that, in fact, caring is not a universal value, nor is being cared for a universally desired state of being.[45] However, an argument can be made that, given the option of a community of caring, the desire to be cared for might be recognized in many who are witness to a community that teaches caring for others as a means to realize that justice is part of the activity of Christian evangelism.

The combining of care ethics and virtue ethics further illustrates the importance of a community that invests in social training. Also, care ethics prioritizes a life view that has been socially construed, or kept in a culturally dark corner of patriarchy, as being deficient in reasoning yet typical of female gender norms. Like Aristotle, Western patriarchy has used socially preferred gender roles not only to limit female contributions to moral discourse, but has used sexist stereotypes to reject specific behaviors as unreasonable because they are seen as representative of only feminine behaviors. Berges writes that such stereotyping has refused "to allow males to consider the gender spectrum as a means of excluding caring and nurture as a grounding component of social organizing and justice." She writes, "We need to know how best to decide between care and justice." [46] Being a caring and nurturing person, as we will see, does not exempt one from employing justice as a response to conflict or oppression. It simply prioritizes the methods of achieving such outcomes.

45. Ibid., 120.
46. Ibid., 7.

CHAPTER 10

Cursed Is One Who Hangs from a Tree

Ethics from "the Other"

Keshia Thomas provided the sort of witness necessary for me to make tangible sense of Jesus and the Bible. I don't know her and haven't spoken with her. I've only seen her in pictures and read stories about her. Yet it is through stories that I know about Jesus, and it is through Keshia Thomas that I know the stories of Jesus and the rest of Scripture are truthful. I know exactly what it means to manifest love for one's enemies in our contemporary setting.

In past years, white supremacist groups gathered annually in Ann Arbor, Michigan, to celebrate Adolph Hitler's birthdate. Such was the case in 1996. While there are a few different perspectives of what occurred at this demonstration, the actions of a counter-protester lends to my understanding of Jesus' ministry and Christian ethics. The white supremacists were demonstrating in a fenced-in area meant to protect them from physical harm at the hand of the counter-protesters who were promoting racial justice and acting as a witness to America's racist history as embodied by groups such as the Ku Klux Klan. Keshia Thomas, an eighteen-year-old Ann Arbor resident, was participating in the counter-protest. Albert McKeel Jr. was also on the outside of the fencing that separated the two groups, thus unprotected from the anti-racist collectives that were going to take issue with his Confederate battle flag, SS tattoo, and other white supremacist regalia. Once everyone became aware of his presence and the absence of police protection, they chased McKeel and began beating him when he fell. Keshia Thomas was part of the group chasing the racist McKeel until she recognized that her enemy—a man who would have called her an enemy and perhaps done worse if the opportunity arose—was potentially in danger of being beaten to death. Thomas's following decision indicates the kind of virtues necessary to embody faith without concern for self-interest or self-preserving outcomes.

Thomas may or may not be a Christian; I do not know. But I do know that her decision to show love toward her enemy, at risk to her own safety, embodied the claims Christians make about the cross, and Jesus' call to carry one's own cross as witness to our belief about messianic truth and justice. Thomas fell to the ground and covered McKeel's body with her own to protect him from the kicks and blows of what was becoming an out-of-control mob.[1] She rescued McKeel, despite his Stars and Bars–decorated clothing and SS tattoos, and the triggers those symbols antagonize. This black teenager embodied the example of Christ, and what I perceive to be most representative of messianic and biblical ethics. She has become representative of what it might look like for me to bear my own cross when notions of God's justice are put to the test or crises of justice arise and invite action on behalf of faith without attention to outcomes. Thomas also becomes a primary example of care ethics in action.[2]

Whether Keshia Thomas knew it or not, her decision is rooted in rather recent history. Mother of Emmet Till, Mamie Till Mobely, committed herself to justice on behalf of her murdered son. "She refused to bear the cross that Money, Mississippi gave her when they lynched her son, and instead sought justice to overcome it, bravely appearing at the trial of her son's accused killers at risk of her own life."[3] Emmet Till was the fourteen-year-old black youth from Chicago who was accused of flirting with a twenty-one-year-old married white woman. His mother insisted on an open-casket public viewing of his body to publicize the terror of lynching.

Baker-Fletcher identifies the courage necessary to attending the trial and making her son's murder a subject of public concern the kind of courage indicative of sacrificial and cross-bearing mandates to seek justice. "If

1. Photos of Thomas coming to the aid of Albert McKeel Jr. are award winning; see *Life Album 1996*. Numerous media reports are available, the most recent an interview from a Michigan reporter. Slaughter, "Former Ann Arbor Resident Reflects," para. 1.

2. Baker-Fletcher, "More than Suffering," 159–60. Baker-Fletcher's concern for self-sacrifice as a healthy personal choice is important when placing Thomas's actions into a messianic ethical context. She writes, "To overcome the cross with Christ, then, includes being willing to risk your own life in the process in the call for justice. Yet, this is not a path that glorifies suffering and rationalizes that suffering is redemptive. Suffering is deepest and most severe when it is the spiritual suffering called despair that leads to cynicism. That is the worst kind of suffering." She adds that such despair and cynicism "perpetuates hatred, injustice, and unnecessary violence. To overcome the cross by taking up one's own cross is to claim divine and personal power over all crosses . . . It is the of confronting evil and staring it in the face. This is the path of life-loving. Resurrection faith is the source of power and courage to say 'No' to evil and destruction."

3. Ibid., 159.

we can ever speak positively about what it means to 'bear one's cross' then she demonstrated it in her Christ-like willingness to risk her own life by making every effort to bring her son's lynchers to justice."[4]

From the actions of a young African-American woman I turn to the work of an African-American theologian to further explore potentially new paradigms for understanding the cross. James Cone's exploration of lynching as being most representative of the social and political meaning behind the cross and the execution of Jesus is one of the most eye-opening theological endeavors I am aware of. Jesus was cursed to hang on a tree just as multitudes of African-American men and some poor whites were hung from trees across the country. Cone draws some conclusions that are integral to understanding the nature of the cross, especially for Americans of European ancestry. Cone sat with Bill Moyer for a television interview in 2007.[5] The interview came during a spate of aggressive placements of empty nooses in public places where blacks gathered.

Cone argues instructively and forcefully that much of American Christendom can read the New Testament and truly recognize the importance of the incarnation by placing Jesus' ministry within the context of being black in the United States. Cone says that American theology and history is never going to be as clean as white Christians want it to be. "If America could understand itself as not being innocent," he tells Moyer, "it might be able to play a more creative role in the world . . ."[6] As it stands, the church cannot fulfill its mission unless it overcomes its commitment to nationalism and American exceptionalism and repents of its paradigm of white supremacy.

"The cross is victory out of defeat and the lynching tree is transcendent of defeat," says Cone. "And that's why the cross and the lynching tree come together. Christians can't understand what's going on at the cross until they see it through the image of a lynching tree with black bodies hanging there . . ." The experience of black America, the reality of slavery and lynching, and Jim Crow are integral to black understandings of the Christ, and the promises of the cross and suffering.[7]

"The cross and the lynching tree interpret each other," says Cone. "Both were public spectacles usually reserved for hardened criminals, rebellious

4. Ibid.

5. Moyers with Cone, "Cross and the Lynching Tree," 2.

6. Ibid., 10.

7. Sims, "Issue of Race and Lynching," 205; citing Apel, *Imagery of Lynching*, 44. "Lynching was used as a weapon to terrorize the black community as a whole in both racial and gender terms. It was an instrument of social disciplining intended to impress all who say or heard about it, not merely to punish the victim; thus innocent black men were sometimes substituted when a fugitive could not be found."

slaves, rebels against the Roman state and falsely accused militant blacks." Cone believes that the cross, within the context of American black religion, "keeps the lynchers from having the last word." Also, he says the lynching tree interprets the cross as it "keeps the cross out of the hands of those who are dominant. Nobody who is lynching anybody can understand the cross."[8]

White Americans might have some clarity on this concern for the cross as the hope of the hopeless if they consider the following exchange between Moyer and Cone. Moyer asks, "Do you believe God is love?" Cone affirms his belief that the God known in Jesus is indeed the God of love. Moyers pushes further, stating, "I would have a hard time believing God is love if I were a black man. I mean, those bodies swinging on the tree. Where was God? Where was God during slavery?"

Cone's response is key to the understanding of how hermeneutics, eschatology, and apocalyptic ethics lead to messianic interpretations of the gospel and the cross. Cone says, "See, you are looking at it from the perspective of those who win. You have to see it from the perspective of those who have no power." That statement is absolutely necessary to my own understanding of the social location from which the Bible must be interpreted, and of the place of rejected privilege in such an interpretation, if a Christian ethic is to be a biblical, messianic ethic. Cone continues, "In fact, God is love because it's that power in your life that lets you resist definitions that other people are placing on you. And you say 'nobody knows the trouble I've seen' . . . But glory hallelujah, that is the fact that there is a humanity and a spirit that nobody can kill. As long as you know that, you will resist."

Narrative discourse and apocalyptic faith are integral to this theology of the cross and lynching tree. Just as Jesus died on a cross and was resurrected in vindication of his faithfulness, Americans must learn from the black church community that the power to identify and respond to evil, and to live faithfully, comes only from an existence outside of, and critical of, sociopolitical power. Such a decision to empty oneself of privilege makes sense only when illuminated by the promise that a believer will be resurrected and vindicated in God's time of redemption and justice. Just

---

8. Moyers with Cone, "Cross and the Lynching Tree," 12. Cone also states, "In fact, biblical scholars, when they want to describe what was happening to Jesus, many of the sad, 'it was a lynching'. And all I want to suggest is if American Christians say they want to identify with the cross, they have to see the cross as a lynching . . . If you identify with the lynchers, you can't understand what's happening. In the sense of resistance, resistance by helpless people (you begin to understand the cross). Power in powerlessness is not something we are accustomed to listening to and understanding. America always wants to think its's going to win everything. Well, black people have a history in which we didn't win. Our resistance is resistance against the odds. That's why we can understand the cross."

as Jesus insisted that Israel repent of its own commitment to an exclusivist interpretation of election and welcome "the other" into the realm of God, so must the American church repent of its commitment to white supremacy, racial injustice, and maintenance of white privilege in order to realize and make credible the promises of the kingdom.

To be clear, this chapter is not meant to be representative of a white scholar attempting to do black liberation theology. I pray this is not a colonization of important theological thought. Rather, I intend to use the American reality of racial injustice and our history of racism to provide a means for a church corrupted by power and privilege to reinterpret the cross, and reimagine the kenotic ethics of Paul's own theological experiences, especially as portrayed in Philippians. This is the attempt of a white theologian to relate to the cross through the American experience of race, and attempt to understand Jesus through the lenses of African-American blackness as it stands in the shadows of American whiteness. It is also an attempt to provide an understanding of redemption, and the reconciliation that occurs between Jew and Gentile, master and slave, and male and female within the context of Christian baptism, and the ethics that display this particular moral vision of brother- and sisterhood.[9]

Cone credits the theology of Reinhold Niebuhr with detailing how faith is so closely connected to the realities of power. Cone views the product of Niebuhr's Christian realism as a positive contribution to American Christian ethics, in firm contrast to my sectarian criticisms of his work. Cone describes the moral vision of Niebuhr as an illustration of "sinful beings seeking justice" in response to the revealed truths of the gospel. "Faith for Niebuhr," Cone states, "is an affect that empowers people to fight in the world. That's what is at stake for him."

This is a key hermeneutical difference from the assumptions of this project, but a difference that provides evidence of how the role of differing experience and hermeneutical lenses can lead to complimentary understandings of Scripture. It also provides evidence of how a community's self-understanding and interpretive maneuvers can make use of apparently

9. Ibid., 3. "Slavery and lynching . . . It's in American culture . . . It's white America's original sin and it's deep. Like for a long time we didn't want to talk about slavery. They (whites) don't like to talk about 246 years of slavery. Then a hundred years of segregation and lynching. America must face up to that we are one community . . . You know, if anybody in this society is brother and sister, it's black people and white people because there is a tussle there you can't get out of. It is deeply ingrained in our relationship to each other in a way that it's not with anybody else in this land." Cone continues, "We built this country. White people know that. After slavery, segregation, and lynching, we still helped built this country. It's a history of violence, a history of black people fighting in every American war."

conflicting accounts of the gospel in order to embody faithfulness in view of others in credible ways. It is Cone's understanding of Niebuhr's work and the American experience of the lynching tree that stands as a measure by which to assess my own theology of the cross and messianic ethics.[10]

Before moving on to a more detailed description of a type of messianic ethic, it is important to explore the nature of womanist ethics. I cannot do justice to the contributions made by black women to Christian theology, but an overview may provide enough support for readers to grasp how understanding Jesus through the history of blackness in the context of American whiteness lead to a fuller expression of messianic care ethics.[11]

To commit to the messianic care ethic is to commit not only to an experience of the world that has largely been buried in America's theological awareness, but to look towards those who have experienced powerlessness and marginalization throughout our history. Yet, black women have clung to Christ and the cross for both hope and an empowering faith that can be fully representative of a historical biblical hermeneutic. I believe that the experience of Africa-Americans within the context of white supremacist culture, especially as experienced by black women in opposition to overbearing standards of whiteness, creates an environment conducive to the type of suffering and faithfulness embodied, and emboldened, at the cross.

Russell refers to the liberation theology standard of praxis—which I present as embodiment ethics. "Action-reflection (praxis) arises out of commitment to Jesus Christ," writes Russell, "and a desire to understand the meaning of the good news in light of the changing world." Russell identifies with Friere's definitive understanding of praxis as "action that is concurrent with reflection or analysis that leads to new questions, actions, and reflections."[12] Such commitment to constant congregational or communal

10. Ibid., 3.

11. Russell, *Human Liberation in a Feminist Perspective*, 54–55. Russell writes, "liberation theologies recognize that persons and societies find themselves in different situations of oppression, and they try to address themselves to concrete experiences that can illuminate their own experience and can be shared with others. They try to express the gospel in light of the experience of oppression out of which they are written . . . Such a method draws on the contributions of many disciplines that help to illuminate the human condition and not just a particular theological tradition." Russell cites Rosemary Reuther's critique of such theological mainstays. She quotes, "these doctrines are no longer taken so much as answers than as ways of formulating the questions." Ruether, *Liberation Theology*, 10.

12. Russell, *Human Liberation in a Feminist Perspective*, 50–51. "Interpretations of the gospel are tested by the experience of Christian communities working with others in society. The actions of the communities are also tested by the biblical witness to the meaning and purpose of human liberation as part of God's plan for all of the groaning creation." She also cites Freire, *Pedagogy of the Oppressed*, 55.

action-reflection is driven by the concept of humanization. Drawing from themes of incarnation, redemption, and indeed human salvation, the concept of praxis or embodied ethics makes the gospel the tangible redemptive component in "situations of broken community, of oppression, of de-futurized minorities and majorities where there is a longing to be whole human beings"[13] Human dignity as measured by the New Testament and the ministry of the Christ can only be realized in a community of care, being accepted as subjects and not objects of someone else's manipulation. In light of sociopolitical realities, the gospel has become almost synonymous with the manipulation of political and social power structures to the benefit of a privileged class. In absence of care, the gospel has been rendered abusive and dictatorial.

"Dorothy Sölle reminds us that sin cannot be understood only as a private matter," writes Russell. When the gospel is reduced to a tool of sociopolitical control, sin becomes an "eminently political, social term."[14] This corporate sin, the use of the gospel as a secular tool of manipulating political outcomes, denies the suffering that is represented in the cross as much as it underwrites the ignorance and willful denial of the suffering of marginalized persons living in the shadows of churches and other institutions that reap the benefit of protected status in support of privilege. When the church is in the service of privilege, it acquiesces to suffering as a tool of social control and evil as a legitimate means of achieving preferred outcomes. However, it is in the gospel that we find the corrective to the heresy. When the privileged take on the suffering of bearing their own cross as an act of repentance, they are liberated from the sinful burden of maintaining

---

13. Russell, *Human Liberation in a Feminist Perspective*, 63.

14. Ibid., 62, citing Sölle, "Gospel and Liberation," 296. "This includes the sins of our own people, our own race, and class . . . we are faced with the responsibility not only for admitting our collaboration in such social sin, but also for working to change social structures that bring it about." As a matter of virtue or care ethics, MacIntyre has a similar concern for historical accountability to corporate or social sin, and particularly the matter of repentance and institutionalized racism in the United States. "From the standpoint of individualism, I am what I choose myself to be . . . I cannot be held responsible for what my country has done unless I choose . . . to assume such responsibility. Such individualism is expressed by those modern Americans who deny any responsibility for the effects of slavery on black Americans, saying 'I never owned any slaves.' It is more subtly the standpoint of those other Americans who accept a nicely calculated responsibility for such effects measured precisely by the benefits they themselves as individuals received from slavery." Such an attitude, states MacIntyre, is "self-detached from social and historical roles and statuses." Such a self, or, individual, "can have no history," writes MacIntyre, thus no responsibility for either repentance or the emptying of privilege. *After Virtue*, 220–221.

privilege and can get to the business of revealing an apocalyptic and divinely inspired response to the truth of societal sin.[15]

Copeland finds Christianity embodied in slave status. "Almost from its emergence," she writes, "Christianity has been described as the religion of slaves." Christian narratives and biblical discourse were powerful resources for American slaves. "Biblical revelation held out formidable power. It offered slaves the 'dangerous' message of freedom, for indeed, Jesus did come to bring 'freedom for the captives' and release for those held in economic, social, and political bondage. It offered them the great parallel event of the Exodus."[16] The view of the gospel, and the truth it reveals, is in considerable conflict when viewed from privileged status as opposed to "slave" status.[17] As persons with access to white privilege, can Americans of European descent find in Jesus and Paul the makings of an image of slave status such as Paul illustrates when he refers to himself as a slave of Christ Jesus? If we follow Copeland, the emptying of privilege allows for a liberating experience of the cross of Christ. "Enslaved Africans sang because they saw the result of the cross, (Jesus') triumph over the principalities and powers, triumph over evil in this world. Slaves understood God as the author of freedom, of emancipation."[18] Contrast such thought with present activities in the church that betray a faith that political power or reasoning, and not voluntary sacrifice, will ultimately liberate humanity from bondage to sin.

15. Copeland, "Wading Through Many Sorrows," 136. Copeland writes, "As a working definition, I understand suffering as the disturbance of our inner-tranquility caused by physical, mental, emotional, and spiritual forces that we grasp as jeopardizing our lives, our very existence. Evil is the negation and deprivation of good; suffering, while never identical with evil, is inseparable from it. Thus, and quite paradoxically, the suffering caused by evil can result in interior development and perfection as well as social and cultural good. African-Americans have encountered monstrous evil in . . . slavery and its legacy of institutionalized racism. Yet from the anguish of our people rose distinctive religious expression, exquisite music and song, powerful rhetoric and literature, practical invention, and art."

16. Ibid., 147–48. She locates the foundations of the black experience in America in religious responses to suffering and oppression. "From their aural appropriation and critical reflection of their own condition, these men and women (slaves) shaped and fitted Christian practices, rituals, and values to their own religious experiences and religio-cultural expectations, and personal needs. The slave community formed a distinctive image of itself and fashioned an inner-world, a scale of values from which to judge the world around them, and themselves."

17. Cone describes American Christendom as being a civic religion from its very beginning. "To the present day, American white theological thought has been 'patriotic,' either by defining the theological task independently of black suffering (the liberal northern approach) or by defining Christianity as compatible with white racism." Cone, *Black Theology of Liberation*, 22.

18. Copeland, "Wading Through Many Sorrows," 148.

All of this attention to suffering, especially when treading the always choppy waters of slavery as an example of suffering, demands a caveat. That being that the acceptance of suffering servanthood must be a voluntary acceptance, and that it must be a sacrifice taken on by persons of privilege, committed to embodying the faithfulness of Christ. For centuries, in the American church no less than other places, the notion of vindicated suffering has in fact been used to keep marginalized persons in their social place, as a foil for resistance or liberation movements throughout history. Do not be mistaken: access to the Bible and the ability to read and interpret its narratives have sparked Christian reform movements and political reform movements alike.

American Christianity, however, has selectively used the Bible to support slavery and segregation, sexism and the maintenance of patriarchy, and social and political hierarchies. Copeland writes that "in [their] teaching, theologizing, preaching and practice, Christians sought to bind slaves to their condition by inculcating caricatures of the cardinal virtues of patience, long-suffering, forbearance, love, faith, and hope." Copeland stresses the absolute necessity of Christian communities of interpretation, regardless of voluntary status or rigidity of practices, to distance itself from "any form of masochism, even Christian masochism.[19]

"A theology of suffering in womanist perspective must reevaluate these virtues in light of Black women's experiences. Such reevaluation engages in a hermeneutic of suspicion and a hermeneutic of resistance, but that reevaluation and reinterpretation must be rooted in a criticism that rejects both naïve realism and idealism."[20] It may be a fine line to walk for those of marginalized communities who have no choice in their suffering.

---

19. Copeland, "Wading Through Many Sorrows," 152.

20. Ibid. "As a mode of critical self-consciousness, Black women's cognitive practice emphasizes the dialectic between oppression, and activism to resist and change it. The matrix of domination is responsive to human agency; the struggle of Black women suggests there is choice and power to act—to do so mindfully, artfully." There is another caveat to the concept of cross-bearing and suffering that is important for persons of privilege to consider as well that will be important for those choosing an ethic of repentance and kingdom building. Yoder insists that some concerns for pastoral care considerations (not related to care ethics) have done considerable damage to Christian ethics and the command to bear one's own cross. "Hosts of sincere people," Yoder writes, "in hospitals or in conflict-ridden situations have been helped by this thought to bear the strain of their destiny with a sense of divine presence and purpose. Yet . . . the validity of this pastoral concern must not blind us to the abuse of language and misuse of Scripture they entail. The cross of Christ was not an inexplicable or chance event, which happened to strike him, like illness or accident. To accept the cross as his destiny, to move toward it and even to provoke it . . . was Jesus' constantly reiterated free choice. The cross of Calvary was not some difficult family situation, not a frustration of

For some women and men, suffering coaxes real freedom and growth, so much that Thurman insists we literally see the change: "Into their faces come a subtle radiance and settled serenity; into their relationships a vital generosity that opens the sealed doors of the heart in all who are encountered along the way. From still others, suffering squeezes a delicious and ironic spirit and tough laughter." Consider the Gullah (woman's) proverb: "Ah done been in sorrows kitchen and ah licked the pots clean."[21]

White Christians cannot relate to or walk a mile in the shoes of African-Americans, refugees from war zones, undocumented Latinos, or American Muslims targeted as "terrorists." Yet, I offer the views of black Americans above to illustrate how we might view the historical person of Jesus within a context that allows for an experience of Ricoeur's "secondary naivete" of Jesus' social location, as well as an understanding of the necessity of emptying oneself of privilege in order to perform as a witness to God's redeeming and reconciling work through incarnational presence. We can begin to unpack the nature of the cross, and what is necessary to the efficacy of the cross in light of resurrection theology. I believe we can embody the moral vision that is part and parcel of this kenotic theology through the development of care ethics grounded in a community's interpretation of the text. Practice will lend itself toward a sanctifying perfection.

---

personal fulfilment, a crushing debt or a nagging in-law; it was the political, legally-to-be-expected result of a moral clash with the powers ruling his society." Yoder, *Politics of Jesus*, 129.

21. Copeland, "Wading Through Many Sorrows"; citing Thurman, *Disciplines of the Spirit*, 136.

CHAPTER 11

Making Sense of the Absurd

I began writing this book in a calving barn in Allegan County, Michigan. The final chapter is being typed in Richmond, Indiana, where I am facilitating a course on peace and justice as an adjunct professor at the Earlham School of Religion during the January intensives. Both the beginning and the end were produced in zero-degree temperatures, though the first chapter was birthed around midnight while waiting for a cow to give birth. I began to write this final chapter in the glint of a bright sunshine on a Saturday morning in a study room at the Lauramoore Mansion, and as I look back over the past year, the gestational period of this project was an experience in contrasts as significant as the contrast between birthing barns, antebellum homes, and seminaries. As it happens, the womb that nourished this project was Flint, Michigan.

It's not that Flint provided a stable and safe (but sometimes dark, nevertheless) place to gestate a book on theology or ethics. Rather, Flint was an environment of spiritual and emotional nourishment that allowed for me to grow personally, and be ministered to by the least of these. And, while Flint was a gestational period for this book, and for my sense of spiritual and religious self to be born yet again, it was also an opportunity to explore what it means to interpret and embody the text as a means of making the rather absurd claims of the gospel credible to others.

Don't be misled by the above statement and assume the gospel stories lacked credibility among the individuals and groups that I worked so closely with in Flint. Rather, the individuals of middle-class and fairly well-educated congregations seemed to me the persons who were most challenged by the attempt to explore the emptying of privilege, and taking healthy spiritual risks. The wonderful relationships that I developed in Flint were not reflected by others that lived outside of that bubble, and the bubble of my congregation. What was received as a gift in Flint was viewed as an act of irresponsibility by some folks back home. Other people had to sacrifice for me to go to Flint, often at great expense. The person I was to pay mortgage to did not get paid. The people I asked for financial support grew weary. My family of five faced difficulties while I was two hours from home three nights a week. I found that the most generous givers were often those who did not share my Christian faith. One humanist couple helped us buy a car.

On the other hand, my own church, Common Spirit Church of the Brethren, consistently helped my family and me with financial, material, and spiritual support at every turn. Yet, not everyone buys into someone's call or vision. None of my work in Flint, and none of my willingness to explore faithfulness and the embodiment of ethics, could have occurred had I not been willing to hear the word "no," and take that as a final answer. I had to receive and accept criticisms that were valid and attacks that misled others about the nature of my beliefs.

Second birth and regenerative sanctifying grace are part of a cycle of life and faith, and the opportunity for me to return to the neighborhood of my first decade of life was a call that was not about me—but then, it was all about me. To act as a minister in the face of a public health crisis related to unsafe water in Flint was a chance to go back to my first experiences of a holy God.

On a winter night a while ago an idea was birthed to write something about faithfulness. Now, in the beginning of another cycle of winter, with temperatures again hovering around zero degrees, I aim to put finishing touches on a project that I hope gives birth to hope. What might it look like for persons in the body of Christ to come together as an apocalyptic witness to possibilities that exist beyond the cycle of Sundays and November elections? As I wrote, I experienced a call to put to the test the kind of theology and messianic ethic that I was attempting to articulate with the written word in cow barns, at the dinner table, at libraries, and in Bill and Mary Lorah-Hammond's spare bedroom north of the corrosive water of the Flint River.

It must be stated that much of this book has been written during what turned out to be the most remarkable election of my own life. I can remember sitting in my grandmother's dining room in Flint while walking home to Arlene Avenue and stopping at her house on Whitney Avenue to spend time with her. On a black-and-white television, Watergate hearings were flickering in the background of our conversation. My earliest understanding of politics, as shallow as my limited exposure would allow for, was rooted in the end of the war in Southeast Asia and the Nixon administration. Now, I am nearly fifty years old and watching this catastrophe of an election result in the Electoral College handing the presidency over to Donald Trump, with nearly 80 percent of Americans of European ancestry who self-identified as evangelical Christians revealing that they voted for him.[1] Trump lost the popular vote by millions, providing more evidence that the great American political divide is cemented. As I have stated early on in this project, the church taking one side or another against the other has been as catastrophic for the body of Christ, as if a meteor had hit and exterminated any last shred of independence it may have had regarding its relationship with American democracy.

If democracy did not fail in the United States in 2016—and certainly it may not have failed—when dissected by historians separated by the distance of time, it will certainly stand out as a turning point of some sort. This book asks the reader to consider the absurdity of the 2016 election, and ponder whether the election is no more than what Americans have been hurdling toward since the 1980s, when the church overthrew one of its evangelical own. Truth did not matter in this election, and much of what was asserted as truth had little to do with credible political, economic, or foreign policy. From the perspective of all sides courageous enough to be honest about 2016, truth was absent. This book suggests that, even in American democracy, for all it is worth, truth has never been present the way we thought is has been. This book states that the church has failed to preach and teach this claim, and in the process of such failure, has somehow become comfortable with politics at the expense of the gospel truth. The gospel preached far too often in the United States is a tame narrative of a rather accommodating God who has been domesticated by the twin towers of privilege and wealth. We are a nation of cheap grace that believes in a God that sheds the divine grace only upon us, and stands in harsh judgment of all things uncomfortable. This American deity is not the God of Scripture, and it is not the God known through Jesus the Christ. It is the biblical Christ that is our salvation, and heaven is not the outcome God wants us to anticipate. Such anticipation is not evidenced by the Bible.

The salvation of the biblical Christ is a salvation in the here and now, a liberation from the institutions of Wall Street, Washington, and the health and wealth priorities of American Christendom. Even the poor white folks voted for Trump, and not because he is a good Christian. Trump's election may very well be, however, due to a shared belief that Hillary Clinton has not proven to be a good Christian. Nor has any presidential candidate represented the love and grace of God in a credible way. Only the church can do that, and we are hidden away, buried beneath layers of red, white, and blue dirty laundry; a replica plastic papyrus constitution; and a television culture that not only provides non-stop political misinformation, but reruns of the

1. Smith and Martinez, "How the Faithful Voted," table 1.

Watergate hearings on demand. We are in dire need of a salvation that reminds us that heaven can wait. We are a broken humanity, and Christ must be made manifest by a church that embodies the love of God, neighbor, and enemy alike in response to the evil of war, poverty, and degradation.

At First Church of the Brethren in Flint, I began to explore those possibilities with Bill and Mary, Jenn Betts, Paul Hammond, and a small Gospel Baptist congregation known as NOW Ministries. I explored what it meant to accept the text as an informant of my preaching and teaching, my ethics and action. Like any good Quaker or Brethren group, we started with meal sharing. Folks from the neighborhood were not going to come to Sunday services. They were, however, coming to the church as we distributed pallet after pallet of bottled water and other health- and nutrition-related items. Food became a big part of our ministry in response to the fact of dangerous levels of lead in Flint's water, the specter of Legionnaire's Disease, poverty and violence, and every other thing on this side of hopelessness.

Mary Lorah-Hammond, the queen of all things ministry at First Church of Brethren, had been regularly attending what she called a "dinner church" on Sunday evenings. She indicated she would like to have the same kind of gathering on Tuesday nights at our own church. A messianic banquet was called for, and flyers were created, printed, and distributed. By 6 p.m. on the inaugural Tuesday, no one came. With the biblical text in mind, and in hand, I left Mary and Jenn cooking and walked around the neighborhood. I went up and down avenues pockmarked with boarded-up houses covered by overgrown greenery, west toward Ballenger Highway, then back east along Corunna Road, where scrub trees witnessed to nature's ability to force life up through the broken glass and blackened beams of burned-out businesses. I mimicked the story of the banquet in which all of the right folks were busy, and all of the wrong folks who I met on my walks were then invited and came to share a meal.

On some evenings I could corral eight or nine folks to come share our food. Other nights, not so many. But one Tuesday evening, I was walking down Arlene with my son Micah, and on the corner of Mann Avenue we saw two women sitting in a minivan. As I got closer, it became evident that there was some sort of misfortune that was being addressed. There were tears on cheeks. I rapped on a window, and when it was rolled down, I told the two women that we had a dinner being served at the Brethren Church on Stocker Avenue. As it turned out, one of the women in the car had just had her food benefits card stolen and they had no groceries. She and her husband and their five children had just moved back into the city, into a house that had been vacant for more than a year and in very poor shape, and they needed food badly. They also needed just a bit of hope.

The whole family came to eat with us. I was able to take the father grocery shopping, and NOW Ministries was able to supply the family with a month's worth of food the next day. For me, this was doing church. It was also an attempt to live biblically under the guide of the positive ethic of Jesus and the gospel stories of his ministry. The gospel vision of the kingdom of God calls for non-violence, and for a peace witness, to make any sense at all. For the peace witness to be received as credible and trustworthy, it must be embodied publicly for the neighbors that you purport to love, and it must be received as trustworthy. Such public embodiment comes with a cost. As the Brethren say, we must count those costs as we head toward the future of a church that is in decline, and a witness that has not only become untrustworthy, but has been discredited as well.

But such stories of joy do not indicate what the church is. There is much, much more that needs doing. My contention is that it is moments of joy that build over time to establish a foundation for the next generation. The church as we knew it in our childhood is dying, and political priorities are both misleading otherwise faithful people and driving others away in droves. It may be that the people most in need of outreach will never be regular church members. But the fact that the church is no longer a credible witness to what it says is true of God is the very fact that keeps other folks looking for a faithful community from exploring their own spiritual leadings, leadings that are of the Holy Spirit and are effectively blasphemed when confronted by American civic religionists. Nowhere else do we find excuses not to feed the poor and house the homeless because they somehow belong on the margins as a consequence of their sins. But sin has treacherous consequences for all of us, and this absence of grace in evidence in the church will result in our condemnation and judgment through the just response of an angry, frustrated, and ultimately distraught and tearful creator God.

This book invites congregations to sit together, share a meal, and read the Bible, then reread it. As you read, with special attention paid to the gospels and Acts, will the group find anything new in the text? Is there anything overlooked by popular understandings of the text? Will anyone begin to notice that the verses that demand care for the poor, the prisoner, the widow and orphan, and the alien vastly outnumber any concern for purity or sexuality? Will anyone throw the question out there: "Are we expected to do all of this?"

Remember Yoder's list of common excuses that pastors and teachers alike give us to avoid loving our enemies, or in fact avoid caring for one another as Jesus instructs in John 15. For much of the American era of civic religious expression and the public love affair with the nation-state and democracy, pastors have been arguing against the strong messianic ethic that I attempt to detail in this project. Yoder asks you and me to consider these assumptions when we read the text together, and then work to overcome them.

First, do we believe Jesus thought the world would end so soon, or that the kingdom of God would be established so quickly, that he did not preach or live an ethic that was intended for others to follow two millennia into the future? Was Jesus only concerned for the behavior of his disciples?

Second, did Jesus only preach to a people of his time without any relevance for future social realties? Was he a country bumpkin with no understanding of what church professionals identify as "complex organizations, institutions, and power"?

Third, can we read the text and state that Jesus was preaching an ethic that was only relevant to persons or communities that lacked political power? This leads us to perhaps the most important question. Now that the church in the United States has a measure of social, economic, and political power, are we obligated to develop an ethic not found in the ministry of Jesus, but rather in the experiences of democracy? A fourth statement takes this one step further. Was the message of Jesus purely spiritual and not intended as an normative ethic of any kind, and in fact useless in the face of social and political realities? And yet another step further, was Jesus preaching a kingdom ethic that was so purely related to God's ideal that it is an impossible ethic for human beings to follow, thus rendering Jesus meaningless as far as his lived-out ministry is concerned? Are we bound to do our comfortable best, accepting grace as an enabling life partner.

Finally, the common pastoral error regarding messianic ethics understood as non-normative Christian ethics is the suggestion that Jesus only came to sacrifice his life for our sins. His ethic is irrelevant, as it is our faith in Jesus that saves us, and we cannot legitimize Jesus or faith with our own behaviors.

Consider these assumptions, and ask whether you have heard such statements in response to questions of loving enemies, non-violence, or feeding the poor. Has anyone ever argued against helping those in poverty by stating that "the poor will always be with us"? When we read the text, is this how we are to understand any messianic ethic—in a manner that renders both the Bible and Jesus' life meaningless as a matter of faith expression?

My next challenge may be harder to discern. Several arguments against sectarian responses to sin and brokenness come to mind. Won't we become more of a cult of religious fanatics? Won't our message be rejected more than it is now, as congregations lose more members every year? Won't we become more insulated and less diverse? Won't this be too hard of an ethic and drive potential new interest elsewhere?

The sectarian response is one of more nuanced embodiment than is often allowed. For starters, we might question what will happen if the church starts preaching Jesus as normative without the expectation of widespread conformity. Does it not make sense that the church encourages people to commit to sharing their gifts and resources in a way that builds a community of servants rather than Sunday services in a building used once or twice a week? Can a congregation begin to talk about selling its building and using the money for outreach? How can small groups follow Jesus, much like those initiated by Wesley and the pietists before him? What if some folks take a wage cut to take a service job or volunteer position that more reflects the ethics of Jesus? Are such steps indicative of a cult mentality or religious fanatics? Indeed, is Jesus representative of fanaticism, or Paul? Perhaps zeal, maybe fanaticism, and perhaps a model of how such zealotry is performed in faithfulness to a God who refuses to allow radical evil to promote sin as normative social behavior, even for the church. The fear in the pulpit is that folks who feel challenged or are insulted by such a gospel will leave. If this is the primary concern, if sacrifice cannot be preached from love, than the pulpit is anti-Christ, no matter how benign it may seem.

As for becoming a cultish representation of truth, remember also that a community of interpretation must always revisit and reinterpret the text. Groups and individuals can only grow spiritually, and only be cognizant of the Holy Spirit's sanctifying presence, when they accept the challenge to change and respond to new understandings of sin, truth, and righteousness. Without new interpretive moves and radical acceptance of a God who works and responds to human need, the church would have never been born. Jesus' teaching indicates that new interpretations are necessary to build the kingdom of God. The Sermon on the Mount comes immediately to mind. If Jesus and his disciples, and if Paul, and Priscilla and her husband, all had to accept the challenge to understand the Hebrew narratives in new ways, so must we. The text tells us that any action undertaken in faith, and in the name of Jesus, will be underwritten by Jesus as we wait for the Holy Spirit to vindicate or reject our insights.

Too often, the church argues over petty concerns about the way we understand both the text and the Spirit, without heeding the warnings of Gamaliel: "Stay away from these people and let them go, for if this is a plan or action of persons, they will be overthrown, but if it is of God, you will not be able to overthrown them; or else you may even be found fighting against God."[2] And from John's epistles we read, "test the Spirit of God: every spirit that confesses that Jesus Christ has come in the flesh is from God;

---

2. Acts 5:38b–40.

and every spirit that does not confess Jesus is not from God."[3] Such a test is contingent, however. Before providing the church with such a simple test, John reminds us that Jesus limits his commands, yet they are integral to faith. God commands that "we believe in the name of . . . Jesus, and love one another, just as he commanded us. The one who keeps his commandments abides in him . . . We know by this that he abides in us, by the Spirit who he has given us."[4] Congregations who confess Jesus understand that love is an indicator of the presence of God's Spirit, and that actions undertaken in love and in Jesus' name will be proven fruitful and Spirit-led, or unproductive, judged, and forgiven. God will not underwrite sin, but healthy spiritual risks undertaken in a Spirit of love will be vindicated because Jesus forgives, and because God works wonders from the mistakes of human beings when performed in love and faithfulness (if not righteousness).

Any action undertaken in Jesus' name is open to critique, and entertaining criticisms are part of the hermeneutic circle. If we are faithful, we will raise our children and teach new members to trust and confirm (to paraphrase a saint of capitalism), to test the boundaries and leadings of the Spirit, and accept support or correction by the community. We always need to ask the right questions before assuming we have any answers. The church must also remind itself that our responses to sin, evil, and brokenness are contingent upon voluntary association and faith in the work we claim is accomplished by God through Jesus. There is another aspect to a New Testament ethic that must be recognized. In the Anabaptist, Quaker, and Puritan/Congregationalist model of polity, congregationalism must emerge as the means of being the church among Protestants. This allows for the epistles written by John to become a blueprint for being a unified though dissonant body of Christ, for there can be no unity without dissent. Dissonance does not refute relationship or mutual aid, nor does it refute love. One must not allow dissonance to become an obstacle to love and healthy relationship. Travelling ministries in the manner of Friends, and missions within the church by congregations of contrasting ethics, are helpful and necessary to dialogue and shared communion in Christ. The act of foot washing facilitates such ministry as loving communication rather than corrective action. Only those communities that cease to confess Christ, or eschew the moral vision of the kingdom of God as normative, would be cast from meal sharing.

This is our contingent ethic, an ethic reliant upon faith in the absurd, and an eschatological and apocalyptic view of the world and culture. This is

3. 1 John 4:2–3. NRSV
4. 1 John 3:23–24. NRSV

our claim of human liberation in Christ. We are not bound to an ethic that is compelled by any outcome or moral vision outside of caring for one another, and "the other." Such absurdities as bearing our own cross, operating from a social location of powerlessness, finding victory in being beaten or lynched, political self-marginalization, and serving the least of these instead of seeking out our own privilege comprise an ethic that invites irrelevance if not ridicule. However, such absurdities are necessary for the liberation of humanity from the unrealized (if not false) promises of the Enlightenment and liberal republican democracy. The only way to represent truth and liberty is to make known a reality that stands in firm contrast to power, corruption, consumerism, and every other -ism that dehumanizes communities by forcing them to compete for resources instead of promoting a means of sharing them. It has become evident that human autonomy is rarely more than individuals competing for resources that should be shared instead of hoarded by autonomous moral agents.

The gospel is the church's opportunity to embody salvation, and it offers an ethic that sets us apart from the domination system of human competition. The problem has become one of confused identity. As stated by Stroup and clarified by Cone in this project, the church identifies more with Americanism and human rights than it does with Jesus and suffering servanthood. Not only does this misrepresent Jesus and the will of God to the rest of the world, it misrepresents the contents of the Bible—the very words of God.

Jesus is the Word, and Bible the words of God. A return to biblical ethics is a return to the embodiment of the Word and the words as normative for the construction of a religious community's identity, faith, and practice. Many may call themselves Christians, or identify as Christians, but it is only through praxis and the practice of the care ethic delineated above that others will know the truth of the gospel, and accept the opportunity for salvation. Cultural Christianity does not impede the gospel, but instead conforms the faith to the culture. Cultural Christianity does impede the witness of what God desires for human relationships, and must be revealed as anti-Christ, an obstacle to human liberation. Indeed, American Christendom has become an obstacle to human liberation as much as it has come to practice the defense of individual or human rights.

As an apocalyptic community, we radically witness to the truth of sin as it lays hidden beneath accepted cultural expressions of stability and utilitarian goods. Such cultural expressions, ranging from the righteousness of democratic ideals and the assumption that human rights are "God-given," are but an opaque layer of enamel covering a reality of violence, oppression, and conformity to that which slowly kills the Spirit of Christ while upholding the letter of individual liberty and autonomy. God did not create human beings to realize autonomous potential outside of a community of under-standing. We are created for relationship, with both God and one another. The prioritization of individual rights over faithfulness has been a demo-cratic ideal that is both productive and important, but just as anti-Christ in its impact on the church. The church has never been called to witness to individual rights, but to God's justice.

While our rights may be valuable, the gospel indicates that care for the other and the pursuit of widespread justice in the name of Jesus is the obligation of the church, and not just the preferred faith expression of a congregation's social justice small group. Reading Ron Sider books as a mo-tivating factor for justice is little more than a self-justifying start. The fact of a whole congregation turning itself over to the will of God is the part of the process aiming toward God's perfecting and perfect kingdom. If the small group is to lead the way, it must be radical and cast judgment on the church, for just as Jesus judged rather than cleansed the temple, the time for the death of Christendom has come. The end is near, and a biblical eschatology is pointing toward the end of the church. Long live the body of Christ. May her name be praised, and her life be lived through each of us who confess him as Lord.

Bibliography

Acts of Philip. Translated by Alexander Walker. In *The Anti-Nicene Fathers*, edited by Alexander Walker, James Donaldson, and Cleveland A. Cox, 8:497–503. Grand Rapids: Eerdmans, 1981.

Alda, Alan, director. "Goodbye, Farewell, and Amen." *M.A.S.H.*, season 11, episode 16. Aired February 28, 1983. Twentieth Century Fox, CBS.

Alter, Robert. *The Art of Biblical Narrative*. New York: Basic Books, 1981.

Anderson, Michelle. "Spring Lake Church Plans to Reinstall Controversial Cross Removed in 2010." *Muskegon Chronicle*, January 23, 2013. http://www.mlive.com/news/muskegon/index.ssf/2013/01/muskegon_area_church_restores.html.

Apel, Dora. *Imagery of Lynching: Black Men, White Women, and the Mob*. New Brunswick, NJ: Rutgers University Press, 2004.

Aristotle. *Nicomachean Ethics*. Translated by H. Rackham. Loeb Classical Library. Cambridge, MA: Harvard University Press, 1934.

Armstrong, Judith. "Deconstruction." *Dictionary of Philosophy*, edited by Thomas Mautner. London: Penguin, 2005.

Baker-Fletcher, Karen. "More than Suffering: The Healing and Resurrecting Spirit of God." In *Womanist Theological Ethics: A Reader*, edited by Katie Geneva Cannon, Emilie M. Townes, and Angela Sims, 155–82. Library of Theological Ethics Series. Louisville: Westminster John Knox, 2011.

Barker, Greg, Julie Powell, and David Espar, writers and producers. "Of God and Caesar." *God in America*, part 6. WGBH, PBS, 2012. http://www.pbs.org/godinamerica/transcripts/hour-six.

Bauckham, Richard. *New Testament Theology*. New York: Cambridge University Press, 1993.

Berges, Sandrine. *A Feminist Perspective on Virtue Ethics*. Houndmills, Hampshire, UK: Palgrave Macmillan, 2015.

Bernstein, Herbert J. "Idols of Modern Science and the Reconstruction of Knowledge." In *New Ways of Knowing: The Sciences, Society, and Reconstructive Knowledge*, edited by Marcus G. Raskin and H. J. Bernstein. Totawa, NJ: Rowman and Littlefield, 1987.

Bird, Phyllis A. "The Authority of the Bible." In *New Interpreters Bible*, edited by Leander Keck, 1:33–64. Nashville: Abingdon, 1997.

Bleich, J. David. "Torture and the Ticking Bomb." *Tradition*, 39/4 (2006) 89–121.

Botti, Catarina. "Feminine Virtues or Feminist Virtues?: The Debate on Care Ethics Revisited." *Etica & Politica (Ethics & Politics)*, 17/2 (February 2015) 107–51.

Bovon, Francois, and Christopher Matthews. *The Acts of Philip: A New Translation*. Waco, TX: Baylor University Press, 2012.

Braaten, Carl E. "Revelation." In *Handbook of Christian Theology*, edited by Donald Musser and Joseph Price, 428–32. Nashville: Abingdon, 2003.

Cahill, Lisa Sowle. "Kingdom and Cross: Christian Moral Community and the Problem of Suffering." *Interpretation* 50/2 (1996) 156–69.

Caputo, John. *Radical Hermeneutics: Repetition, Deconstruction and the Hermeneutic Project*. Bloomington, IN: Indiana University Press, 1987.

Carlin, Dan. "Prophets of Doom." *Hardcore History* 48. http://www.dancarlin.com/product/hardcore-history-48-prophets-of-doom/.

Cartwright, Michael G. *Practices, Politics, and Performance: Toward a Communal Hermeneutic for Christian Ethics*. Princeton Theological Monographs 57. Eugene, OR: Wipf and Stock, 2006.

Charry, Ellen T. "A Sharp Two-Edged Sword: Pastoral Implications of Apocalyptic." *Interpretation* 53/2 (1999) 158–72.

Chrystal, William G. "Reinhold Niebuhr and the First World War." *Journal of Presbyterian History* 55/3 (1977) 285–98.

Cone, James. *A Black Theology of Liberation*. C. Eric Lincoln Series in Black Religion. Philadelphia and New York: Lippincott, 1970.

Copeland, M. Shawn. "Wading Through Many Sorrows: Toward a Theology of Suffering in a Womanist Perspective." In *Womanist Theological Ethics: A Reader*, edited by Katie Geneva Cannon, Emilie M. Townes, and Angela Sims, 135–53. Library of Theological Ethics Series. Louisville: Westminster John Knox, 2011.

Davis, Ellen F. "Reasoning with Scripture." *Anglican Theological Review* 90/3 (2008) 513–19.

Didache. Translated by M. B. Riddle. In *The Ante-Nicece Fathers*, edited by Alexander Walker, James Donaldson, and Cleveland A. Cox, vol. 7. Grand Rapids: Eerdmans, 1981. http://www.earlychristianwritings.com/text/didache-roberts.html.

Dorrien, Gary. "Rauschenbusch's *Christianity and Social Crisis*." http://www.religion-online.org/showarticle.asp?title=3501.

Driver, John. *How Christians Made Peace with War: Early Christian Understandings of War*. Peace and Justice Series 2. Scottsdale, PA: Herald: 1988.

Dunn, James. *Jesus Remembered: Christianity in the Making* Vol. 1. Grand Rapids: Eerdmans, 2003.

Ellul, Jacques. *Anarchy and Christianity*. Translated by Geoffery W. Bromily. Grand Rapids: Eerdmans, 1991.

Evans, C. Stephen. Introduction to *Fear and Trembling*, by Søren Kierkegaard. Edited by Evans and Sylvia Walsh. Cambridge, UK: Cambridge University Press, 2006.

Faith in Public Life. "Release of Poll on Southern Evangelicals' Attitudes on Torture." September 2008. http://www.faithinpubliclife.org/newsroom/press/page/40/.

Fee, Gordon, and Douglas Stuart. *How to Read the Bible for All It's Worth*. Grand Rapids: Zondervan, 1981.

Feuerbach, Ludwig. *The Essence of Christianity*. Translated by George Eliot. New York: Harper and Row, 1957.

Frei, Hans. "Apologetics, Criticism, and the Loss of Narrative Interpretation." In *Why Narrative?: Readings in Narrative Theology*, edited by Stanley Hauerwas and L. Gregory Jones, 45–64. Grand Rapids: Eerdmans, 1989.

Freire, Paulo. *Pedagogy of the Oppressed*. Translated by Myra Ramos. 30th Anniversary Edition. New York: Bloomsbury, 2014.

Frend, W. H. C. *The Rise of Christianity*. Philadelphia: Fortress, 1984.

Funk, Robert W. *Language, Hermeneutic, and the Word of God: The Problem of Language in the New Testament and Contemporary Theology*. New York: Harper and Row, 1966.

Gadamer, Hans-Georg. *Truth and Method*. New York: Seabury, 1975.

Gilligan, Carol. *In a Different Voice: Psychological Theory and Women's Development*. Cambridge, MA: Harvard University Press, 1982.

Godzich, Wlad. Afterword in *The Postmodern Explained*, by Lyotard, Jean-Francois 109–36. Edited by Julian Pefanis and Morgan Thomas, translated by Barry Don, Bernadette Maher, et al. Minneapolis: University of Minnesota Press, 1992.

Goldberg, Michel. *Theology and Narrative: A Critical Introduction*. Philadelphia: Trinity, 1991.

González, Justo. *The Story of Christianity*. Vol. 1, *The Early Church to the Dawn of the Reformation*. San Francisco: HarperSanFrancisco, 1984.

Gushee, David. "Five Reasons Why Torture Is Always Wrong." *Christianity Today* 50/2. (2006) 32.

———. *The Future of Faith in American Politics: The Public Witness of the Evangelical Center*. Waco, TX: Baylor University Press, 2008.

———. "What the Torture Debate Reveals about American Evangelical Christianity." *Journal of the Society of Christian Ethics* 30/1 (2010) 79–98.

Gutierrez, Gustavo. *A Theology of Liberation: History, Politics, and Salvation*. Translated and edited by Sister Caridad Inda and John Eagleson. Maryknoll, NY: Orbis, 1988.

Hamm, Ken. *Answers in Genesis*. https://answersingenesis.org.

Harink, Douglas. *Paul Among the Postliberals: Pauline Theology beyond Christendom and Modernity*. Grand Rapids: Brazos, 2003.

Hart, Megan. "Spring Lake's Christ Community Church Removes Cross, Changes Name to C3Exchange." *Muskegon Chronicle*, June 23, 2010. http://www.mlive.com/news/muskegon/index.ssf/2010/06/spring_lakes_christ_community.html.

Hauerwas, Stanley. *A Community of Character: Toward a Constructive Christian Ethic*. Notre Dame, IN: Notre Dame University Press, 1981.

———. "The Democratic Policing of Christianity." *Pro Ecclesia* 3/2 (1994) 215–31.

———. "On Being a Church Capable of Addressing a World at War: A Pacifist Response to the United Methodist Bishops' Pastoral 'In Defense of Creation.'" In *The Hauerwas Reader*, edited by John Berkman and Michael Cartwright, 426–58. Durham, NC: Duke University Press, 2001.

———. "On Keeping Ethics Theological." In *The Hauerwas Reader*, edited by John Berkman and Michael Cartwright, 51–74. Durham, NC: Duke University Press, 2001.

———. *The Peaceable Kingdom: A Primer in Christian Ethics*. Notre Dame, IN: University of Notre Dame Press, 1983.

———. *War and the American Difference: Theological Reflections on Violence and National Identity*. Grand Rapids: Baker Academic, 2011.

Hauerwas, Stanley, and William H. Willemon. *Resident Aliens: Life in the Christian Colony*. Nashville: Abingdon, 1989.

Hawkins, John. "Seven Political Differences between Liberals and Conservatives." *Townhall.com*, January 25, 2011. http://townhall.com/columnists/johnhawkins/2011/01/25/7_non-political_differences_between_liberals_and_conservatives/page/full.

Herzog, William R., II. *Jesus, Justice, and the Reign of God: A Ministry of Liberation.* Louisville: Westminster/John Knox, 2000.

Hobbes, Thomas. *Of Man, Being the First Part of Leviathan.* Edited by Charles W. Eliot. Volume 34, part 5. Harvard Classics. New York: P.F. Collier & Son, 1909–14.

hooks, bell. *Feminist Theory: From Margin to Center.* Cambridge, MA: South End, 1984.

Huebner, Chris K. *A Precarious Peace: Yoderian Explorations on Theology, Knowledge, and Identity.* Waterloo, ON: Herald, 2006.

Heidegger, Martin. "Hölderlin's Earth and Heaven." In *Elucidations of Hölderlin's Poetry,* translated by Keith Hoeller. New York: Humanity Books, 2000.

Helgeland, John, Robert J. Daly, and J. Patrick Burns. *Christians in the Military: The Early Experience.* Philadelphia: Fortress,1985.

Horwitz, Josh. "Thomas Jefferson and the 'Blood of Tyrants.'" *HuffingtonPost.com,* September 1, 2009. http://www.huffingtonpost.com/josh-horwitz/thomas-jefferson-and-the_b_273800.html.

Howard, Brian Clark. "Shark Gives Rare 'Virgin Birth' to Three Pups." *National Geographic,* June 16, 2016. http://news.nationalgeographic.com/2016/06/leopard-shark-virgin-birth-aquarium-australia/.

Hume, David. *The Natural History of Religion.* Edited by H. E. Root. Stanford, CA: Stanford University Press, 1957.

Husserl, Edmund. *Ideas.* Translated by Boyce Gibson. New York: Macmillan, 1931.

Ingraffia, Brian D. *Postmodern Theory and Biblical Theology.* Cambridge: Cambridge University Press, 1995.

Jewison, Norman, director. *Fiddler on the Roof.* United Artists, 1971.

Justin Martyr. *Dialogue with Trypho.* In *The Anti-Nicene Fathers,* translated and edited by Alexander Walker, James Donaldson, and Cleveland A. Cox, vol. 1. Grand Rapids: Eerdmans: 1981.

———. *First Apology of Justin.* In *The Anti-Nicene Fathers,* vol. 1.

———. *Second Apology of Justin.* In *The Anti-Nicene Fathers,* vol. 1.

Kierkegaard, Søren. *Fear and Trembling.* Edited by C. Stephen Evans and Sylvia Walsh, translated by Sylvia Walsh. Cambridge: Cambridge University Press, 2006.

Kiner, Richard, T. Jerry L. Kernes, and Therese M. Dautheribes. "A Short List of Universal Moral Values." *Counseling and Values* 45 (2000) 4–16.

Kitcher, Philip. "Truth or Consequences." *Proceedings and Addresses of the American Philosophical Association* 72/2 (1998) 49–63.

Kohlberg, Lawrence. *Essays on Moral Development.* Vol. 1, *The Philosophy of Moral Development.* San Francisco: Harper Collins, 1981.

Lacoste, Jean-Yves. *Experience and the Absolute: Disputed Questions on the Humanity of Man.* Translated by Mark Rafferty-Skehan. New York: Fordham University Press, 2004.

Lawler Michael, and Todd Salazar. "Virtue Ethics: Natural and Christian." *Theological Studies* 74/2 (2013) 442–73.

Life Album 1996: Pictures of the Year. New York: Time-Life, 1997.

Lindbeck, George A. *The Nature of Doctrine: Religion and Theology in a Postliberal Age.* Louisville: Westminster/John Knox, 1984.

Lear, Norman, creator and writer. "Sammy's Visit." Directed by John Rich. *All in the Family,* season 2, episode 21. Aired February 19, 1972. Bud Yorkin Productions, CBS.

Long Jr., Edward Leroy. "The Use of the Bible in Christian Ethics: A Look at Basic Options." *Interpretation* 19/2 (1965) 149–52.

Lovin, Robin W. *Reinhold Niebuhr and Christian Realism.* Cambridge: Cambridge University Press, 1995.

Lyotard, Jean-Francois. *The Postmodern Condition: A Report on Knowledge.* Translated by Geoff Bennington and Brian Massumi. Edited by Wlad Godzich and Jochen Shulte-Sasse. Theory and History of Literature 10. Minneapolis: University of Minnesota Press, 1984.

———. *The Postmodern Explained.* Edited by Julian Pefanis and Morgan Thomas, translated by Barry Don, Bernadette Maher, et al. Minneapolis: University of Minnesota Press, 1992.

MacIntyre, Alasdair. *After Virtue: A Study in Moral Theory* 2nd ed. Notre Dame, IN: Notre Dame University Press, 1986.

Malina, Bruce J. "Exegetical Eschatology, the Present, and the Final Discourse Genre: The Case of Mark 13." *Biblical Theology Bulletin* 32/2 (2002) 44–59.

Manoussakis, John P. "The Anarchic Principle of Christian Eschatology in the Eucharistic Tradition of the Eastern Church." *Harvard Theological Review* 100/1 (2007) 29–46.

McClendon, James William. *Ethics: Systematic Theology.* Vol. 1. Nashville: Abington, 1986.

Meeks, Wayne. *The Origins of Christian Morality: The First Two Centuries.* New Haven, CT: Yale University Press, 1993.

Metz, Johann Baptist. "A Short Apology of Narrative." In *Why Narrative?: Readings in Narrative Theology,* edited by Stanley Hauerwas and L. Gregory Jones, 251–62. Grand Rapids: Eerdmans, 1989.

Miller, R. Scot. "*Pistous Iesous Christous*: The Faithful life of Jesus Christ and Covenant Fulfillment in the Judeo-Christian Narrative." *The Paul Page.* August 12, 2008. http://www.thepaulpage.com/new-perspective/from-the-paul-page/articles/.

Moyers, Bill, interview with James Cone. "The Cross and the Lynching Tree." Transcript. *Bill Moyers Journal.* Directed by Ken Diego, produced by Bill Moyers. Aired November 23, 2007. PBS. http://www.pbs.org/moyers/journal/11232007/transcript1.html.

Mudge, Lewis S. Introduction to *Essays on Biblical Interpretation,* by Paul Ricoeur. Minneapolis: Fortress, 1980.

Nash, James A. "The Bible vs. Biodiversity: The Case against Moral Argument from Scripture." *Journal for the Study of Religion, Nature and Culture* 3/2 (2009) 213–37.

National Association of Evangelicals. *An Evangelical Declaration Against Torture: Protecting Human Rights in an Age of Terror.* January 1, 2007. http://nae.net/an-evangelical-declaration-against-torture/.

Niebuhr, H. Richard. "The Story of Our Life." In *The Meaning of Revelation.* New York: MacMillan, 1941. Reprinted with permission in *Why Narrative?: Readings in Narrative Theology,* edited by Stanley Hauerwas and L. Gregory Jones, 21–44. Grand Rapids: Eerdmans, 1989.

Niebuhr, Reinhold. *Children of Light and Children of Darkness: A Vindication of Democracy and a Critique of its Traditional Defense.* New York: Scribner, 1944.

———. "Civil Rights Climax in Alabama." *Christianity in Crisis* 23/5 (1965) 61.

———. "The Crisis in American Protestantism." *The Christian Century* 80/49 (1963) 1498–1501.

————. "The Mounting Racial Climax." *Christianity in Crisis* 23/12 (1963) 121–22.

————. "Must We Do Nothing?" In *War in the Twentieth Century: Sources in Theological Ethics*, edited by Richard B. Miller. Louisville: Westminster/John Knox, 1992.

————. "Why the Christian Church Is Not Pacifist." In *War in the Twentieth Century: Sources in Theological Ethics*, edited by Richard B. Miller. Louisville: Westminster/John Knox, 1992.

Nietzsche, Friedrich. "On Truth and Lie in an Extra-Moral Sense." In *The Portable Nietzsche*, edited and translated by Walter Kaufmann, 39–46. New York: Viking, 1954.

Noah, Timothy. "The Imperial Vice-Presidency." *Slate*, December 23, 2004. http://www.slate.com/articles/news_and_politics/chatterbox/2003/12/the_imperial_vice_presidency.html.

Nozick, Robert. *Anarchy, the State, and Utopia.* Oxford: Blackwell, 1974.

Ogden, Schubert M. *Christ Without Myth: A Study on the Theology of Rudolph Bultmann.* New York: Harper, 1961.

Ogletree, Thomas W. *The Use of the Bible in Christian Ethics.* Philadelphia: Fortress, 1983.

Okure, Therese. "What Is Truth?" *Anglican Theological Review* 93/2 (2011) 405–22.

Olsen, Matthew. "Scientific Proof of the Virgin Birth." October, 2, 2014. https://answeringprotestants.com/2014/10/02/scientific-proof-of-the-virgin-birth/.

Pambrun, James R. "Hermeneutical Theology and Narrative." *Theoforum* 32/3 (2001) 273–301.

Powers, Richard G. *Not Without Honor: The History of American Anticommunism.* New York: Free Press, 1995.

Ramsey, Paul. "Is Vietnam a Just War?" In *War in the Twentieth Century: Sources in Theological Ethics*, edited by Richard B. Miller. Louisville: Westminster/John Knox, 1992.

Rauschenbusch, Walter. *Christianity and the Social Crisis.* New York: Macmillan, 1907. https://archive.org/stream/christianityando1rausgoog#page/n5/mode/2up.

————. *Christianizing the Social Order.* New York: MacMillan, 1912. https://archive.org/stream/christianizingso1rausgoog#page/n14/mode/2up.

————. *Theology for the Social Gospel.* New York: Abingdon, 1917.

Rawls, John. *A Theory of Justice.* Cambridge, MA: Belknap, 1971.

Ricoeur, Paul. *Symbolism of Evil.* Translated by Emerson Buchanan. New York: Harper and Row, 1967.

Rieger, Joerge. *Christ and Empire: From Paul to Postcolonial Times.* Minneapolis: Fortress, 2007.

Rorty, Richard. *Contingency, Irony, and Solidarity.* Cambridge: Cambridge University Press, 1989.

Rossing, Barbara R. *The Apocalypse Exposed: The Message of Hope in the Book of Revelation.* New York: Basic Books, 2005.

Roth, Robert P. *Story and Reality.* Grand Rapids: Eerdmans, 1973.

Reuther, Rosemary Radford. *Liberation Theology: Human Hope Confronts Christian History and American Power.* Glen Rock, NJ: Paulist, 1972.

Rocco, Christopher. "Between Modernity and Postmodernity: Reading Dialectic of Enlightenment Against the Grain." *Political Theory* 22/1 (1994) 71–97.

Ruf, Henry L. *Postmodern Rationality, Social Criticism, and Religion.* Paragon Issues in Philosophy. St. Paul: Paragon House, 2005.

Russell, Letty. *Human Liberation in a Feminist Perspective: A Theology.* Philadelphia: Westminster, 1974.

Sales, John, director. *Matewan.* Cinecom Pictures, 1987.

Sandlin, Mark. "I Want My Religion Back—You Can Keep the Ugly Baggage." *Patheos,* July 27, 2014. http://www.patheos.com/blogs/thegodarticle/2014/07/i-want-my-religion-back-you-can-keep-the-ugly-baggage/.

Saskice, Janet Martin. *Metaphor and Religious Language.* Oxford: Clarendon, 1985.

Scruton, Roger. *From Descartes to Wittgenstein: A Short History of Modern Philosophy.* London: Routledge and Kegan Paul,1981.

Seidman, Steven. "The End of Sociological Theory: The Postmodern Hope." *Sociological Theory* 9/2 (1991) 131–46.

Shakespeare, Steven. *Derrida and Theology.* London: T. & T. Clark, 2009.

Siker, Jeffrey. *Scripture and Ethics: Twentieth-Century Portraits.* Oxford: Oxford University, 1997.

Sims, Angela D. "The Issue of Race and Lynching." In *Womanist Theological Ethics: A Reader,* edited by Katie Geneva Cannon, Emilie M. Townes, and Angela Sims, 203–16. Library of Theological Ethics. Louisville: Westminster John Knox, 2011.

Slaughter, Martin. "Former Ann Arbor Resident Reflects on Saving Man from Beating at KKK Rally." *Ann Arbor News,* June 24, 2016. http://www.mlive.com/news/ann-arbor/index.ssf/2016/06/saving_man_from_beating_at_kkk.html

Smith, Gregory, and Jessica Martinez. *How the Faithful Voted: A Preliminary 2016 Analysis.* Pew Research Center, November 9, 2016. http://www.pewresearch.org/fact-tank/2016/11/09/how-the-faithful-voted-a-preliminary-2016-analysis/.

Spong, John Shelby. "Bishop Spong Q&A on Revelation." Attributed response to forum question. April 14, 2007. http://www.christianforums.com/threads/bishop-spong-q-a-on-revelation.5169368/.

Sölle, Dorothee. "The Gospel and Liberation." *Commonweal* 41/20 (1972) 270–75.

Sproul, R. C. *Essential Truths of the Christian Faith.* Carol Stream, IL: Tyndale, 1992.

Starnes, Todd. "Are We Still One Nation under God?" *Fox News,* Opinion, July 2, 2012. http://www.foxnews.com/opinion/2010/07/02/todd-starnes-barack-obama-united-states-christian-nation/.

Stroup, George W. *The Promise of Narrative Theology.* Louisville: John Knox, 1981.

Sykes, Stephen. *The Identity of Christianity.* Philadelphia: Fortress, 1984.

Taylor, Jessica. Citing 'Two Corinthians,' Trump Struggles to Make the Sale to Evangelicals." *NPR,* January 18, 2016. http://www.npr.org/2016/01/18/463528847/citing-two-corinthians-trump-struggles-to-make-the-sale-to-evangelicals.

Thiel, John E. *Nonfoundationalism.* Guides to Theological Inquiry. Minneapolis: Fortress, 1994.

Thurman, Howard. *Disciplines of the Spirit.* Richmond, IN: Friends United Press, 1977.

Tillich, Paul. *Systematic Theology.* Vol. 1, *Reason and Revelation, Being and God.* Chicago: University of Chicago, 1951.

Tooley, Mark D. "The Evangelical Left's Nazi Obsession." *FrontPage Magazine,* October 30, 2008. Republished with permission at https://juicyecumenism.com/2009/10/08/the-evangelical-lefts-nazi-obsession-2.

United Nations. "A Universal Declaration of Human Rights." New York: United Nations, 1948.

Van Buren, Paul Matthews. *The Secular Meaning of the Gospel Based on an Analysis of Language.* New York: McMillan, 1963.

Walker, Alice. *In Search of our Mother's Gardens: Womanist Prose*. San Diego, CA: Harcourt, 1984.

Wilson, Jonathan R. *Living Faithfully in a Fragmented World: Lessons for the Church from MacIntyre's After Virtue*. Christian Mission and Modern Culture 13. Harrisburg. PA: Trinity, 1997.

Wink, Walter. *Engaging the Powers: Discernment and Resistance in a World of Domination*. Minneapolis: Fortress, 1992.

Wright, N. T. *Jesus and the Victory of God*. Minneapolis: Fortress, 1996.

———. *The New Testament and the People of God*. Minneapolis: Fortress, 1992.

Yoder, John Howard. *The Priestly Kingdom*. Notre Dame, IN: University of Notre Dame Press, 1984.

———. *The Politics of Jesus: Vicit Agnus Noster*. 2nd ed. Grand Rapids: Eerdmans, 1994.

Ziziouslas, Johan. "Toward and Eschatological Ontology." Unpublished paper delivered at King's College, 1999.